The Historic Gardens of England Series

Historic Gardens of Cambridgeshire and the Isle of Ely

Opposite: Plenipotentiary, winner of the 1834 Epsom Derby.

Horseheath Lodge

The Historic Gardens of England Series

Historic Gardens of Cambridgeshire

and the

Isle of Ely

Timothy Mowl

Laura Mayer

For Michael Richardson

The publication of this volume has been made possible by a grant from
THE LEVERHULME TRUST
to cover all the necessary research work

The title page from
David Loggan's
Cantabrigia Illustrata,
1688. *Reference Library,*
Bristol Central Library

First published in 2013 by Redcliffe Press Ltd.
81g Pembroke Road, Bristol BS8 3EA
T: 0117 973 7207
E: info@redcliffepress.co.uk
www.redcliffepress.co.uk

ISBN 978-1-908326-32-4`

British Library Cataloguing-in-Publication Data
A catalogue record for this book is available from the British Library

Designed by Stephen Morris, smc@freeuk.com www.stephen-morris.co.uk

Printed and bound by Zenith Media

Contents

Acknowledgements

As with the last nine books in this series, my first thanks go to Professor Gordon Marshall and his Trustees at the Leverhulme Trust, whose benevolent funding of the research has made visiting the gardens of Cambridgeshire a pleasure rather than a financial strain. Their generosity has made it possible for Dr Laura Mayer, a former PhD student of mine, to be appointed as consultant for *Cambridgeshire and the Isle of Ely*. She has undertaken all the research and co-ordinated the site visits, with thoughtful support from her Cambridge-based parents, in a coolly professional manner. I should also like to thank Marion Mako, my co-author on *Cheshire* and *Somerset* and Research Fellow of the project, who has overseen the progress of the work with efficiency, and her predecessor Dr Clare Hickman, co-author of *Northamptonshire*, for setting Laura off on the right foot.

Jamie Carstairs has photographed most effectively the archival images from the University of Bristol's Special Collections and I must thank most warmly Michael Richardson, to whom this book is dedicated, for bringing many important texts to my notice. My publisher, John Sansom, has been a thoughtful editor, and Stephen Morris has achieved yet another elegantly designed volume. Alexandra Denman has proofed the typescript most thoroughly, while Douglas Matthews has produced yet another definitive index. I must also thank Chris Gibson for help and advice on technical matters, and for his support of Laura.

We are grateful to the conscientious staff at Cambridgeshire Archives, Cambridge University Library, Cambridgeshire Collection in Cambridge Central Library, Cambridge University Collection of Aerial Photography, English Heritage Archives in Swindon, Bristol University Library, Bristol Central Library, the British Library, the National Trust and the Bodleian Library.

Laura and I must also pay tribute to the late John Drake, founder of the Cambridgeshire Gardens Trust and, until recently, its Chair. In failing health, John walked us around his own intensely atmospheric garden just before he died, and the Trust's *Gazetteer*, for which he was largely responsible, has been a valuable resource.

Owners, gardeners, archivists, colleagues and friends who have shared their time, knowledge and hospitality include Prof John Adamson, Howard & Fiona Anderson, Lord Jeffrey & Dame Mary Archer, Tony Arnold, Peter Balaam, Helen Barlow, Dr Dianne Barre, Duncan Baxter, Helen Beaton, Ian & Kate Beaton, Esther Bellamy, Michael & Valerie Berkson, Diana Boston, Frank Bowles, Simon Bradley,

Dr Jane Bradney, Michael & Margaret Braithwaite, Robert Bramley, Adrian Bridgewater, Richard & Frankie Bridgwood, Nicholas Browne, Caroline & K C Carr-Briggs, Paul & Arabella Chambers, Amanda Chapman, Francis & Charlotte Clarke, Stephen Coates, Dr Claire Cockcroft, Rt Revd Stephen Conway, Dr Karen Cook, Eustace Crawley, Louisa Dare, Paul Davis, Lord & Lady De Ramsey, Emmah Duffus, Dr Peter & Ann Duncumb, Dawn Dyer, Dr Kay Elder, Nigel & Anne Elgood, Steve Elstub, Lord & Lady Fairhaven, Hazel Farrow, Chris & Sarah Field, Dennis Footman, Christopher Francis, Doug & Margaret Fuller, Peter & Janet Garner, Elizabeth Gilbert, Steve Griffiths, Dr Mike Gross, Michael Herbert, Debbie Hodder, Lee & Laura Hughes, Peter & Fleur Hughes, Tom Hughes, Peter & Gay Johnson, Jonah Jones, Christoph Keate, David & Liz Kendrick, Arabella Killander, Revd Canon Philipa King, Kate Lancaster, John & Jane Lewin Smith, Peter & Susan Lewis, Dr Roger Lovatt, Vince Lucas, Terry & Margaret Lynch, Matt Mace, Adam Magee, Anna Markwell, John Marlar, Sir Michael & Lady Marshall, Alun Martin, Sue Martin, Dr Christopher & Wendy Mayer, Dr Patricia McGuire, Julian & Sarah Metherell, Gillian Moore, Paula Morrin, Andrew Myson, Dr Michael Nedo, Robin Newman, Barry Norman, Sandra Norman, Sir & Lady Nourse, Richard Parsonson, Kate Pateman, David Payne, Richard Pemberton, Melanie Pluck, Jim & Hilary Potter, Tony & Lissi Puckridge, Faith Raven, Jane Readman, Dr Jane Renfrew, Ben Rickett, Stephen & Denise Rivers, Philippa Rose, Sharon Sanderson, Jane Sansom, Ben & Sue Shephard, Gavin Smith, Samantha Smith, Prof Peter Spufford, Jamie Stevens, Jennifer Talbot, Ian, Bron & Angela Taylor, Sidney Taylor, Stephen & Sarah Tebboth, Beverley Thompson, Dr Kate Thompson, Anne Thomson, Pam Thornhill, Christopher & Lady Linda Vane Percy, Lucy Waitt, Fred Waters, Philip Whaites, Jane Whitaker, Shirley Whittering, Dr Peter Willis and Richard & Angela Wright.

Cambridgeshire and the Isle of Ely was researched during my final year of teaching on Bristol University's MA in Garden History and written alongside the launch of Buckingham University's new Research MA in the field, so I must thank my fellow university colleagues for their support. My agent, Sara Menguc, has continued to encourage the project with affectionate enthusiasm. The staff at Madingley Hall gave Laura and I a warm welcome and provided a perfect base for garden visits in the west of the county, Judy Rossiter was a kind and informative hostess at Springfield House, Linton, while Gill & Peter Pedersen at The Old Vicarage, Isleham helped us negotiate the deserted fens of the Isle of Ely.

After twelve years of garden visiting and writing it is time for me to take a break and to look forward to new publishing ventures. Consequently, this is the last book in the present series.

Timothy Mowl,
Bristol, May 2013

Introduction

Fenlands, horses, literary figures and a university

Bishop's Palace, Ely · Wandlebury Ring · Horseheath Lodge
Harston House · Hemingford Grey Manor · Southernwood · The Grange
Kings Mill House · The Guildhall, Whittlesford
Lucy Cavendish College

EVEN THOUGH THE NATIONAL TRUST CLAIMS ON ONE OF ITS DISPLAY boards at Wicken Fen National Nature Reserve, north-east of Cambridge, that there is less than 0.1% of the original East Anglian fenland left, this is not immediately apparent when driving across the Isle of Ely. Wide expanses of peaty black fields stretch out under low skies, while narrow roads, bordered with warning signs urging drivers to 'Think Don't Sink' in the deep, water-filled ditches either side, lead northwards to the great cathedral ship of the fens. While this land has provided fuel and food for centuries it has not encouraged the creation of gardens or designed landscapes. As a result, there are precious few sites between Cambridge and Ely that will detain the garden historian. The lost early eighteenth-century house and layout at Fordham Abbey, just south of Soham, is the last central outrider before the fenland, while the formal canals at Chippenham Park mark the eastern boundary of garden influence in the area. To the west lie the old county of Huntingdon and the Soke of Peterborough, which for reasons of county boundary consistency within this series, have been left for a later volume, though they are now included within the modern Cambridgeshire.

Staying overnight at The Old Vicarage, Isleham, was like stepping back into a rural community straight out of *Kilvert's Diary*. All the Ordnance Survey map names signified fenland occupation. 'Prickwillow Road', with an angular grid of narrow droves radiating from it over Isleham Fen, took us to Ely past 'Walnut Tree Farm', 'Burn Foot Tree Farm' and 'Elderberry

Farm', and all the while to the east the ruler-straight, canalised reach of the River Lark ran parallel to us. The draining of the Cambridgeshire fens in the seventeenth and eighteenth centuries, by the creation of the Old and New Bedford rivers in an attempt to connect the Great Ouse with the sea at King's Lynn, is not within the scope of this study. However, while the 4th Earl of Bedford and his gentlemen adventurers managed to reclaim vast tracts of land for cultivation, in the process creating a remarkable productive landscape, they were not in the business of encouraging historic gardens. In respect of this land management, there is a Rococo wall monument in the south porch of Ely Cathedral with a portrait bust of Humphry Smith, which records his 'Superior Abilities in Draining Fenny and Marsh Lands/Witness his Performances in Thorny Level in the Isle of Ely'. In the original county this has inevitably resulted in a garden void to the north, alleviated a little by two sites within the confines of Ely: Abbey Park to the south of the Cathedral (*colour 1*) and the walled enclosure by the former Deanery, which is now the **Bishop's Palace Garden** (*1*), the original across the road having been sold off.[1] However, the majority of historic sites are in and around Cambridge itself, together with a swathe of important landscapes to the south of the university town. As a result, this present survey ranges geographically throughout the county, but its focus is south of Cambridge, from Humphry Repton's abortive proposals to rebuild Waresley Park in either Gothic or Grecian style on the Huntingdon border by Gamlingay, to the great moat of Kirtling Tower in the east on the edge of Suffolk, whose yew-shaded ramparts Queen Elizabeth walked in 1578 and in whose vaulted chambers she enjoyed a banquet which included '4 stags made into 48 pasties'.[2]

While the fens make an all-encompassing visual impression in the Isle, it is easy to miss the great circular hill fort at **Wandlebury** in Stapleford parish, as the A1307 Babraham Road from Cambridge dips down into a leafy stretch of dual carriageway and speeds past the entrance to the site. The drive is obscure, set back from the road, and has no sign, but the entry point is signalled by brick gate piers supporting ironwork gates and a retiring gate lodge, Regency in date and circular in form, with pointed-arched windows and a conical slate roof. This is the drive to Wandlebury Country Park and Nature Reserve, where the signage informs the visitor

1 Box-edged rose beds in the grounds of the former Deanery at Ely, now the Bishop's Palace, are overshadowed by the great west tower of the Cathedral

that 'four miles of footpath including a nature trail give access to the public all year round'. The Cambridge Preservation Society was first involved at Wandlebury in 1937 when a 'Save the Gogs' fund was set up to protect the area from unsympathetic development. In 1954 Terence Gray donated the land and buildings within 'Wandlebury Ring' to the Trust in memory of his parents Sir Harold and Lady Gray, thereby ensuring their preservation for posterity. All this is proudly displayed on boards at the car park, though any further signs of a faintly municipal guardianship fade as leafy and slightly unkempt paths lead to the brick stable block, now converted to housing, and the inner enclosure beyond the archway.

The circular hill fort (2) was first inhabited in the third century BC, when a timber-faced rampart with a ditch guarded its inner enclosure.[3] Thereafter, it was in habitation until a period of decay before it was strengthened as a stronghold for the Iceni against the Belgae in the first

2 This aerial view of Wandlebury Ring shows the circular hill fort and the surviving stable range of Gogmagog House. The site of the house is marked out as a platform, from which descend the terraces of the lost formal garden. *Copyright reserved Cambridge University Collection of Aerial Photography*

century AD. The inner enclosure was levelled in the eighteenth century to make way for Gogmagog House, built by Francis, 2nd Earl Godolphin, which was begun in 1729 and completed in 1735. Before the Godolphins took over, Celia Fiennes rode to the site on her way to Cambridge in 1697. Her description gives some impression of the great ditch and the views from this unnaturally high vantage point in an otherwise flat county. She approached the

> Hodmogoge [Gogmagog] hills which looks at a distance like a long Barn, but when you approach near you see it is a great fortification or ruines of a Castle with great trenches one within another, and all the buildings there is only a long string of Stables to keep the king's hunting horses; the hill is of a great height from whence you have a great prospect of the whole Country and of Cambridge.[4]

3 The grave of 'The Godolphin Arabian' underneath the central arch of the stable range at Wandlebury

The original stables had been built by James II in about 1685 and survived until 1980; they were subsequently leased in the 1720s from the dean and chapter of Ely by Tregonwell Frampton, who held the official post of 'Master or Inspector of the King's Running Horses at Gog Magog'.[5] This long association of Wandlebury with horses was continued by Lord Goldophin who, after completing his house in 1732 and creating the gardens within the inner ramparts, built a new stable block to the south-west. His complex is shown in a contemporary watercolour (*colour 2*) which, even allowing for a little artistic licence, gives a good impression of the inner enclosure and the deep encircling ditch.[6] The visitor enters the demesne under the archway of this range, where a stone tablet is set in the cobbled floor (*3*). This is the grave of 'The Godolphin Arabian', which died in 1753 aged 29. It is likely that Lord Godolphin built the new stable block at the same time as a memorial to his great horse, said to have been one of three founding stallions of modern thoroughbred horse racing bloodstock.

From the archway the great inner enclosure opens up, walled in stock brick and dramatised by some tall cedars and other, much younger, deciduous trees. To the right a stone sundial embellished with a dolphin and a ducal coronet centres the grassy platform of the vanished house, which was demolished in the 1950s, while further out by the garden wall is the timber-framed and clay-tiled Tadlow Granary, dismantled by the Avoncroft Museum of Buildings at Bromsgrove in 1971 and re-erected here at Wandlebury in 1980 by the Cambridge Preservation Trust. In the middle of the enclosure is a rectangular pool, which might be a relic of the early eighteenth-century formal landscape, but it is the deep-delved walk, encircling the inner ramparts like an ancient hollow way, that makes the most striking impression. Here, it is recorded in 1200, a ghostly warrior haunted the ditch, while in the 1620s Cambridge scholars are said to have cut or re-cut the figure of the legendary giant Gogmagog on the bank. It was reported to be visible, lying within the ramparts, in 1720.[7] Much later, in 1955, figures of a sun goddess, two men and a chariot cut into the slope of the bank were found by local archaeologist T C Letherbridge; they are still just visible in the shrubberies. Certainly there is a numinous atmosphere about the place, particularly in the shadowy ditch. Ring counts date some of the trees on the banks to 1795, suggesting that this Gothic, gloom-filled walk overhung with yews is a conscious expression of the Savage Picturesque (*4*). This landscape campaign and the subsequent replanting of the inner enclosure was probably carried out by Lord Francis Godolphin Osborne, who inherited in 1785 and died at Gogmagog House in 1850.

Not surprisingly, with Newmarket as the important focus of horse racing in the county, at least one other Cambridge house has an important historic racing association. This is **Horseheath Lodge**, not to be confused with Horseheath Hall. The Lodge is a stock brick Regency building set within a small landscaped park through which flows a tributary of the Granta. Both house and park are charming, if unremarkable historically;[8] the interest of the site is in Plenipotentiary, winner of the 1834 Epsom Derby, bred and trained by Stanlake Batson at the Lodge, where there was a training ground called the Gallop. Inside the house there is a plaque, based on an engraving by the Newmarket artist John Frederick Herring, of the great horse with his jockey Conolly aboard. The horse is reported to have 'always looked like a fat bullock in training', but was 'much admired for his beauty and racing points'.[9] The Derby win was the high point of Plenipotentiary's career. It is thought that the horse was doped at the following classic of that season, the St Leger, raced at Doncaster, thereby ruining his constitution; as a result Plenipotentiary never won another classic race. He has pride of place on the village sign, which was presented to the village in 1988 by Sir Arthur Marshall of Horseheath Lodge in memory of his wife, Rosemary Wynford, Lady Marshall.

Another theme in the county's gardens is the association of certain sites with important literary figures and the influence those gardens have had on the creative process. The novelist Graham Greene spent many of his early summer holidays, particularly during the First World War, at his

4 The atmospheric yew walks on the banks of the ditch at Wandlebury probably date to the 1790s and are characteristic of the late eighteenth-century Picturesque aesthetic

uncle's house at **Harston**, south-west of Cambridge on the A10 to Royston. The early eighteenth-century red-brick house is set back from the road within its walled enclosure and on its front lawn is a beautiful Art Nouveau fountain dated 1897. Sir William Graham Greene lived here from 1893 until 1952, but was never at the house when the future novelist was there, being 'very remote'; he stayed 'safely away from any family turbulence' in his bachelor flat off Hanover Square in London.[10] In August 1914, when the future novelist was aged nine, he remembered being sent out from Harston with a basket of apples, freshly picked from the orchard, for tired soldiers resting on Harston Green.[11] That Harston made a strong impression on the young boy is borne out by Greene's desire to be buried alongside the other Greenes in the parish churchyard,[12] and the fact that the garden, or at least an idealised version of it, appears in several of his novels, most notably *The Ministry of Fear*, published in 1943.

To the side of the house is a small rose garden, enclosing a sundial, which has been laid out by the present owners, Francis and Charlotte Clarke, and from here the garden advances into a more heavily planted area and down to a stream bristling with yellow irises. Beyond this is a shadowy walk of yews, box and holly and, further out, the site of an old tennis court. Early Ordnance Survey maps of 1885 and 1903 show the house with walled enclosures to the rear, an orchard beyond and an oval, tree-shaded pool to the north-west. These are the grounds that Greene would have known and loved and they are close to the garden at the convalescent home described in the chapter entitled 'Conversations in Arcady' in book two of *The Ministry of Fear*:

> The garden was of a rambling kind which should have belonged to childhood and only belonged to childish men. The apple trees were old apple trees and gave the effect of growing wild: they sprang unexpectedly up in the middle of a rose-bed, trespassed on a tennis court, shaded the window of a little outside lavatory like a potting-shed which was used by the gardener ... A high red brick wall divided the flower-garden from the kitchen-garden and the orchard, but flowers and fruit could not be imprisoned by a wall ... Beyond the orchard the garden faded gradually out into paddocks and a stream and a big untidy pool with an island the size of a billiard-table.[13]

While Greene is known to have stayed at Harston and fictionalised its grounds, both Lucy M Boston and Rose Macaulay actually lived in the county, at Hemingford Grey Manor and Southernwood, Great Shelford, respectively. The textured manor house at **Hemingford Grey** became the inspiration for Boston's classic set of children's books set in Green Knowe, and it was where she laid out a garden after buying the house in

1937. Its setting could not be more idyllic, right on the banks of the Great Ouse, south-west of St Ives by the Huntingdon border. A gate in the towpath wall leads into a garden scattered with topiary animals and chess pieces centred by a gravel walk leading to the gable end of the brick house of the Paynes, built in 1130 and reputed to be the oldest continuously inhabited house in England. The 'Hemingford Garden Room' is open to the public for a small entrance fee payable to the black honesty box; appropriately, children are free. As well as the topiary shapes, there is a 'Hidden Garden' to the rear of the house past a medieval stone sculpture of St Christopher, while there is a productive kitchen garden alongside one of the surviving arms of the original moat. There is a charming homespun atmosphere to the garden, which is mirrored in one of Boston's fictional passages in *The Chimney of Green Knowe*:

> Tolly went out with dignity, too proud to run, and renewed his acquaintance with the big statue of St. Christopher against the house wall, wrapped around with new strands of tiny bronze ivy leaves ... It stood there gigantic and immovable with stone eyeballs that had been seen but unseeing ever since they were carved in the thirteenth century ... Tolly ran in the garden along the track beside the moat under the trees, and found the green deer cut out of yew, whose leafy neck he rumpled, and the green hare and the green squirrel and the green peacock.[14]

When Rupert Brooke was an undergraduate at Cambridge he was a frequent visitor for Sunday lunch at **Southernwood**, and often went boating with Rose Macaulay on the river at the bottom of the garden. After Somerville College, Oxford, and a time spent in London writing novels and living in a flat with a female friend – her 1913 *The Lee Shore* was a prizewinner – Macaulay had returned home to live with her parents, who had retired to Great Shelford.[15] Her father was a distinguished medieval scholar, a fellow of Trinity who taught English in the University when Brooke was up at King's. He also had a connection with the young poet through Rugby public school, where he had been a master, though before Brooke's time there. The 1906 Ordnance Survey map shows the house just after it had been built, at the end of its entrance drive,

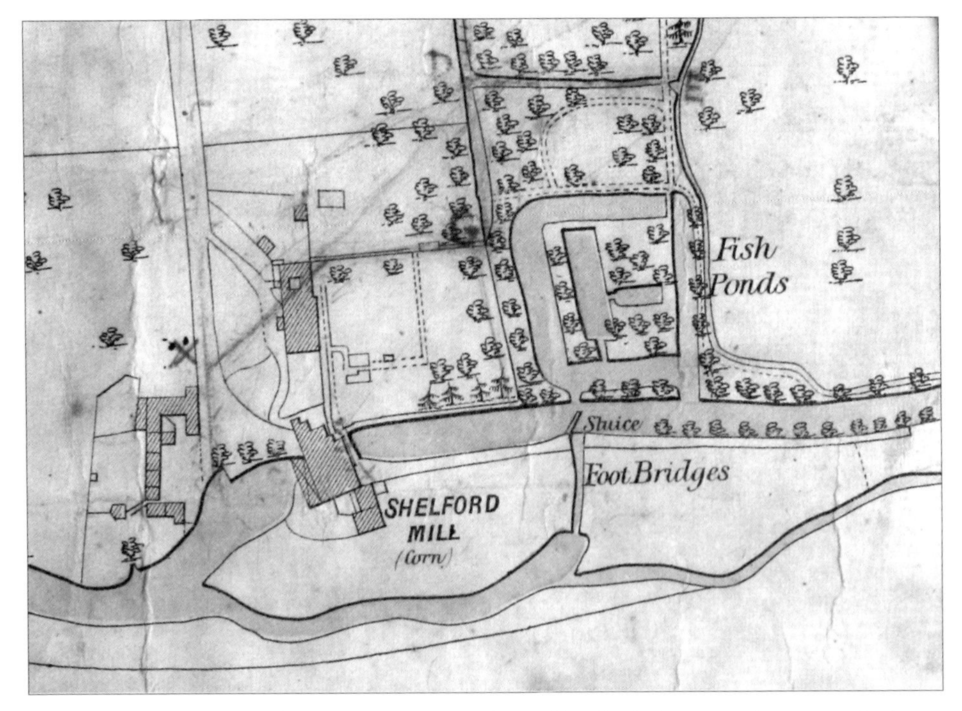

5 The complex water garden at The Grange, Great Shelford, from an 1890 map. *By kind permission of Nicholas Browne*

surrounded by open fields leading down to the river. Lawns and an orchard survive from the original layout, but the land by the river has since been developed for housing. Before this encroachment, Macaulay used the river setting for a garden in her 1909 novel, *The Secret River*, which, appropriately enough, has a blue flower border on its grey cloth hard cover. Brooke was to be similarly inspired by the Cam for one of his most powerful poems on transcendental landscape, 'The Old Vicarage, Grantchester'. However, we must leave Grantchester for a later chapter, to consider the sculpture garden laid out there by Jeffrey, Lord Archer and his wife Dame Mary Archer.

Just along the road from Southernwood, to the south of Church Street, the garden of **The Grange** extends via an ornamental parterre as far as the Cam to take in part of a large moated water garden. This is marked as 'Fish Ponds' on an 1890 map (5), but its design, which incorporates an inner canal, suggests that it was intended to be as much ornamental as productive and is likely to date from the later medieval period.[16] Much of this is fenced off, as the greater section is now part of the adjacent **Kings Mill House** garden, also at Great Shelford. This beautiful brick house of 1825 has a walled garden at the rear in which there is a gate leading to the water garden; its wide, angular reaches are overhung with trees. The children's author Philippa Pearce was brought up here in Great Shelford and it is recorded that this riverine setting was the inspiration for her 1958 book, *Tom's Midnight Garde:* 'Of the four sides of the garden, Tom had already observed that three were walled' and through a hedged tunnel on the fourth side he 'found himself looking out over a meadow'.[17] It might be that the water garden suggested the pond in Tom's garden, but 'the octagonal summer-house with an arcaded base' which overlooked it is likely to be a fictional embellishment more appropriate to an enclosed pleasure garden.

As a final theme in the county's sites, Cambridge University looms large, with the vestiges of many historic gardens surviving within its walled enclosures and an important botanical garden at its heart, not to mention a diaspora of academics, like Emeritus Professor Peter Spufford at **The Guildhall, Whittlesford**, who have found their way out of the town and are now safely billeted in one of the many delightful villages to the south where they tend their own plots. The gardens of the University will find their chronological place in a separate chapter on the seventeenth century, and also in the last chapter, where twentieth-century interventions in the historic cores, across the Cam and wider afield, are treated. But one University garden will serve as a fitting end to this short profile of the county.

As one would expect from a respected archaeologist and palaeoethnobotanist, the **Lucy Cavendish College Physic Garden** is a faithful recreation of a small Anglo-Saxon garden of physical plants. Before she embarked upon the garden at Lucy Cavendish, Dr Jane Renfrew had already designed the Redegund Garden at Jesus College to commemorate the patron saint of the twelfth-century nunnery that pre-dated the founding of the college. On the north side of the hall at Jesus she laid out two flowerbeds of apothecaries' roses and violets, saffron crocuses, Madonna lilies and a selection of trees: pears, crab apples and a bay to signify the miracle St Radegund performed with a bay tree. But the Lucy Cavendish Physic Garden came about when Dr Renfrew took on a doctoral student, Debbie Bannen, an archaeologist with a botanical bent who was working on the uses of plants in the Anglo-Saxon period. Excavations in Winchester, which Dr Renfrew supervised, and the creation of another garden in Shaftesbury led, via the re-planting with herbs of the Master's Garden at Jesus, to the Physic Garden at Lucy Cavendish. In the small, hedged enclosure, set out in four quadrants and lined with narrow brick paths, all the plants are those proven by archaeology to have been grown for medicinal and healing purposes in the Anglo-Saxon period. At the centre is a modern cast of a Pictish carved stone, made by a firm in Glasgow, which conveys the correct air of scholarly historicism.

Such attention to accurate detail is rare in the county and almost unheard of in the University, whose historic garden enclosures have been allowed generally to revert to lawns edged with suburban flower borders. The scholarly recreation of an Anglo-Saxon garden at Lucy Cavendish brings early gardens to mind, but there are none surviving in the county. However, this lack of physical horticultural evidence is more than made up for by the complexity of many of Cambridgeshire's early moated sites, where surrounding earthworks can often give a clue, at least, to the form and purpose of the original garden layouts.

1

Wimpole Hall – 'a flower in the desert'

CAMBRIDGESHIRE CONSPICUOUSLY LACKS MAJOR COUNTRY HOUSES SET within landscape parks or, indeed, significant gardens. The anomaly is Wimpole Hall, eight miles south-west of Cambridge and six miles north of Royston, the development of which reads like a veritable *Who's Who* of garden and landscape history. Wimpole presents, as the National Trust claims in its guidebook, almost a 'case-book history of English gardening from 1690 to 1830'.[1] Well-known names associated with its successive landscape campaigns include George London and Henry Wise, Charles Bridgeman, Robert Greening, Sanderson Miller, Lancelot 'Capability' Brown, James 'Athenian' Stuart, William Emes and Humphry Repton, who produced one of his Red Books for Wimpole in 1801. This exhaustive roll-call appears to have depleted Cambridgeshire's entitlement to celebrated garden designers and landscape architects, leaving the rest of the county largely bereft. The parkland that survives today is a complex overlay of the work of these important designers. Wimpole's last private owners, Captain George Bambridge and his wife Elsie, completed the landscaping in the twentieth century.

The house (*colour 3*) stands within 20 acres of garden and 500 acres of formal and landscaped park, with walled kitchen gardens and a working farm to the far north-east. Wimpole's estate straddles the junction of flat clay lands that extend west from the city of Cambridge, with steepening chalk grounds leading south-west to the Chilterns.[2] This topographical siting takes advantage of dramatically diverse vistas from the Hall, a rarity in a predominantly level county. To the south, the land opens out and rolls away towards Royston; to the north and east it slopes steadily upwards to Johnson's Hill, the highest point of the estate. Perhaps the most impressive feature of the Hall's setting is Bridgeman's replanted South Avenue, which runs towards the main entrance. The original line of trees was planted around 1720, a similar avenue to the north having been removed when the grounds were landscaped in the eighteenth century.

Wimpole's architectural history is just as complex as the development of its gardens. The red-brick house is easily the largest and most impressive in the county, comprising a vast south front flanked by five-bay extensions to either side. The oldest section, the seven-bay central façade, is the work of Sir Thomas Chicheley, owner, architect and staunch Royalist, and was completed around 1650.[3] This house was extended at the end of the seventeenth century under the 2nd Earl of Radnor. His scheme was recorded in a 1707 engraving by Jan Kip, taken from a lost drawing by his business partner, Leonard Knyff. The engraving depicts a large range of eleven bays with a pediment above, which was never built. However, the two projecting wings, each nine windows wide, were realised. Radnor sold Wimpole to the Duke of Newcastle, who died only a year later in 1711 following a hunting accident. Edward Harley, 2nd Earl of Oxford and Earl Mortimer, then inherited the estate through his wife, Henrietta Cavendish-Holles, the duke's daughter. It was Oxford's protégé James Gibbs who extended Wimpole's frontage, also adding the western library wing and chapel between 1713 and 1721. At the same time, Gibbs designed carved urns and busts for the northern gardens. These were moved to the front of the house in the nineteenth century and now dramatise the south-eastern and south-western corners of the south railing screen.[4]

In 1740, Philip Yorke, 1st Earl of Hardwicke and Lord Chancellor, who had acquired Wimpole the previous year, commissioned Henry Flitcroft to carry out work on the house. Both Radnor and Oxford before him had been forced to sell Wimpole to pay off increasing debts, but as one of England's leading lawyers, expense was of no consequence to Lord Hardwicke. Flitcroft refaced the old house in red brick to match Gibbs' newer

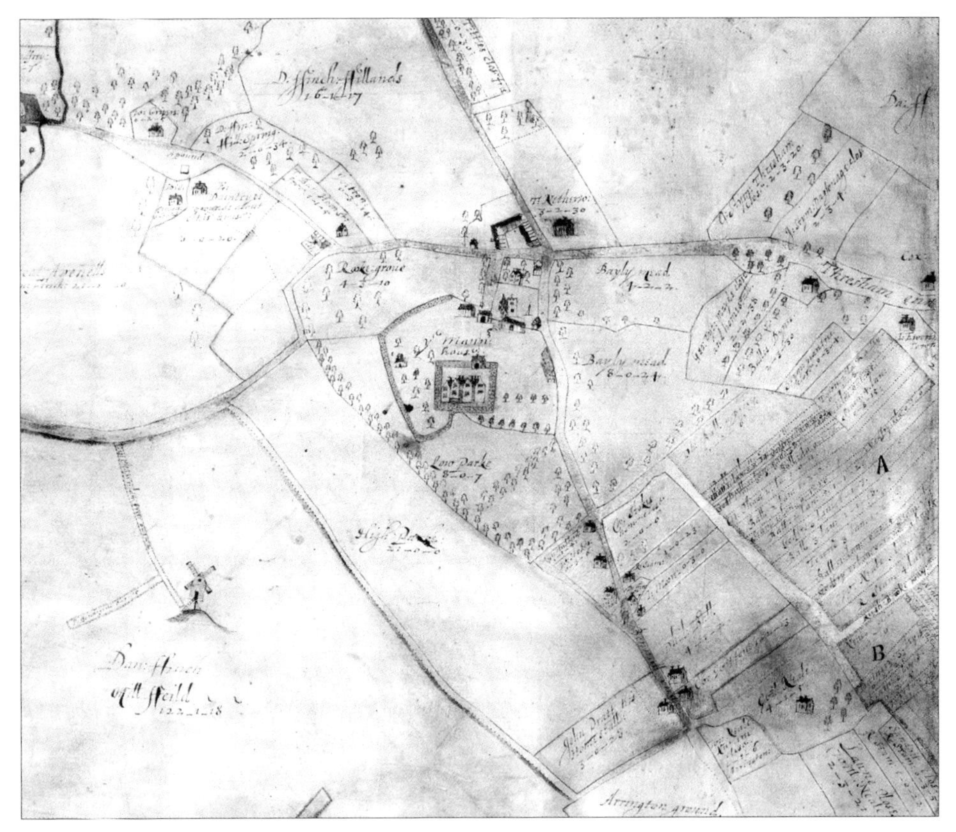

6 Benjamin Hare's 1638 map of the Wimpole estate shows the moated site of the original house. *Cambridgeshire Archives*

wings, a job which had been left unfinished when Oxford ran out of funds. Under the Hardwickes, Wimpole was then altered by a succession of notable architects. These included James Thornhill, Sir John Soane and H E Kendall, whose towered wings, which had been built for the 4th Earl, were fortunately demolished in 1953.[5] The 5th Earl, known as 'Champagne Charlie' because of his lavish lifestyle, was the last of the Hardwickes to live at Wimpole. In 1894 he sold the estate to the 2nd Lord Robartes and 6th Viscount Clifden, a direct descendant of Earl Radnor, who had owned Wimpole two hundred years previously. The Hall finally left private ownership in 1976, when Elsie Bambridge, Rudyard Kipling's daughter, gifted it along with 3,000 acres to the National Trust.

Before Thomas Chicheley began work on the present Hall in the seventeenth century, Wimpole was a small medieval manor, set in a modest deer-park of 200 acres. To the north and south of this were three medieval villages called Bennall End, Thresham End and Green End. The earliest visual reference to the estate is Benjamin Hare's map of 1638, unconventionally orientated with east at the top (*6*).[6] This estate plan was commissioned by Chicheley only two years before building work started on his new house, and records the original gabled building approached by a pair of gatehouses, described as an 'old faire house'. It was sited in a rectangular moat to the north of the Hall, with a 'High Parke' and 'Low Parke' marked by banks containing avenues of trees to the north and west of it. By 1641, the county historian John Layer noted that 'Thomas Chicheley Esq lord of this village is now constructing an extraordinary curious neat house near the ancient site',[7] and all traces of Wimpole's medieval moated manor were subsequently lost.

We know little of Chicheley's garden scheme for his new house, which he built in a modern style with a central Dutch gable and hipped roof. He might have laid out a rectangular formal garden around the house, but he certainly enclosed the park and planted a grand avenue to the south.[8] Extravagant and provocative, as a politician Chicheley was expelled at one time or another from both the Long Parliament and the Privy Council, relying on his tennis prowess to regain courtly favour. Charles II supposedly had himself weighed after a match with Chicheley to gauge just how much weight he had lost during the game.[9] Samuel Pepys described Chicheley as living 'in mighty great fashion' and eating 'in the French manner'.[10] Not surprisingly, like several future owners of Wimpole, he ended his life in financial embarrassment.

Earl Radnor was similarly deemed to be 'mad good-nature, bounty misapplied', this time by Alexander Pope.[11] Radnor was one of the principal supporters of the new king, William III, and Kip's engraving suggests that by the end of the seventeenth century he had carried out a grandiose transformation of Wimpole's gardens, to complement his extension of the house (*7*). In the absence of any seventeenth-century architectural drawings for Wimpole, Kip's engraving is an important record of the improvements made by Chicheley and Radnor. First the Earl mapped out a rectangular formal garden on the north-south axis, presumably on the foundations of Chicheley's original plot. Then he dug out a water garden to the south-west of the Hall, the banks of which survive today, and hollowed out a series of formal fishponds to the far north of the park, towards Johnson's Hill. Between 1693 and 1705, Radnor sought professional advice from one of the greatest partnerships in

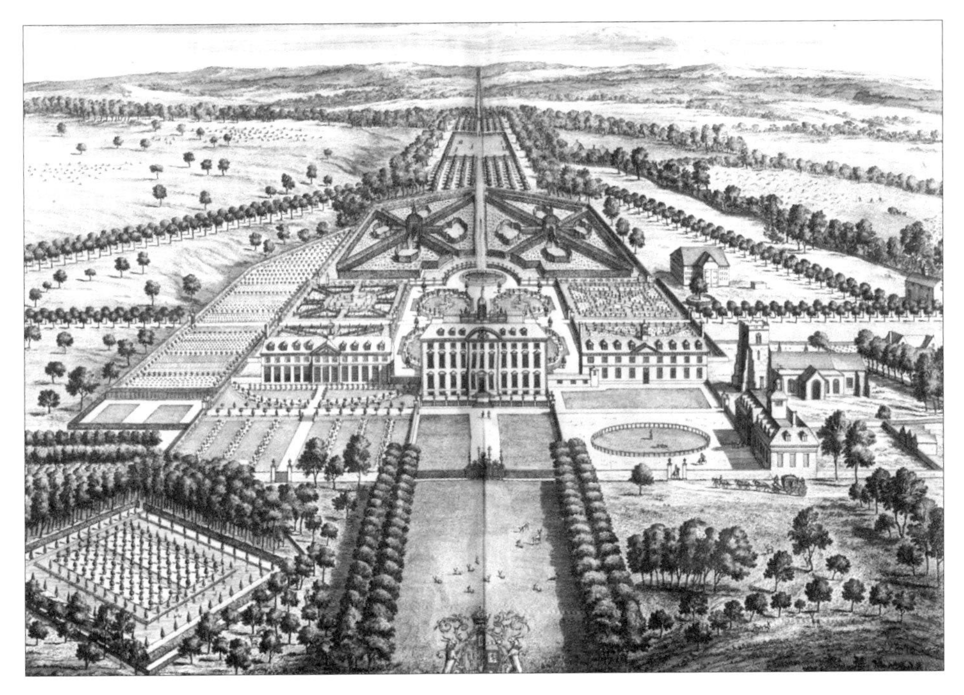

7 A bird's eye view of Wimpole from Leonard Knyff and Jan Kip's 1707 *Britannia Illustrata* – the most elaborate Franco-Dutch formal layout in the county. *Bristol University Special Collections*

British gardening: George London and Henry Wise. They extended Wimpole's northern garden in a Franco-Dutch style, with vast parterres, box hedging, intersecting alleys and magnificent statuary. As nurserymen, London and Wise held the monopoly on such large-scale gardens, as they could first design for, and then supply landowners with, the thousands of trees needed for avenue planting. Daniel Defoe described Wimpole's garden at this time as 'adorn'd with all the Natural Beauties of Situation;

and to which was added all the most exquisite Contrivances which the best Heads cou'd Invent to make it artificially as well as naturally pleasant'.[12] Together with Radnor's vision for the house, London and Wise brought a continental Baroque grandeur to Cambridgeshire.

As each owner of Wimpole left his mark on the architecture of the Hall, so they extended and revised the gardens. Under the 2nd Earl of Oxford, Wimpole flourished as a late Baroque estate, a grand setting from which to entertain fellow Tory sympathisers and house his great collections. Zachary Grey's memoir describes Lord Oxford as 'indeed rich, but thankful; charitable without ostentation; and that in so good-natured a way as never to give to the persons whom he obliged in that respect'.[13] From 1721 onwards, Lord Oxford employed Charles Bridgeman to rework and extend London and Wise's layout. Bridgeman had trained at the Brompton Park Nursery alongside the two men, and later became Wise's partner in the role of joint Chief Gardeners to George I, responsible for Hampton Court, Kensington, Newmarket, Windsor and St James's Palace. There is also some evidence to suggest that Bridgeman's father had been Lord Oxford's head gardener and still lived on the Wimpole estate. To the south of the Hall, where Gibbs was busy extending the house with symmetrical wings, Bridgeman laid out new gardens in his transitional style, 'straddling the divide between the formality of the previous age and the "natural style" of the succeeding one' with paths, bosquets and clipped hedges.[14] He recorded his intentions in a series of surveys of the park, variously dated 1720 and 1721.[15]

Bridgeman's most noted feature, the three-mile long South Avenue, was planted with double lines of elms 50 feet apart, across a central space of 90 yards. It originally stretched from the south front of the Hall to beyond the Cambridge road, encircling a large octagonal basin fed by the River Cam. As successive generations of landscape gardeners naturalised Wimpole, this avenue stubbornly survived; a truncated version exists today as rows of limes, grafted from trees on the estate. As Humphry Repton wrote in his 1801 Wimpole Red Book, the avenue was 'on too vast

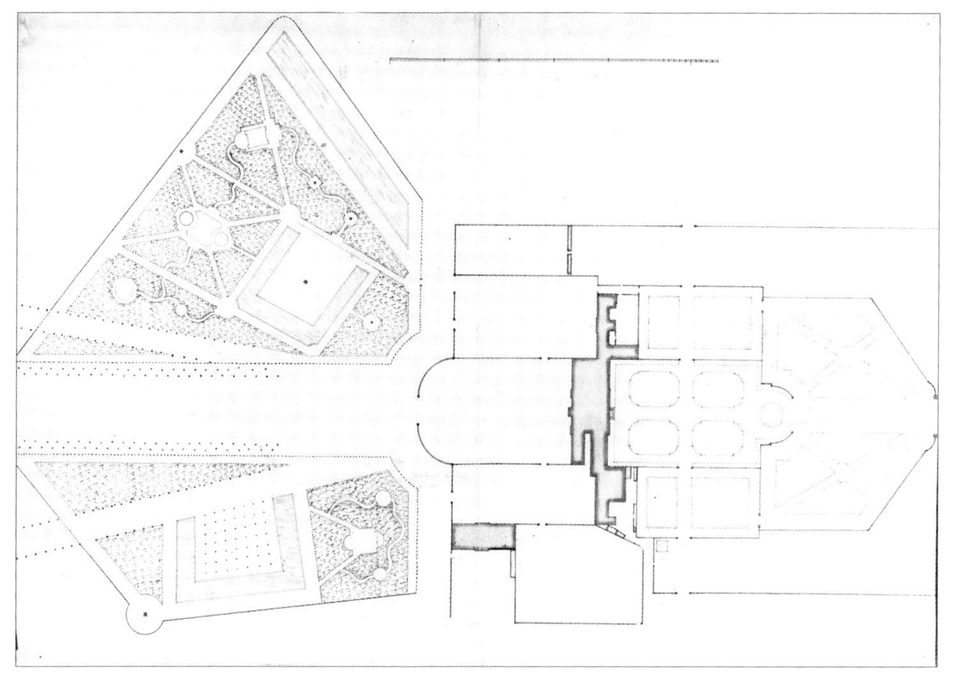

8 Charles Bridgeman's map of Wimpole, recording a geometrically formal area by the house and two, more informal, enclosures with serpentine paths set within a notional *patte d'oie*. *National Trust*

a scale to be destroyed by the new system and therefore it remains as a specimen of former Magnificence'.[16] Together with this main double avenue, Bridgeman also created two diagonal vistas flanking a smaller, narrower avenue laid out at the end of the previous century by London and Wise for Earl Radnor (*8*).

Unfortunately for Lord Oxford, his wife's excessive fortune was not enough to keep him in the manner to which he had become accustomed. As a Tory he was excluded from office, and a combination of political inertia and spiralling debts forced him to take solace in drink. On 4 November 1739, the Wimpole estate, heavily mortgaged, was sold for £86,740 to Philip Yorke, 1st Earl of Hardwicke and Lord Chancellor.[17] For the frustrated Lord Oxford this would have been a heavy blow, for Hardwicke was one of the most successful of all the Whig party leaders. Sure enough, Mrs Delany wrote that Lord Oxford 'has of late been so entirely given up to drinking, that his life has been no pleasure to him or satisfaction to his friends ... He has had no enjoyment of the world since his mismanagement of his affairs; it has hurt his body and mind, and *hastened his death*'.[18] Similarly, Lady Mary Wortley Montagu believed that he had advanced his own end 'by choice, refusing all remedies till it was too late to make use of them. There was a will found dated 1728 in which he gave everything to my Lady, which has affected her very much, notwithstanding the many reasons she has to complain of him'.[19] At his death, Lord Oxford's library totalled 50,000 items, with the additions of 41,000 prints and 350,000 pamphlets.[20] Just like Radnor and Chicheley before him, the expansion and enhancement of the Wimpole estate had significantly contributed to his ruin.

Unlike Lord Oxford, who was survived only by a daughter, Chancellor Hardwicke had five sons, and over the next 150 years Wimpole remained in the stable hands of five generations of the same family. Hardwicke also enjoyed one of the most brilliant political careers of the eighteenth century, with even George II failing to recognise him after he left office, so seldom had he been seen without his judicial robes and powdered wig.[21] Contemporary opinion of the Hardwickes was sharply divided. Horace Walpole complained of the 'miserable and pernicious turn of the whole family, than which nothing can be more illiberal and wretched, though possessed of immense wealth and the children matched in to the most wealthy families'.[22] The Chancellor needed a fashionable estate to enhance his family's standing in society; a house and garden so imposing that his political position would be unquestionable. The antiquated Baroque interiors favoured by his predecessor's despondent Tory set were duly ripped out, and in 1742 Henry Flitcroft was charged with re-facing the jumbled hotchpotch of styles which characterised the south front of the Hall.

Once the house was elegant and uniform, Lord Chancellor Hardwicke turned his attention to the pleasure grounds. London and Wise's northern parterres and gravelled walks, which had largely survived Bridgeman's wider landscape interventions of the 1720s, were by this time deemed woefully unfashionable. The Chancellor therefore decided to

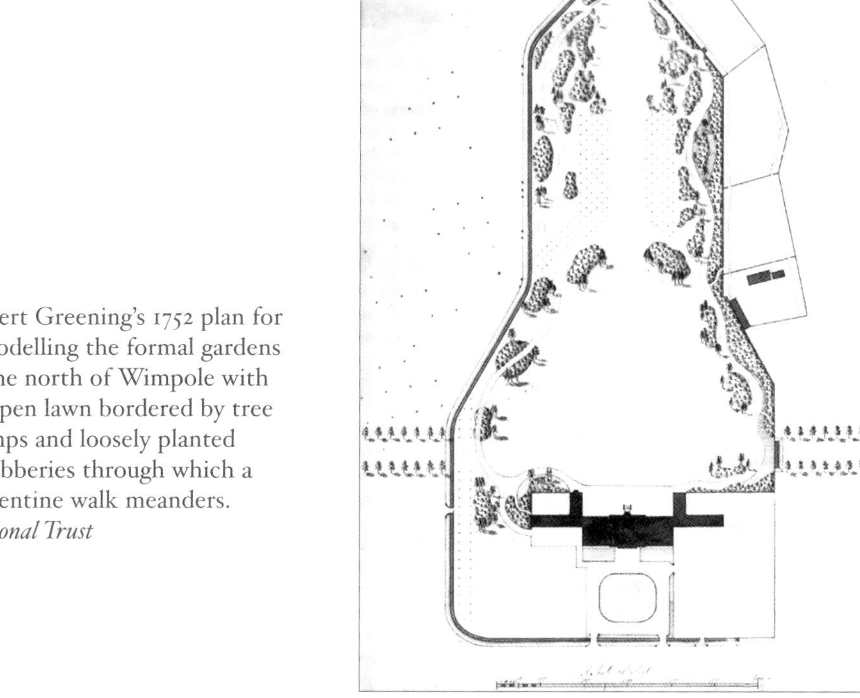

9
Robert Greening's 1752 plan for remodelling the formal gardens to the north of Wimpole with an open lawn bordered by tree clumps and loosely planted shrubberies through which a serpentine walk meanders.
National Trust

employ Robert Greening of Brentford, son of the successful nursery gardener Thomas Greening, to redesign the layout to the north of the Hall. Greening, like Bridgeman before him, came to Cambridgeshire bearing royal credentials, having previously worked for Princess Augusta at Kew. His plan for Wimpole, dated 1752 (9), shows how he replaced London and Wise's geometric plats with informal lawned areas, naturalised the symmetrical bosquets and bowling green beyond, and added a serpentine walk around the perimeter.[23] Views to the west of the house were created by cutting through axial rows of trees 'to form the horse chestnuts into clumps, so as to open the view up the side of the hill from the house and garden'.[24] Greening also moved the walled kitchen gardens to the east of this new layout, enabling the Hardwicke family's gardeners to grow exotic fruits against a new heated hot wall.

By mid-century, the estate covered 11,000 acres of this part of the county, as well as another 8,000 in the fens, extending into parts of Hertfordshire, Hampshire and Suffolk.[25] Under Chancellor Hardwicke's direction, Greening and an army of gardeners had transformed Wimpole's old gardens from the formality of parterres and fenced enclosures into an emergent landscape park with sunken ha-has. In 1753, some fourteen years before Lancelot Brown arrived at Wimpole, the Chancellor's daughter-in-law, Jemima, Marchioness Grey, wrote to her friend Mary Talbot describing this radical change:

> I have found here quite a New Place, my Lord having now completed his Gardens, & nothing ever made a greater change or a more different scene. Instead of straight Gravel walks with Borders & Cross plots surrounded by walls, & views into the Park through Iron Gates, there is now a large green Lawn behind the House, bounded by Clumps of Trees & flowering shrubs, a broad serpentine walk through them, & enclosed with a Sunk Fence that lets the Park quite into the Garden.[26]

This increasing fashion for informality was the catalyst for Wimpole's most important garden building, the Gothick Folly (*colour 4*). As early as 1749, while Flitcroft was still busy rebuilding the parish church, the Chancellor simultaneously employed the gentleman architect Sanderson Miller to design a romantic ruined castle. Sited to the far north of the house, this would be the focus of a spectacular view from the Hall. The Chancellor had been inspired by Miller's Sham Castle at Hagley in Worcestershire, built in 1747, which gained Walpole's praise as bearing 'the true rust of the Barons' Wars'.[27] In 1749, George Lyttelton, owner of Hagley, wrote to Miller with the news that Chancellor Hardwicke 'wanted to see the Plan of my Castle, having a mind to Build one at Wimple himself ... but differing in many respects, particularly in this, that he wants no House or even room in it, but mearly the Walls and Semblance of an Old Castle to make an object from his House'.[28] Miller drew a series of elevations for the Wimpole Folly between 1749 and 1751, but building work only began in about 1768; it was eventually realised by the Chancellor's son and daughter-in-law.

10 Sanderson Miller's drawing of the Folly at Wimpole – a direct descendant of his Sham Castle at Hagley Hall, Worcestershire. It is a welcome visual focus in an otherwise dull Brownian park. *National Trust*

Sir Joshua Reynolds, painter and first president of the Royal Academy, proclaimed: 'we have naturally a veneration for antiquity, whatever building brings to our remembrance ancient customs and manners, such as the Castles of the Barons of Ancient Chivalry, is sure to give ... delight'.[29] As an early example of revived Gothic, Wimpole's Folly was consciously designed by Miller to trigger the imagination with an association of ideas (*10*).[30] Composed of three circular towers linked by false walls, with doors, pointed openings and one ecclesiastical window, the Gothick Folly continues to capture the imagination. Built after twenty or so years of planning, it involved two generations of patrons and designers: Chancellor Hardwicke and Miller, and his son Philip Yorke, the 2nd Earl, with Capability Brown, aided by the Cambridge antiquary and pioneering scholar of the Gothic Revival, James Essex.[31]

Together with his wife, the brilliant Marchioness Grey, the 2nd Earl toured England's most cutting-edge gardens, recording their developments methodically in a travel journal. These included Shugborough in Staffordshire, where his brother-in-law, Thomas Anson, was busy creating a Chinese island complex complete with oriental planting, teahouse and junk. On succeeding to the title in 1764, the couple took up permanent residence in Cambridgeshire, bringing to Wimpole their enthusiasm for landscape improvements. They had already employed Brown at Wrest Park in Bedfordshire, the estate Jemima had inherited from her grandfather. It is not surprising that they charged Brown and Essex with the resurrection of the Folly plans when Miller was unable or unwilling to continue the project. On 30 October 1767, Lady Annabel Yorke, the Earl's eldest daughter, wrote: 'I ought in justice to afford as much paper to the great Mr Brown, who has been two days here surveying his Improvements, [which] as yet furnish no great matter for Description, nor the Tower neither, tho' that our architect Mr Essex promises will make a figure next year.'[32]

Essex was right, and upon its completion Wimpole's Folly was hailed as a textbook exemplar of the architecture of the Gothic Revival. The Marchioness, however, was not overly impressed. She was a lover of the emerging Picturesque aesthetic, and called into question Brown's alteration of the original intention, complaining:

> The Tower is better for being raised, but the additions Mr. Brown has [made have] quite changed [it] from our plan [Miller's original plan], though he undertook to follow it, and said he liked it. That is, he has 'Unpicturesqued it' by making it a mere continuous solid object, instead of a Broken one. The wall – which is still going on – is continued entire at the bottom from the whole Tower to the Broken one, and is to be fractured only in the upper half of the Gateway, which is, I believe to resemble our design. However as it makes altogether a greater object it won't do ill, and the upper part of the wall, if well done, may yet be sufficiently varied.[33]

As with all garden buildings erected in this style, political readings of the Gothick Folly have been suggested. David Adshead argues that in the

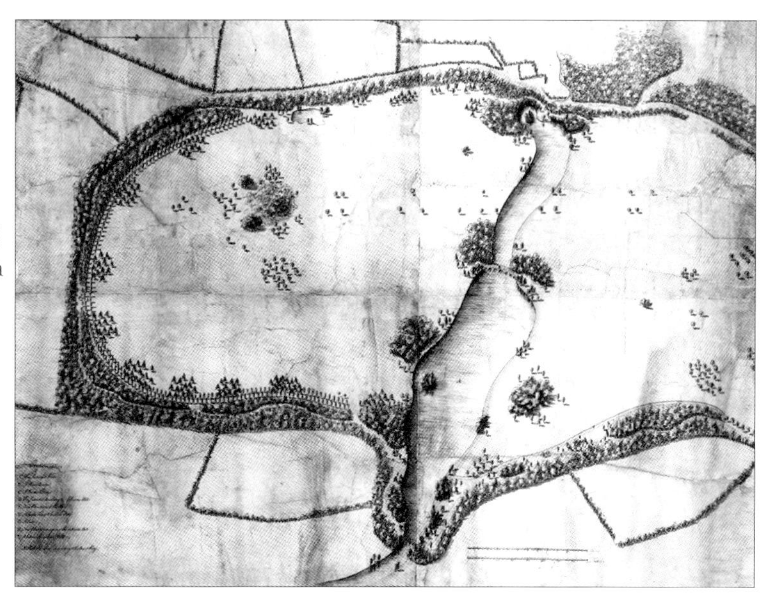

11
Lancelot Brown's proposals to remove the hedges and field boundaries from the farmland at Wimpole, replacing them with smooth grass, and to create a tree-lined ride on three sides of the park.
National Trust

eighteenth century medieval defensive architecture could be associated with the notion of political opposition,[34] although it was also confusingly co-opted by political opponents. The most famous example of Gothick being used to symbolise a political agenda is, of course, James Gibbs' 1741 Temple of Liberty at Stowe in Buckinghamshire, which was built for Lord Cobham, who supported the Whigs in opposition to their First Minister, Sir Robert Walpole.[35]

At the time of the 2nd Earl's succession, Wimpole's estate was considerable, but the gardens around the house were still of a 'comparatively modest size'.[36] Consequently, while work was being completed on the Folly, Brown set about landscaping Wimpole's northern parkland. This had previously been leased as arable land to Zachary Moul and William Ratford, tenant farmers of Chancellor Hardwicke. Writing to Brown on Christmas Eve 1767, the young Earl expressed the hope that the landscape gardener might 'have the leasure in the Holy days to make out the minute for our proceedings at Wimpole'.[37] Brown's subsequent plan of the same date (*11*) shows how he tore down the hedges and field boundaries of the previously farmed land and laid the whole area to smooth grass.[38] Finally, he bounded the eastern, northern and western sides of the considerably extended parkland with a three-mile-long, tree-lined ride.

To the north of the park, Earl Radnor's two surviving square fishponds were naturalised into a chain of serpentine pools linked by a wooden Chinese bridge. These survive today and lie in the shallow valley to the north-west of the house, between the ha-ha and the Gothick Folly. The third lake, which does not appear on the 1767 plan, and for which Brown received an extra £980, was added some time later to the east.[39] Lastly, he cut gaps through the old North Avenue to allow vistas through the trees whilst still focusing the eye on the Gothick Folly and Johnson's Hill, the highest point of the estate. Marchioness Grey was at once exulted and exhausted, writing to Catherine Talbot in 1769 that

> Mr. Brown has been leading me such a Fairy Circle, & his Magic Wand has raised such landscapes to the Eye – not visionary for they were all there but his Touch has brought them out with the same Effect as a Painter's Pencil upon canvass that after having hobbled over rough Ground to Points that I had never seen before, for two Hours, I return half Tired, & half Foot sore, & really must break off, it being just Dinner-time & post time.[40]

After the Gothick Folly's completion, and in a conscious attempt to revive the architecture of the ancients within their pleasure grounds, Yorke and his wife employed the archaeologist and dilettante James 'Athenian' Stuart. One of the pioneers of neo-Classicism, Stuart had worked at Shugborough for the Earl's brother-in-law throughout the 1760s. At Wimpole he was commissioned to build a classical temple, which was demolished in the late nineteenth century, on the slopes to the west of the main house.[41] This building was known variously as the 'Hill House', 'Prospect House', 'Palladian Building' or 'Belvedere', and functioned as a summerhouse and viewing station. Wimpole's status as one of the greatest landscape gardens of its time was cemented by the inclusion of illustrations of both the Prospect House and the Gothick Folly in

Josiah Wedgewood's 1773-4 Imperial Russian dinner service made for Catherine the Great. The contrast between the two buildings was mirrored by others at Hagley, where Stuart had in 1758 built a Temple of Theseus in direct contrast to Miller's earlier Gothick Castle. In the nineteenth century, Humphry Repton would adapt the Prospect House somewhat prosaically, filling in the elegant open loggia on the ground floor and converting the whole into a labourer's cottage. At the same time, he transformed the Gothick Folly into a more practical keeper's lodge.

From 1790 onwards, Sir John Soane was employed extensively at Wimpole by 'Philly' Yorke, the 3rd Earl of Hardwicke, who had inherited the title through his father, the Hon Charles Yorke, younger brother to the 2nd Earl. Soane had met and impressed his future patron during the younger man's tour of the Continent, as a letter dated 31 January 1779 from Philly to his uncle back home at Wimpole testifies: 'The three temples of Paestum of the old Doric order are magnificent buildings and I was astonished to find how perfect they are. An English architect by name Soane who is an ingenious man now studying at Rome accompanied us thither and measured the buildings'.[42] Soane's first work for Philly was undertaken during the 1780s at his Hertfordshire home, Hamels. This gained him the much greater Cambridgeshire commission upon his patron's elevation to the earldom. Soane carried out various internal alterations to the house at Wimpole, the most impressive being his two-storey Yellow Drawing Room, which he inserted ingeniously into the north-western corner of the oldest block.

During this time, the 3rd Earl consulted William Emes, a professional improver of estates who worked in an essentially Brownian manner, as a landscaping foil to Soane's architectural works. His 'Survey and part proposal for the Park at Wimpole' (*colour 5*) is dated 1790 and was hugely ambitious.[43] In reality, Emes achieved much less than he proposed, but he did move Greening's kitchen garden, built for Chancellor Hardwicke, to its present location to the north-east of the Hall. He also planted up the area between the two extensively, and encircled the walled kitchen gardens with a belt of trees to screen them from the growing farmyard. Emes also removed Greening's shrubberies to the north of the Hall, where they had been planted to conceal the outlines of London and Wise's complex parterres, demolishing all evidence of the nurserymen's work. In addition, as the plan shows, he proposed widening and extending Brown's series of pools, as well as digging out a new serpentine lake to extend across the southern part of the park from east to west. Neither of these proposals was realised, and Bridgeman's South Avenue was once again saved.

As well as holding the office of Lord Lieutenant of Cambridgeshire between 1790 and 1834, the 3rd Earl was passionately keen on agricultural advancements, as was the fashion at the end of the century, and commissioned Soane to design Home Farm for the estate. This was built to the far north-east of the Hall, beyond Emes' new kitchen gardens. William Cobbett described the 3rd Earl as 'a gentleman chiefly distinguished for his good library in St. James's Square, and understanding the fattening of sheep as well as any man in Cambridgeshire'.[44] Soane's various drawings for the Home Farm, along with assorted cottages, are dated 1793-4. They incorporated cow stalls, stables for draught-horses and the surviving Great Barn, as well as an elaborate octagonal dairy and farmhouse, neither of which was built to his designs. Previously, Soane had constructed a similar dairy-cum-tearoom at Hamels for the Earl's wife, Elizabeth Lindsay, where she ate strawberries and pored over romantic novels.[45] This rustic building functioned both practically, as a working dairy, but also aesthetically, as a picturesque evocation of the pastoral within the landscape. Despite the fact that Wimpole's Home Farm was never as extensive as the original plans had intended, it nevertheless served a similar purpose. Soane's complex was simultaneously modern and productive, as well as being a nostalgic reminder of the simple life of the Ancients.

Sadly, in the nineteenth century Wimpole Hall's Home Farm was diminished still further when some of the carefully designed rustic buildings were pulled down to accommodate more cowsheds. At this time, Soane's *Castello d'Acqua* or reservoir-house, which was built in about 1795 and sited at the southern end of Brown's eastern ride, also disappeared, along with Stuart's Prospect House.[46] Today, the Great Barn houses a museum, while the Home Farm is one of the largest rare breed centres in the country, where Grand White Park cattle once again graze the parkland.

In 1801 the 3rd Earl, now Lord Lieutenant of Ireland, called in Repton to modernise Wimpole's gardens still further. This commission was most likely the result of personal recommendation, as in 1792 Repton had produced a Red Book for Edward Craggs-Eliot, 1st Baron Eliot, who was the father-in-law of Caroline Yorke, the 3rd Earl's stepsister. At Wimpole, Repton extended the shelterbelt of trees, planted by Brown around the perimeter of the estate, to the north-east of the park, in order to accommodate new carriage drives. He also advocated that the entire Hall be whitewashed. This last recommendation was ignored, along with many others, including placing a boat on the lakes so that the water would be visible from the house.

Repton's main concern with Wimpole, as with many other estates that he worked on, was its lack of formal garden areas. He wrote fervently: 'there is no part of Mr. Brown's system which I have had more difficulty in correcting than the absurd fashion of bringing cattle to the windows of a house. It is called natural, but to me it has ever appeared unnatural that a palace should rise immediately out of a sheep pasture'.[47] Repton wanted to re-introduce an enclosed garden area to the north of the Hall (*colour 6*), and argued for an iron railing to be inserted between the outer corners of the two wings, with a central gateway leading out into the park.[48] Something resembling this garden was eventually laid out around 1825 by the 3rd Earl's land agent, Robert Withers. However, Lady Elizabeth quashed Repton's idea for a wall of railings, noting firmly in the margin of the Red Book that 'This would cost too much money – and the effect doubtful'. The Earl's wife might have enjoyed playing milkmaid at Hamels, but despite her romantic leanings she was also a pragmatist, and was not to be persuaded.

Repton's proposal for re-instating a formal garden between the two northern wings is not, as is frequently presumed, the gaudy area of parterres edged with box that visitors can wander around today (*colour 7*), which was laid out by The National Trust in the 1990s. Rather, with minimal 'improvements' carried out (and the Great Conservatory, which he built with his son to adjoin the western end of the house, long since demolished), Repton's only legacy at Wimpole is his realignment of the eastern drive. It was left to Henry Edward Kendall to erect the troublesome iron railings, during his work for Charles Yorke, the 4th Earl, in the 1840s, albeit further away from the house than Repton had suggested. During this time the area enclosed by Withers was taken up with a Victorian formal garden of flowerbeds and herbaceous borders. Other than replanting this garden, no new landscaping schemes were devised under either the 4th or the 5th Earls of Hardwicke.

Without a doubt, the most successful of all the National Trust's restoration projects is the spectacular renovation of Emes' walled Kitchen Garden. Accessed via the shrubbery to the north-east of the house, it is, in fact, a double-walled enclosure of two acres. The first gated entry, concealed amidst evergreen plantings, leads into an expansive orchard with flower borders flanking the outside of the inner walls (*colour 8*). The interior walls support espaliered fruit trees and enclose productive vegetable beds. These are divided into quadrants, set around a fountain pool in the centre. There is also an abundance of herbaceous borders, running along the two main axes and inner walls, brimming with lavender, iris, echinacea and dahlia. These beds are formal and symmetrical, as are many productive plots, serving to frame the garden's structural focus: Soane's elegant glasshouse, designed in 1793 while he was still at work inside the Hall.

During springtime, the shrubbery is quilted with many varieties of narcissus and daffodil, all planted by Elsie Bambridge in the twentieth century. Apart from her yearly additions of these bulbs, Wimpole's gardens were relatively ignored by its last private owners; instead the Bambridges concentrated on knocking down Kendall's wings and restoring the inside of the Hall, which had been left bare by the 7th Viscount Clifden, to its former magnificence. The complex chronology of the estate's development and the roll-call of distinguished architects and landscape gardeners who worked there is almost unprecedented in England.

Repton might have been prone to obsequious exaggeration when attempting to flatter prospective patrons into commissioning one of his designs. However, at Wimpole he came near to the truth when he wrote to the 3rd Earl of Hardwicke that

> The counties of Cambridge and Huntingdon consist generally of flat ground and cornfields with few hedges or trees; while the few hills are yet more naked; but Wimpole abounds in beautiful shapes of ground and is richly clothed with wood – it is therefore like a flower in the desert, beautiful in itself but more beautiful by its situation.[49]

2

Watery enclosures and the progresses of a queen

Guilden Morden Hall · Kingston Wood Manor · Landwade Manor
Burwash Manor · Lopham's Hall · Manor Farm, Great Eversden
Castle Farm, Castle Camps · Bury Farm, Meldreth
Rippington Manor, Great Gransden · The Old House, Eltisley
Little Linton · Catley Park · Harlton Garden Remains
Swaffham Bulbeck Abbey · Denny Abbey · The Burystead
Kirtling Tower · Sawston Hall · Childerley Hall · Haslingfield Hall

EARLY GARDENS ARE NOTORIOUSLY DIFFICULT TO PIN DOWN AND, WHERE they do survive, as tantalising earthworks often associated with moats, their remains are difficult to interpret precisely. Cambridgeshire is rich in such moated sites, with 63 examples in west Cambridgeshire alone. The Royal Commission on Historical Monuments has defined these as homestead moats, garden moats and unclassified moats.[1] While it is the garden moats that will be worth pursuing here, there are several other sites, such as that at Harlton, where water forms an important feature of what might have been a designed landscape. At other moated sites there is always the distinct possibility that the inner enclosure contained a garden laid out around the environs of the house. One such is the idyllic setting of **Guilden Morden Hall** (*colour 9*). An early plan (*12*) shows that it had a garden within the moat and an orchard outside the inner enclosure, but still bounded by water.[2] There was a similar arrangement at **Kingston Wood Manor**, originally Kingston Wood Farm, just south of Bourn close to Ermine Street. An estate map of 1720 shows the gabled Tudor house, just before it was given a classical front, set within its D-shaped moat,

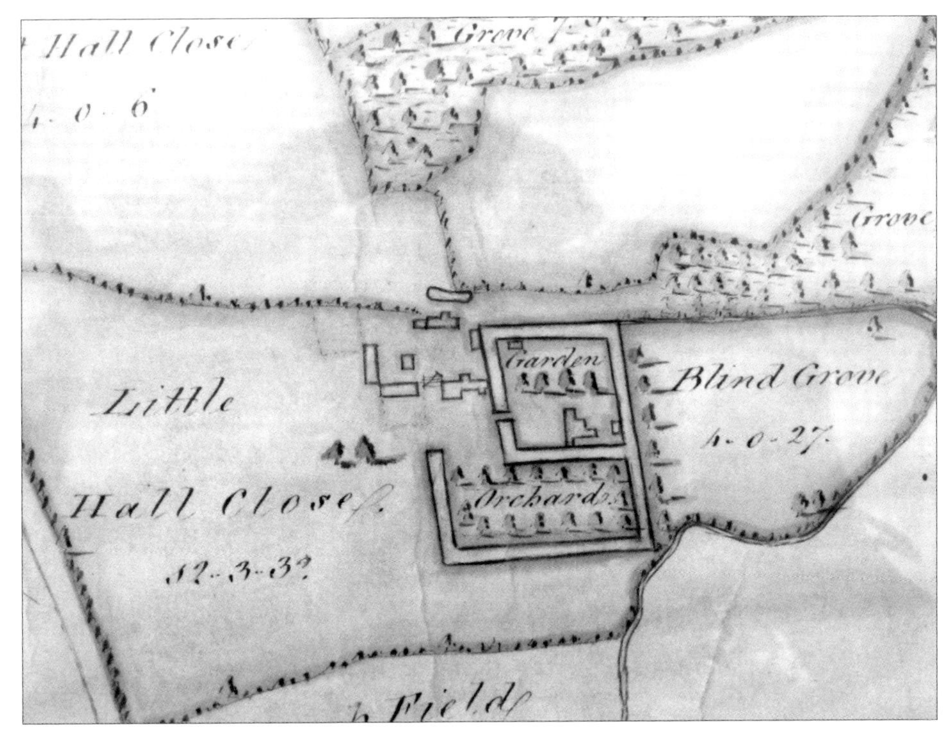

12 This 1797 estate map of Guilden Morden Hall shows the moated enclosure around the house and a further canalised area surrounding an orchard. *Cambridge University Library Ms. Plans 273*

while the field to the south is marked 'Orchard'.[3] Today the moated site survives, its inner enclosure alive with topiary shapes and a hedged rose garden, which was laid out by Sir Alexander and Lady Reid between 1964 and 1992.

Other sites embraced by deep waters include the romantic moated enclosure of the former **Landwade Manor** north of Newmarket. This is now subsumed within the grounds of Landwade Hall, close to the parish church of St Nicholas (*13*). The house of the Cottons has long gone, but the stone-revetted rectangular moat survives with an arched brick causeway bridge; a modern circular Doric temple has been placed within its enclosure. Much less romantically idyllic, as its farm buildings have been taken over by a complex of independent shops, is **Burwash Manor** at Barton, west of Cambridge, though the house still composes beautifully above its dark waters. Sadly, all vestige of the original oval moat

13

The grounds around Landwade from the air. The rectangular moated site of the original manor house is north-east of the church. *Copyright reserved Cambridge University Collection of Aerial Photography*

surrounding **Lopham's Hall**, south of Carlton in the east of the county, has disappeared, though it is shown clearly on a 1799 map which marks the inner enclosure as 'Yard and Garden'.[4] More survives at **Manor Farm, Great Eversden**, including a water-filled arm to the front of the house and a deep ditch to the rear (*14*). There is a further watercourse in the fields to the north and west, though its date and purpose are conjectural. At **Castle Farm, Castle Camps**, there are the impressive remains of a moat associated with the medieval castle of Aubrey de Vere, Earl of Oxford, sited between the church and the house, while within the enclosure there are runs of Tudor garden walling. Similar, though more modest, remains of a twelfth-century moated site survive at **Bury Farm, Meldreth**, where Margaret Lynch has contrived modern formal gardens with parterres and a pergola. These are centred by a circular box enclosure within which are tall box 'trees' denoting the site of the medieval manor house.

14 A surviving arm of the moat, with its causeway bridge, at Manor Farm, Great Eversden

Of more consequence are the grounds of Rippington Manor, Great Gransden, and at The Old House, Eltisley. **Rippington Manor** was originally built by Robert Audley in about 1560, its timber frame being encased in brick in 1631, when it was bought by Charles Aldemare-Caesar.[5] The house remained in Caesar ownership until 1823, after which the Revd William Webb, Master of Clare College, lived there. During the Second World War, Gordon Welchman, one of the Bletchley Park Enigma code breakers, lived at Rippington and features the house in his *The Hut Six Story*: 'the walled garden sloping down to the monk's carp pond, was and is one of the most peaceful places I have ever known'.[6] The house terrace gives onto the lawned garden, centred by a hedged enclosure, which still slopes down to the waters of what is left of the moat. **The Old House at Eltisley** is also timber-framed, though its piebald cladding still provides a striated reflection in the dark waters of the moat. The house is slightly later than Rippington Manor, being built in 1612 for James and Elizabeth Disbrowe, whose initials are proudly carved on a timber next to the rear door. This is significant, as the moat around the house is developed into a larger watercourse in the form of a letter 'J', perhaps signifying the owner's initial. Such conceits are not uncommon in the late Tudor and Elizabethan period, both in house plans and garden layouts. The present owners, Peter and Fleur Hughes, have done much to retrieve the water garden from a tangle of dense undergrowth. Eltisley village is rich in moated sites, the *RCHM* recording as many as five in the vicinity.

Little Linton is a particularly interesting site and shares with Harlton, and also with The Grange and Kings Mill House at Great Shelford, mentioned in the Introduction, a complex water garden. At the back of the converted barn at Little Linton there are two moats: one enclosing a garden by the house and another to the side, which is now overgrown but whose canals can be traced. Both appear on a 1600 map (*15*), which marks the existing barn on one side of the moat, and the courtyard house within its enclosure on the other.[7] The water garden is depicted as having a rectangular arrangement of canals within the outer moat.[8] This area was described in 1771-2 as 'summer house, boathouse, land, orchard and fishpond',[9] combining leisure with productivity. Indeed, these water complexes must all have functioned as fish larders. The closest in type to this garden is that constructed at Tackley in Oxfordshire by John Harborne in 1620.[10]

Little Linton has a close kinship with **Catley Park** (sometimes known as Catley Orchard), an intensely atmospheric relict site about a mile-and-a-half distant to the south-west.[11] It is reached by a long track on the other side of the Cambridge Road, which passes a grain store and then heads out into the fields. As the hedges close in, the track narrows and then opens out into a grassy clearing dominated by a ruined eighteenth-century barn complex. Next to this is the original walled enclosure of the sixteenth-century house, which is also shown on the 1600 map with the main building at its centre. On the northern corners of the wall there are pavilions, while to the south-west corner, alongside a canal, there is another small building. The stone and flint footings of this pavilion survive by the canal today. This was where Thomas Sclater was busily

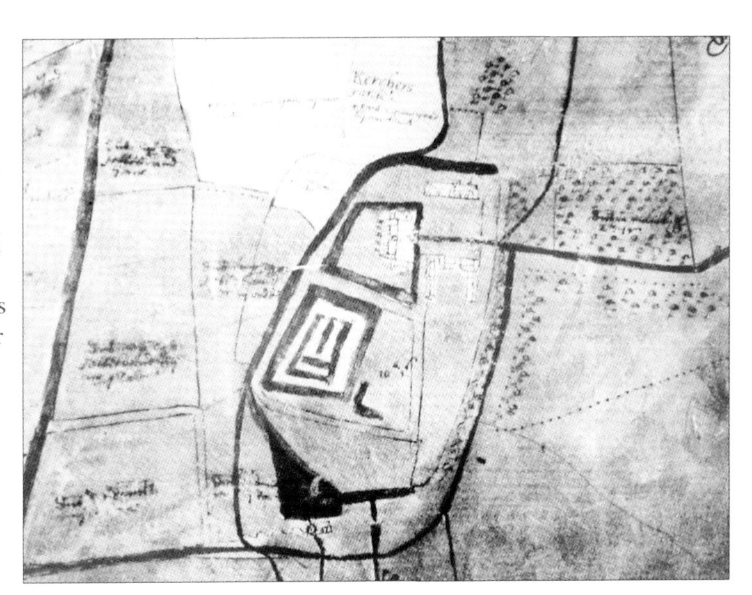

15
This 1600 map of Little Linton shows the original house set within its moat, as well as the adjacent water garden, both of which survive today. *Cambridge University Library, Maps.bb.53(1). 95.25-33*

planting fruit trees between 1674 and 1682, as will be discussed later in connection with a similar planting campaign at Horseheath Hall. In the planting records for 1675 there is a useful description of the enclosure: 'The front of ye Howse viz ye inward wall from ye Dovecoat to the Corner where there was a little Brick Howse is all a *South* wall to be planted with peaches, Apricock & Nectarines being in length in all 10 pole besides the door & 10 foot distance for every tree, in all 31 trees viz Apricock trees 9 Peaches 9 Nectarincs 8 Vines.'[12] Further entries mention the brewhouse, which must have been one of the corner buildings, and an orchard outside the walls. The wall by the 'Mote or pond' was planted up with five varieties of cherry.[13]

The garden remains at **Harlton** are more obscure, though even more extensive than the water garden at Little Linton. Access to the site is on Washpit Lane via a gate opposite the Manor Farm and along a public footpath, which skirts the village cricket pitch. At the hedgerow boundary of the field, the watercourse that fed the layout can still be seen. At this point there is a moated enclosure in the field beyond, visible on the aerial view as a rectangular wooded area (*16*). A path alongside the hedge to the north leads to a stile into the next field where a series of embankments and

16
The earthwork remains of an extensive garden with water features at Harlton, seen from the air. There is a further moated site, now covered in woodland, at the top of the photograph. *Copyright reserved Cambridge University Collection of Aerial Photography*

ditches, some filled with standing water, can be discerned (*colour 10*). In the distance hawthorn bushes line a ditch and on the horizon, their dishes upturned to the sky, are the radio telescopes of the Mullard Radio Astronomy Observatory at Lord's Bridge. The *RCHM* speculates that the earthworks are of two distinct sites, one to the north, of a moated sixteenth- or seventeenth-century house with 'gardens and pools', and the other, southerly moat, probably defensive, surrounding 'a medieval manor house'.[14]

Earthworks at former ecclesiastical sites are often more suggestive of garden remains but might, in fact, be nothing of the sort. Complex earthworks close to the remains of the Benedictine priory at what is now known as **Swaffham Bulbeck Abbey** could be part of a designed landscape, but the *RCHM* entry suggests that they 'are probably not associated with the priory but may represent post-medieval farm buildings'.[15] At another monastic site, the surviving fragment of **Denny Abbey** north of Waterbeach, there are further extensive earthworks. While there is no firm evidence to prove that these were, in fact, horticultural spaces, the *CGT Gazetteer* states that the 15-acre site, which includes 'the remains of fish-ponds and some unusual rectangular ditched plots', were 'probably once gardens tended by individual monks'.[16]

One last ecclesiastical fragment is worth a digression for the possibilities of the earthworks there and the unbridled enthusiasm of the current owners, Stephen and Sarah Tebboth, who have lovingly restored the former medieval chapel at **The Burystead**, west of Sutton, close to the New Bedford River. A brick range of 1742 is attached to the ochre-washed chapel with its blind, two-light cusped windows and diagonal stone buttresses. The Prior and Convent of Ely originally owned Burystead Manor and after the Dissolution it was given to the Dean and Chapter. The property was considered to be a valuable asset in the fourteenth century and it is likely, therefore, that the moated area in the field beyond the present house was part of a designed landscape. The rectangular ditched area is lined at points with mature trees (*colour 11*), indicating, according to the *CGT Gazetteer*, 'that here was a C17th garden and moat. There would seem to be no reason for laying out such a large moat for defensive requirements at some distance from the Manor'.[17]

There remain four further sites in this review of possible early garden survivals where documentary and archaeological support for the presence of horticultural features are more in evidence. Three of these – Kirtling Tower, Sawston Hall and Haslingfield Hall – have documented royal connections, while Childerley Hall has surviving walled enclosures, originally laid out for both productivity and leisure.

The great entrance gatehouse and mansion of **Kirtling**, set dramatically high upon a platform and guarded by a rectangular moat, at points some 65 feet wide, was built by a successful Tudor courtier, Edward North. He had made his money as Chancellor of the Court of Augmentations, set up by Henry VIII to administer the estates of the dissolved monasteries. He bought the medieval castle on the site in 1533 and in 1554 Mary Tudor elevated him to the peerage as Lord North. Soon after, he built his red-brick quadrangular house on the site of the motte of the castle. Until it was demolished in 1801, Kirtling Hall was the most impressive and important sixteenth-century building in the county.[18] Even today, with only the turreted gatehouse (*colour 12*) and its adjacent 1872 Gothic Revival wing standing, it is a place that exudes real power. In recent years, Lord and Lady Fairhaven have added a modern addition to the complex, designed in scholarly and sympathetic style by Digby Harris.[19] Kirtling Tower, as it is now known, is still bordered on three sides by the original Tudor moat, watery to the north and east, dry to the west. To the south, where the moat has been filled in, extensive lawns reach out to the wider landscape and are flanked to the west by a walled kitchen garden. On the lawn, set against dark green yew hedging, are copies of the statues from the Temple of Concord and Victory at Stowe that now dramatise the inexorable vistas of Anglesey Abbey.

A causeway bridge on the entrance drive crosses the western sector of the deep-delved moat, which has a wide grassy ledge cut into the bank along its whole length (*17*). This is called Tudor Walk, presumably after Mary Tudor, and may once have been lined with an avenue of yews; a solitary tree survives on the embankment. There are further yews on the other side of the moat and a copper beech, underplanted with *Tulipa sylvestris*, which were first identified by a Miss Rhodes in 1952. Tulips are generally thought to have been introduced to this country in 1578; coincidentally the year of an important royal visit to Kirtling.[20] The Fairhavens' gardener, Richard Ayres, has also found in the grounds a rare Tudor daffodil with a distinctive double row of petals.[21] In much the same way as a long gallery provided exercise in an Elizabethan house when the weather was inclement, the Tudor Walk would have offered similar activity outside, with views across the moat to the house set within its garden enclosures and beyond the water to the parish church. Kirtling was one of the few places in Cambridgeshire that Queen Elizabeth visited on one of her progresses into the country en route to Norfolk, accompanied by Lord North's son, Roger, who had inherited as 2nd Lord North in

1 Ely: the great cathedral ship of the fens seen from Abbey Park, once a medieval deer park overlooked by a twelfth-century castle on Cherry Hill belonging to the bishops of Ely

2 Richard Relhan's watercolour of Gogmagog House, now demolished, set within the iron age hill fort at Wandlebury. *Cambridge University Library, Relhan Views 1, no. 10*

3 The garden front of Wimpole Hall as seen from Lancelot Brown's park. The site is a palimpsest of garden history through four centuries

4 The grazing longhorn cattle compose with Sanderson Miller's Gothick Folly at Wimpole, as in a painting by Claude Lorrain

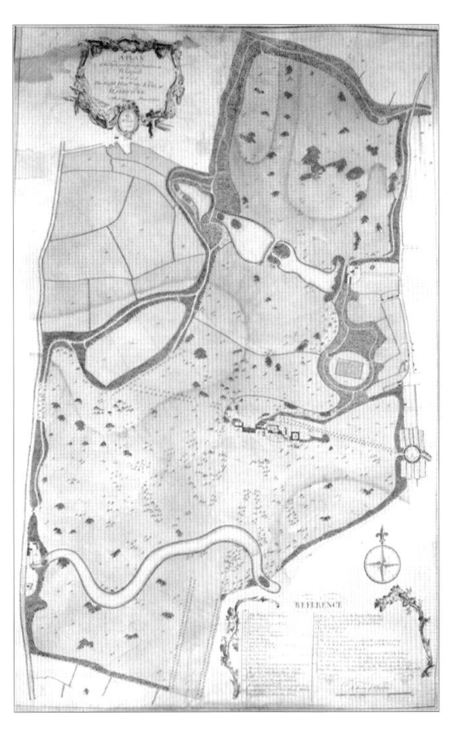

5 William Emes' 1790 survey of Wimpole containing his proposals for the park, which include the removal of Robert Greening's kitchen garden and his shrubberies on the north front of the Hall. *National Trust*

6 Humphry Repton's 1801 scheme for re-establishing a garden to the north of the Hall at Wimpole. *National Trust*

7 The garishly planted parterres to the north of Wimpole Hall are not survivors of Repton's 1801 scheme; they were laid out by the National Trust in the 1990s

8 The most impressive restoration at Wimpole is the walled Kitchen Garden with its orchard and luscious borders planted up against the inner walls. The National Trust has also restored Sir John Soane's elegant 1793 glasshouse

9 A typical Cambridgeshire moated site – Guilden Morden Hall set within its homestead moat, while alongside there is another garden moat, which encloses an orchard

10 The atmospheric site at Harlton retains its ditches, some of which are filled with water in high summer, while hawthorns line the structural bones of the former garden enclosures

11 The Tebboths lend scale to the great ditches in the fields at The Burystead – a possible garden dating from the pre-Dissolution ownership of the Prior and Convent of Ely

12 The great gatehouse of Kirtling Tower is all that survives of Edward North's Tudor mansion where Queen Elizabeth was entertained in 1578

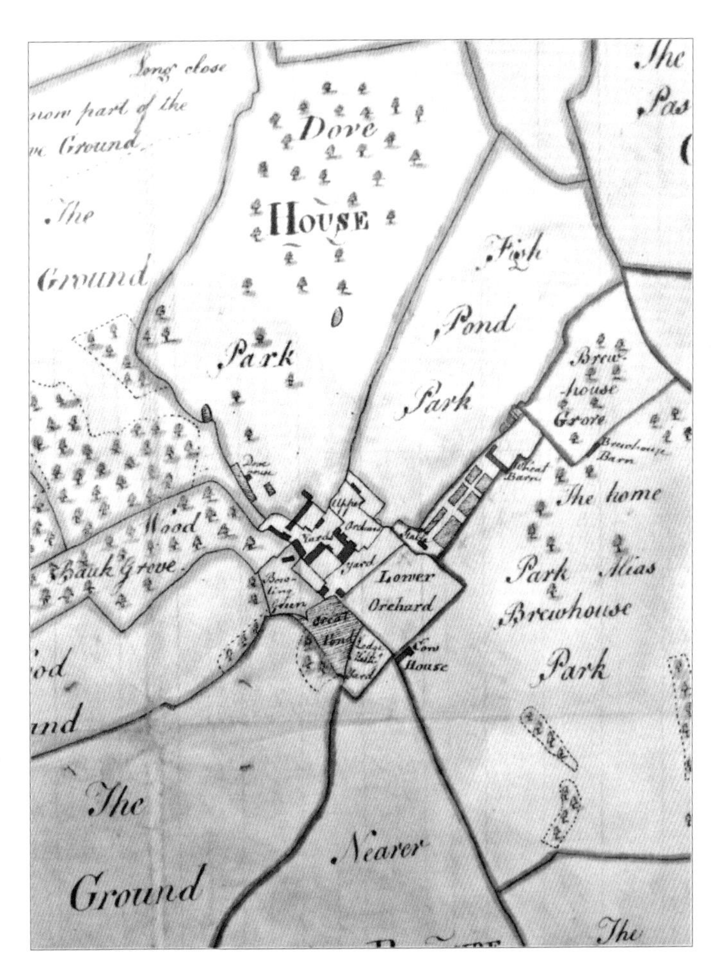

13
This 1808 map of Childerley shows the original walled garden, now transformed into an orchard, and a series of fish-ponds. *Cambridge University Library, Ms. Plans 552*

14
The causeway Bridge at Haslingfield crosses a moat, which extends around three sides of a brick-walled complex that has Elizabethan and mid-seventeenth-century ranges

15 Rudolph Ackermann's 1815 *History of the University of Cambridge* contains several views of simplified college gardens, such as that at Peterhouse. *University of Bristol Library, Special Collections*

17 Queen Elizabeth may well have promenaded along the Tudor Walk, which overlooks the moat at Kirtling Tower, when she visited the house on her progress into the county of 1578

1564. Her vast entourage of diplomats, courtiers and statesmen arrived at Kirtling on 1 September 1578:

> Hir Highnesse came to my lorde Northes, who was no whit behind any of the best for a franke house, a noble heart, and well ordered entertaynement; and there was an oration made by a gentleman of Cambridge, and a stately and fayre cuppe presented from the University, all the ambassadors of France beholding the same; and the gentlemen of the shire (as in many other places) did beare the Queene's meate to the table, whiche was a great liking and gladnesse to the gentlemen, and a solemne sighte for strangers and subjectes to looke upon.[22]

Although the house was big enough to accommodate her retinue, a 'banckettting howse' for her entertainment and a stand in the park for viewing the hunt had to be constructed for the three-day visit, which cost the 2nd Lord North a staggering £762 4s 2d.[23] This sum included a £120 jewel for the Queen and at least one lavish banquet, the menu for which listed twenty-five sorts of birds, a cartload and two horse loads of oysters, and sixteen bucks that had been made into 128 pasties.[24] For comparison, Sir Nicholas Bacon spent £577 when the Queen visited him for four days in May 1577, while Lord Burghley spent £337 7s 5d on her four-day visit in 1578; this was at a time when his household expenses were approaching £2,000 per year.[25]

Nothing survives on the site today of the complex of walled gardens that Lord North must have devised around his new house once the motte had been levelled for building. It is likely that the privy garden was sited to the east of the Hall, which is where excavations were carried out in the autumn of 1991 by the Cambridge Archaeological Unit. J Miller supervised the work and the report was completed in November 1992.[26] Trenches dug to the east of the Victorian wing uncovered the remains of garden walls built of handmade, deep red bricks with 'angular flint inclusions bonded with creamy sandy mortar', and gave some indications of the layout of the Tudor garden in relation to Lord North's 1554 house.[27] One significant find was the brick foundation at the south angle of the moat of a possible 'ornamental garden feature'.[28] If the interpretation of the brickwork is correct this might well be the banqueting house, providing a garden venue for the banquet course of the feast, while offering views out over the expansive landscape towards Wickhambrook in the south-east. Further evidence of walling was found beneath the front lawn, suggesting 'a formal system of walled gardens with walls running east-west from each of the front (south) towers'.[29] This is confirmed by eighteenth-century illustrations of the house at Kirtling. However, the report makes the additional claim that 'the style of its construction suggests the wall may have been relatively high or included more substantial features than a simple garden wall, such as castellations or corner turrets'.[30] All these features accord closely with garden layouts of the late Tudor period, particularly at royal palaces such as Hampton Court, where walled garden compartments were laid out between 1529 and 1538.[31] In his official capacity as an important and trusted courtier, Lord North would have been familiar with such royal layouts.

Walled enclosures were a typical feature around the skirts of most sixteenth- and early seventeenth-century houses and are recorded in a painting of the south front of Croxton Park, the house built for Dr Edward Leeds, who died in 1589.[32] Similar walls laid in English bond survive in part at The Berristead at Wilburton, close to the late sixteenth-century house, but while much more of the Tudor house survives at **Sawston Hall** than at Kirtling, there is no evidence on the site above ground of its original enclosed compartments. Like Kirtling, the Hall was originally surrounded by a moat, only one arm of which is visible to the south-east of the house. However, there are canals and fishponds in the woodland beyond, suggesting that there was a complex water garden here close to the house owned by Sir John Huddleston. This was burnt down in 1553 by members of the Lady Jane Grey faction after Mary Tudor had spent a night in the house. Apparently she was sleeping in the Tapestry Room when the Duke of Northumberland's men advanced upon the house; she escaped dressed as a milkmaid. After the collapse of Northumberland's plot, Huddleston was repaid for his loyalty and was given a licence by the Queen to take stone from Cambridge Castle to rebuild his house.[33] Date stones in the inner courtyard record Sir John's campaign, which began in 1557, and the completion of the building by his son, Sir Edmund, in 1584.

Today the grounds comprise open lawns to the north and east, while new gardens have been laid out to the south. The *CGT Gazetteer* records that the elaborate sixteenth-century gardens that surrounded the house 'are shown as parch marks on the lawns in an aerial photograph which revealed geometric planted compartments separated by straight paths on a grand scale, with a raised terrace walk aligned on the north front of the Hall'.[34] A survey of 1580 confirms this, stating that there was 'a large Corte beinge quadrant' in front of the house.[35] It is not known how the garden enclosures were planted up, but it is possible that the striking figure of Atlas, now relocated to the inner courtyard, might once have been a focal point in the gardens.

Rather more of the original garden layout survives at **Childerley Hall**, east of Cambridge beyond Madingley. This is yet another moated site, with a rectangular enclosure to the south, between the house and the Great Park, which has been restored by the present owners.[36] Unfortunately for this study access was not allowed, but the *CGT Gazetteer* mentions raised 'walkways and viewing mounts at two corners'.[37] Furthermore, the four-acre garden is thought to have been 'divided by paths into smaller knot gardens, mazes and arbours', which have not survived.[38] It is likely that these features date from the fourth Sir John Cutt's tenure of the house; he died in 1615. None of this can be verified here, but an aerial view via Google Earth combined with an 1808 map of Childerley (*colour 13*) shows the original rectangular layout in what was once the 'Lower Orchard'.[39] The 'Great Pond' to the south-west is now known as Church Pond, while the series of rectangular fishponds to the east have completely disappeared under woodland adjacent to a field known in 1808 as 'Fish Pond Park'. A Richard Relhan drawing, also of 1808, shows part of the walled enclosure to the east front.[40]

Another Relhan watercolour (*18*), this time of about 1814, shows the vast walled enclosure surrounding **Haslingfield Hall**.[41] This is an intensely evocative site where three arms of the moat, together with the towering brick walls of the garden, survive to give a clear impression of the whole layout.[42] While the house has been reduced in size, the causeway bridge (*colour 14*) is still in place and both the Dovecote and Well House shown in the Relhan painting still stand outside the moat. The Elizabethan garden complex is without question the most important remaining in the county, though there is some debate as to its precise dating. What is not in doubt is that Dr Thomas Wendy was royal physician to three sixteenth-century monarchs: Henry VIII, Edward VI and Queen Mary. Henry granted him the manor of Haslingfield in 1541 and he was building his new house on the site in the 1550s: a chimneypiece from the house carrying the date 1555 was relocated to Bourn Hall in the early nineteenth century. Quite what survived from the medieval moated site is unclear, but runs of walls around the enclosure constructed of bricks laid in English bond are, no doubt, of the 1550 period. However, other walls,

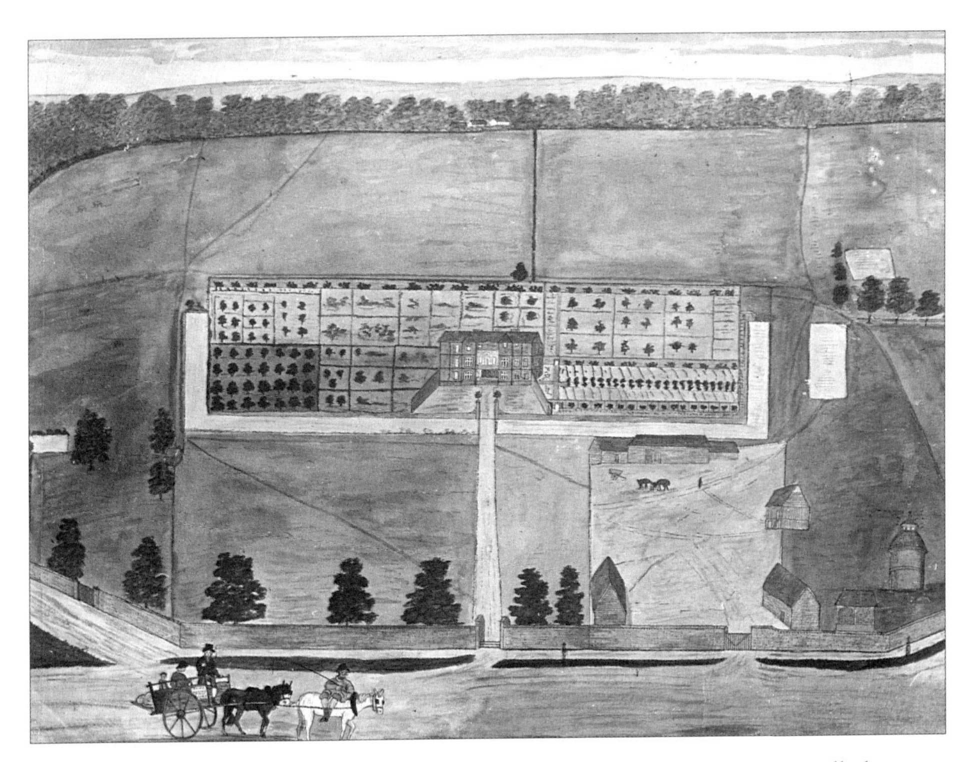

18 Richard Relhan's 1814 watercolour of the part-Elizabethan, part-Carolean walled complex at Haslingfield Hall. *Cambridgeshire Archives, 23/z929*

particularly those to the east of the house, are laid in Flemish bond and probably date from the ownership of Sir Thomas Wendy (an indirect descendant of the original owner) in the seventeenth century; he died in 1673. The stately monument in the parish church has him standing proudly in contemporary dress.

The Relhan watercolour depicts the site after Sir Thomas had remodelled it post-1660 and suggests that little was done in the intervening 150 years. The *RCHM* entry for Haslingfield states that 'the grounds were also much improved, most of the surviving walls and other features ... being substantially of the Restoration period'.[43] Certainly the arched and buttressed doorway (*19*) in the wall and the rusticated brick gate piers giving access from the rear of the house to the moat appear to be of the latter half of the seventeenth century. Relhan depicts all the surviving walls, though the walled forecourt giving onto the Bridge has gone.

19 This section of the walled enclosure around the surviving fragment of Haslingfield Hall dates from Sir Thomas Wendy's ownership in the mid-seventeenth century

Almost the whole enclosure is divided up into orchards, though there appear to be vegetable beds at the top right-hand corner, while the smaller walled compartment to the side of the house has a tree-lined walk extending as far as the gate piers. No doubt the 2.5-acre enclosure was originally laid out with ornamental gardens, as well as more productive areas. The compartmented gardens close to the house must once have been filled with knots, parterres and gravel walks for maximum display, as Queen Elizabeth was the guest of yet another Thomas Wendy, the nephew of Dr Thomas, on an earlier progress than that of 1578, when she travelled to the county to address the University in 1564. This historic event is still marked in Haslingfield by a carved image of her on horseback, which dramatises the village sign.

3

Hortus Sociorum and Hortus Magistri – seventeenth-century Cambridge

LIKE ITS SISTER UNIVERSITY OF OXFORD, CAMBRIDGE HAS LOST ALMOST ALL of its original historic gardens, opting instead for a minimalist treatment of lawns and flower borders where once the lawns were dotted with cypress trees (*20*) and enriched with parterres, living sundials, mounts, arbours, canals and garden houses, while its private gardens across the Cam have been subsumed within later building. Indeed, most of the intricately designed spaces within the college walls had reverted to grass scattered with a few trees when William Custance published his plan of Cambridge in 1798.[1] The colourful plates (*colour 15*) of Rudolph Ackermann's 1815 *History of the University of Cambridge* confirm this process of simplification. In one case alone, at Christ's College, an eighteenth-century garden pavilion fronting a plunge pool survives, along with a famous mulberry known as Milton's Mulberry Tree, named after the famous poet John Milton, who went up to Christ's in 1625 and graduated in 1629. Few colleges have attempted to recreate any vestige of their once historic enclosures, though in 1960 a diagonally planned Elizabethan-style perennial herb garden, designed by John Codrington, was laid out in New Court at Emmanuel College. What the colleges do offer, however, are several interesting and atmospheric twentieth-century gardens, but these will be treated in their chronological place in the last chapter of this book.

Though long gone, former layouts within the college walls can be retrieved through a series of early maps and seventeenth-century engravings. These include John Hammond's map of 1592,[2] which gives a bird's eye view of the walled gardens; John Speed's 1610 map of Cambridge,[3]

20 The Principal Court at Peterhouse was once planted up with cypresses and conifers, as seen in Loggan's 1688 *Cantabrigia Illustrata*. *Reference Library, Bristol Central Library*

which extends to the other side of the Cam to record the gardens in that area; a 1634 map of the city from Thomas Fuller's 1655 *Church-History of Britain*,[4] which gives more detail of these private spaces; and finally David Loggan's map and exquisitely delineated plates for his *Cantabrigia Illustrata* of 1688.

The detail on Speed's 1610 map (*21*) is fairly notional, but it does record the main garden areas of the principal colleges. Working anti-clockwise from east to west, these start with Jesus, where just below the 'Kinges dich' there is a tree-lined area with rectangular fishponds, later appropriated by the Master of St John's. Marked 'E' on the map, St John's has six parterres extending as far as the Cam and then a bridge over to a tree-lined enclosure called 'St John's Walkes' alongside a garden of rectangular fishponds. At this period Trinity, Trinity Hall and Clare College seem only to have had orchards in their walled sectors close to the Cam, whereas King's has two distinct garden areas: the lawn by the great Chapel, which has tree avenues and two parterres that must be Elizabethan, for they are

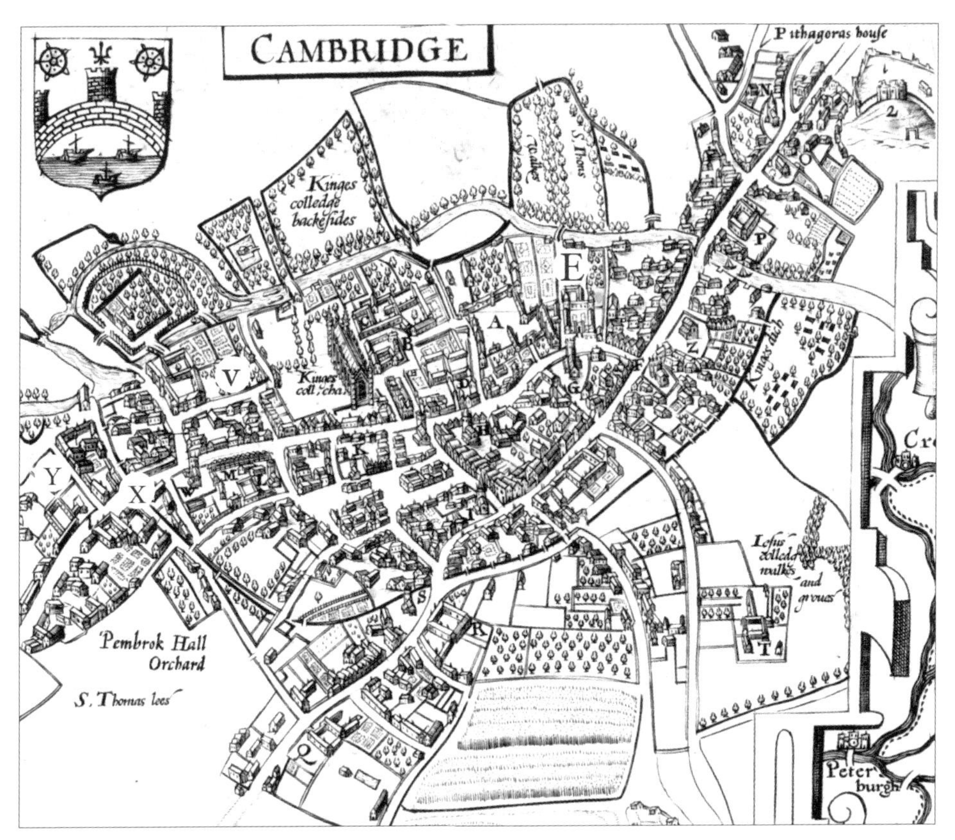

21 John Speed's 1610 Map of Cambridge shows few college gardens, but marks the more private fellows' garden areas across the Cam at King's and St John's. *University of Bristol Library, Special Collections*

shown on the 1592 Hammond map, and a bridge across the Cam giving access to 'Kinges colledge backesides'. These last are tree-lined, with the southerly section centred by a rectangular moat with a summerhouse or fishing pavilion. Next comes Queens' College ('V'), which has several parterres and orchards by the main college buildings, though the half-timbered 1540 President's Gallery in the Cloister Court (*22*), which may once have provided elevated views over Tudor knots, now commands a space enlivened only by a single tree. There is another extensive garden across the Cam, accessed by two bridges. This moated enclosure, which partly survives today with Cripps Court at its heart, has a walled garden and beyond that a tree-lined palisade; it is liberally planted with trees. The

22 The loggia and gallery of the President's Lodging at Queens' College may once have provided views over formal parterres or knots

only other colleges shown with significant garden enclosures are Peterhouse, marked 'Y', and Pembroke ('X'), with seven compartments and a walled orchard beyond.

The 1634 map illustrated in Thomas Fuller's *Church-History* is far less informative as regards gardens (*23*), though at first glance it appears to show a domed garden building on the lawn by the west door of King's College Chapel. This is drawn with a conical roof on Richard Lyne's map of Cambridge, published in 1574.[5] Unfortunately for garden history studies, it turns out to have been a makeshift bell tower that was erected when the grand building planned by Henry VI was never realised; it was demolished in 1739.[6] David Loggan's 1688 map shows its rectangular footprint at the head of a diagonal path across the lawn leading to a new bowling green, first mentioned in 1658,[7] which had supplanted one of the parterres. Next to it was a gallery, built in 1468-9, for views over the meadows across the Cam.[8] In fact, apart from the re-design of some of the parterres and an expansion of some college gardens, the ubiquity of

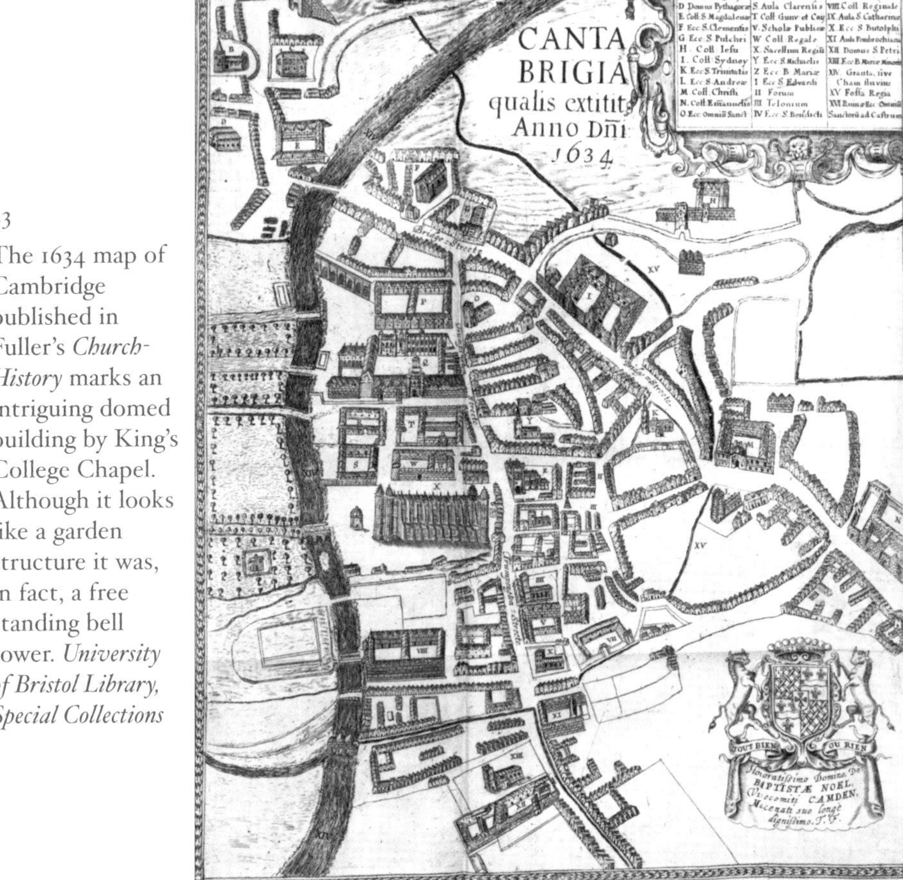

23
The 1634 map of Cambridge published in Fuller's *Church-History* marks an intriguing domed building by King's College Chapel. Although it looks like a garden structure it was, in fact, a free standing bell tower. *University of Bristol Library, Special Collections*

bowling greens is the main difference between the grounds depicted in 1634 and those on Loggan's 1688 map. This was due, in part, to the appearance of books on country leisure pursuits, such as Gervase Markham's *Country Contentments*, which was published in 1615.[9] Markham writes of the 'art' and 'cunning' of the game, but also stresses the therapeutic aspect of playing in the open air, as long as it is 'exercised with moderation'.[10] Queens' appears to have had the first green in the University, for it was already in existence in the Fellows' Garden in 1608–9.[11] A typical example is that at Jesus (*24*), where one sector of the orchard has been cleared for bowls. The green at Trinity College was laid out between 1647 and 1648.[12] Some of these new bowling greens were given pavilions or covered settles

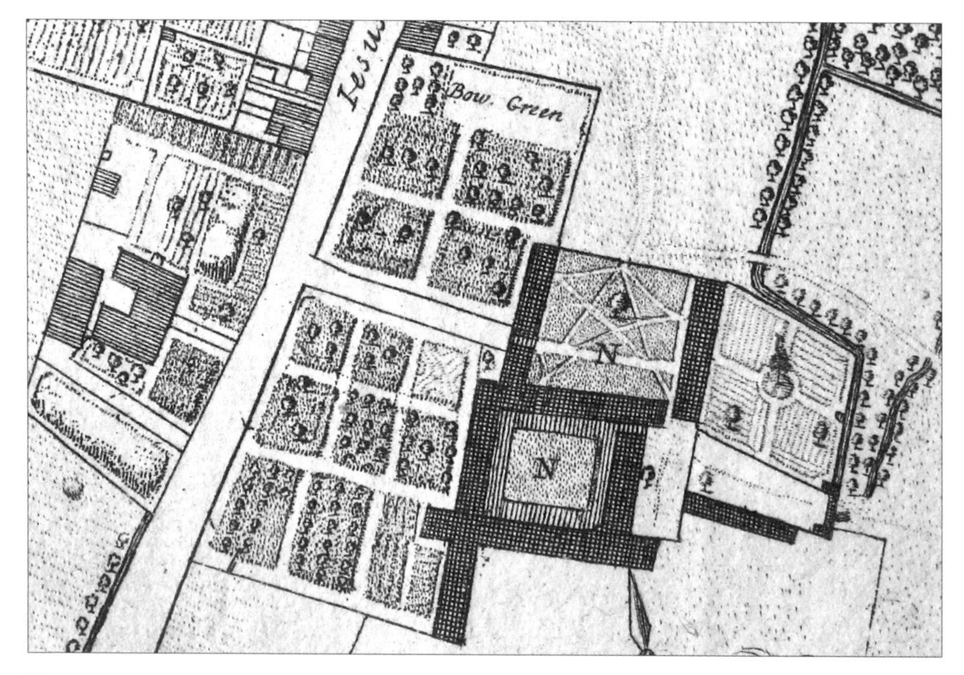

24 The compartments around Jesus College from Loggan's 1688 map of the town contain one of the ubiquitous bowling greens that sprang up in college gardens during the Jacobean period and beyond. *Reference Library, Bristol Central Library*

where fellows could shelter to watch the sport; two of these are apparent at King's and the adjacent green at Clare College, both shown on the previous illustration. At Jesus the detail of the walled enclosures is more precise, with diagonal paths across grass in one and a quadripartite arrangement centred by a tree set on a mound in another. It is, however, the individual plates of the colleges that provide the most detail as to how these courts and enclosures were laid out horticulturally.

The college views reveal a perfect blend of polite ornamentation and productive husbandry, as one would expect by the late 1680s after the earnest pronouncements of the Commonwealth for England to become self-sufficient, and the tendency to formalise gardens after the Restoration. All colleges had kitchen gardens. That at King's was laid out between the college and the river, where in 1362-3 the workman was making the beds, or *herbaria*, while at Peterhouse the kitchen garden was being cultivated in the 1370s with parsley, cress, garlic, leeks and saffron.[13] There are many records of saffron cultivation in the college account rolls, both for consumption and for medicinal purposes. The crocus which produces it (*Crocus sativus*) was growing by the river between King's College Bridge and Clare College in the 1460s, and in the following century a portion of the Grove (*virgultum*) at Peterhouse was set aside for its production.[14] Vines were grown for the production of 'verjuice' for consumption, the arched trellises over which they were trained creating shady galleries for contemplative walking.[15] At Queens' College the vineyard (*ortus vinearum*) is specially mentioned in the 1520s, while frames for the vines were being constructed in 1538-9.[16] Indicative of the theme of good husbandry, promoted in the next century by Samuel Hartlib, Walter Blith and John Beale, one Loggan view shows a sloping vegetable garden at Sidney Sussex, while in the fellows' garden at Christ's College, ornamental buildings were accompanied by a dovecote and bee skeps (*25*). It is no coincidence that William Lawson's *Country House-Wives Garden*, re-issued in 1648, included a section on the 'Husbandry of Bees', or that Hartlib was to publish in 1655 a detailed study of apiary entitled *The Commonwealth of Bees*.

Christ's garden temple was cruciform in plan with four gabled openings providing seated views within the garden and to the fields beyond. In 1682, just before Loggan published his view, this 'Summer house in ye Coll. Orchard' had six chairs and a table.[17] It has long gone, but an arcaded eighteenth-century Summerhouse and plunge pool (*26*) survive in the present Fellows' Garden, which is reached via a gateway through the Fellows' Building. Thomas Salmon first mentioned a bath at Christ's in 1748, at the height of the current fashion for cold bathing as part of a gentleman's physical regimen.[18] It was noted soon after in a description of the grounds published in 1763:

> The Fellows Garden is well laid out, and one of the pleasantest in the University: There are both open and close shady Walks, beautiful Alcoves, a Bowling-green, and an elegant Summer-house: beyond which there is a Cold-bath, surrounded with a little Wilder-

25 Husbandry was an essential element of mid-seventeenth-century gardens, hence the presence of bee skeps in the gardens at Christ's College. *Reference Library, Bristol Central Library*

26 A rare survival in Cambridge college gardens – the eighteenth-century Summerhouse at Christ's College

ness. It may not be improper to mention in this Place that there are several other Baths in the University; but the best, and which is a public one, is in a little Wood two Miles West of the Town, near the Village of Madingly.[19]

Thomas Wright described the garden and its therapeutic complex a century later, in 1847:

The chambers in Inigo Jones's building are chiefly occupied by fellows. A gateway in the middle leads to the fellows' garden, the most celebrated in the university, both for its picturesque beauty, and for its mulberry tree, said to have been planted by the hand of Milton, while a student at the college. At the south-eastern corner of the garden is a bath, with an elegant summerhouse, and by the water side two or three pedestals, one of which supports a bust of the great poet, and the other an urn to the memory of Joseph Mede. The view towards the north-west corner, is one of the most picturesque that can be conceived.[20]

Not only do the Summerhouse and Bath, now transformed into a swimming pool, survive, framed by busts of Milton, Nicholas Sanderson, Ralph Cudworth and Joseph Mede,[21] but so too does the famous mulberry tree, though it is reported to have been planted in 1609, long before Milton went up to Cambridge.[22] Emmanuel also had a summerhouse, doubling as a bath house, which was already in the garden by 1680.[23] It is shown clearly in Loggan's view of the college and was mentioned in a 1748 account of the grounds:

The Gardens are very extensive, and well planted with Fruit. There is a Bowling-Green and Cold-Bath in the Fellows Garden, over which is a neat Brick Building, sash'd in Front, and containing also

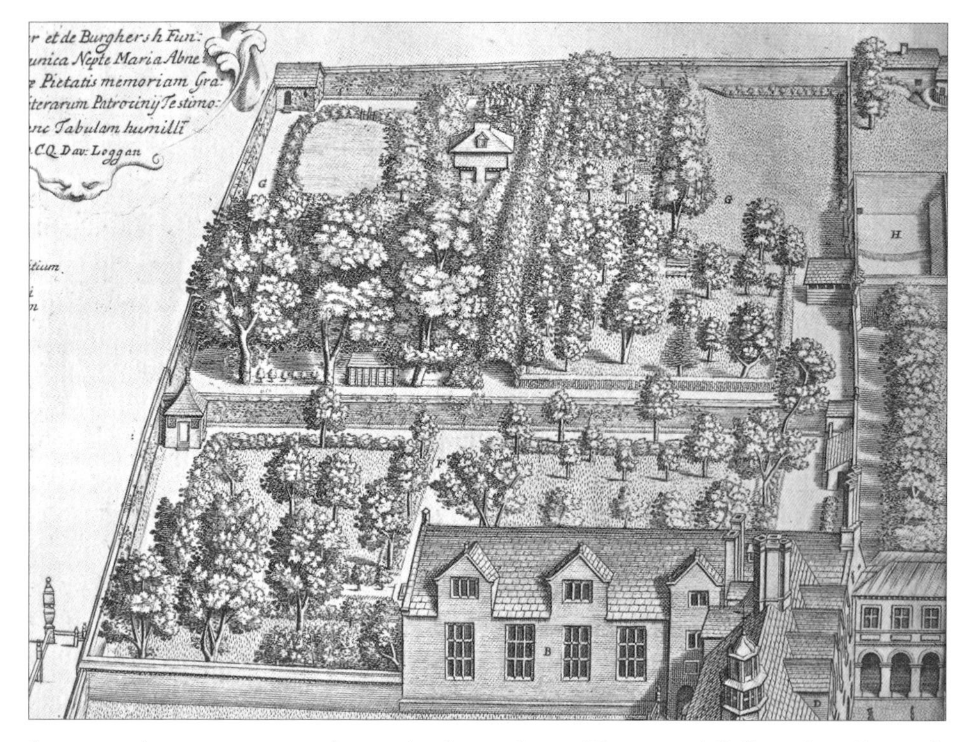

27 Seventeenth-century summerhouses in the gardens of Emmanuel College from Loggan's 1688 *Cantabrigia Illustrata. Reference Library, Bristol Central Library*

> a commodious little Room to dress in. The Curious take notice of a fine young Cedar-tree in this Garden.[24]

The pool survives, though reshaped, in the present Fellows' Garden. Emmanuel also had another, less medicinal, summerhouse in the Master's Garden, which George Dyer saw in 1814: 'The master's garden has in it nothing remarkable, except it may be a summer-house, of some antiquity, surrounded with the prints of our principal old poets, a very agreeable nook, in which either a pipe or a poem will go very pleasantly.'[25]

Loggan's plates record further summerhouses at Corpus Christi, where there was also a green arbour; those at Emmanuel, one with a typical late seventeenth-century conical roof (*27*); one at Gonville and Caius, which was a substantial structure that may have doubled as a gardener's bothy; two at Queens', accompanied by several settle-type seats arranged around

28 An ornamental mount garden at Sidney Sussex College. *Reference Library, Bristol Central Library*

the bowling green; and a two-storey octagonal building with a conical roof and projecting porch, which overlooked a decorative mount topped by a columnar sundial at Sidney Sussex (*28*). In the Fellows' Garden at Trinity Hall inscribed tablets dated 1619, but reset in the walls in 1708, are the only reminders of the summerhouse depicted in Loggan's view.[26]

The most intriguing garden buildings of this period in the University were in the grounds at Peterhouse. In the Grove on Loggan's map (*29*) there was a tennis court, marked number 39, and close to it by the river bank, a structure built in 1544-5, known from the account rolls as the 'spectaculum or New-work'.[27] It was built of freestone and paved, and was repaired in 1589-90;[28] Hammond shows it with battlemented walls overlooking Choe Fen. It is likely, therefore, to have been a look-out. Further west there was a part-walled area divided into quadrants of what look to be vegetable beds interspersed with trees. At the centre of this garden were identical twin structures. It is unlikely that they were merely gardeners'

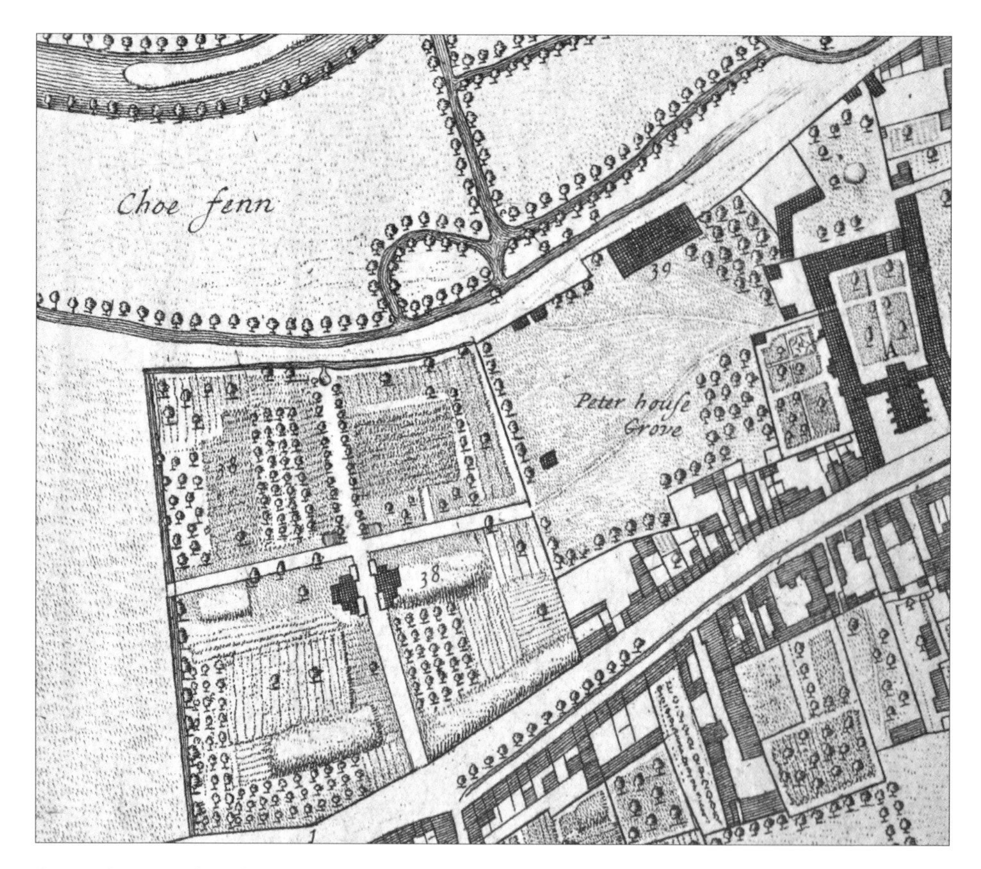

29 Loggan's 1688 plan shows two mysterious buildings facing each other on either side of a central gravel path in the walled garden at Peterhouse. Their symmetrical alignment suggests that they were ornamental classical structures. *Reference Library, Bristol Central Library*

houses, for they are perfectly symmetrical and have a polite air about them. The buildings are present on the 1763 Plan of Cambridge, which also shows a bath house on the western boundary by the river, 'much frequented by Students',[29] but by 1798, when William Custance published his plan, the two garden buildings had been amalgamated into one and the site was then owned by 'C Pemberton Esq'. Thereafter, the site is marked on the 1904 Ordnance Survey map as Grove Lodge, perpetuating, in the name at least, its original function as a polite garden building.

Another seventeenth-century garden feature, albeit somewhat rare, which is present in Loggan's views at both Queens' and Pembroke, was the

30 Living sundials were usually made of box with a wooden gnomon. This example was sited behind Christopher Wren's chapel at Pembroke. *Reference Library, Bristol Central Library*

living sundial, usually laid out in clipped box with a wooden gnomon. There was a famous example at Wollaton Hall, Nottingham, and another at New College, Oxford; this last was an embellishment to the Mount Garden there.[30] Most colleges had dials on their walls, often set on their halls, as at Pembroke, where dials were set up in 1552.[31] But its garden dial was sited in the Master's Garden (*Hortus Magistri*) to the east of the Wren Chapel amongst flowerbeds and low bushes (*30*). The Queens' College garden dial was in the Fellows' Garden (*Hortus Sociorum*), adjacent to the bowling green.

As we have seen, the main colleges on the Cam had extensive riverine gardens on the north bank, the most complex of which was the one at St John's. Its meadows were laid out in a series of enclosures bordered by hedges (*31*). This area of enclosed walks was created in 1602-3, and accessed via a formal avenue leading from the Cam next to the tennis court (marked 'I'). This last was originally constructed in 1573-4, but rebuilt as part of the early seventeenth-century garden improvements.[32]

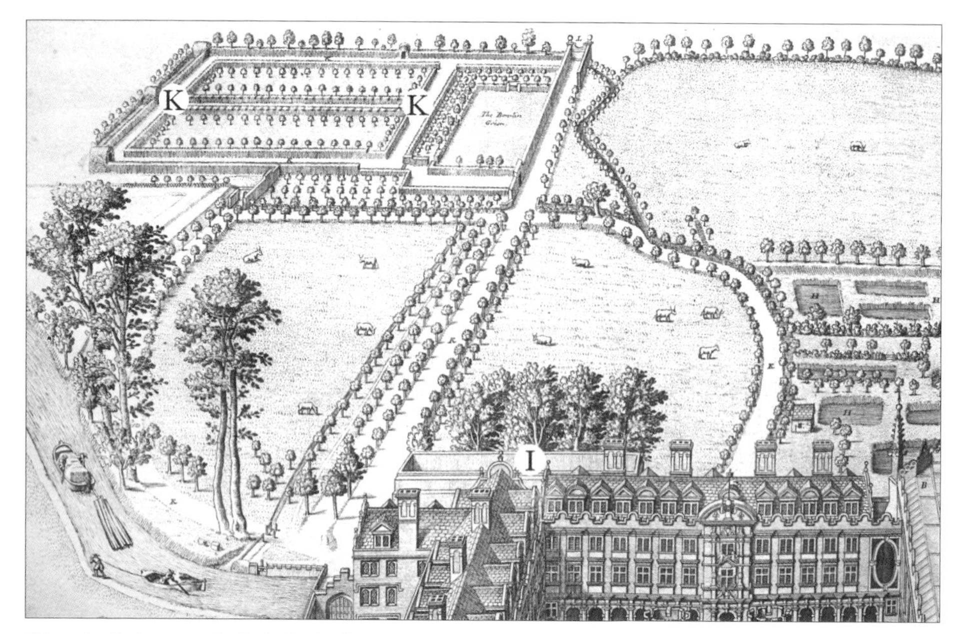

31 The *Ambulacra* in St John's College Walks on the other side of the Cam from the College. The complex also included green arbours and a bowling green. *Reference Library, Bristol Central Library*

The avenue led through a pasture meadow, and on to a bowling green and the '*Ambulacra*', marked 'K'. The Latin term denotes an area of courtyards and colonnades in front of a basilica, exactly the impression given by the tree-lined, hedged walks, which were punctuated by green arbours. All the grass compartments were hedged on the outside, but the bowling green had a sturdy wall, which was constructed in 1648-9, while its strengthening buttresses were added 1666-7.[33] Celia Fiennes was particularly taken with the college grounds when she visited the University in 1697: 'St Johns College Garden is very pleasant for the fine walks, both close and shady walks and open rows of trees and quickset hedges, there is a pretty bowling green with cut arbours in the hedges.'[34] Adjacent to the meadows was the extensive area of rectangular fishponds shown on Speed's map, but now furnished with fishing houses for the fellows to enjoy their sport. St John's also owned the fishponds below the King's Ditch; by the time Loggan surveyed the city in 1688 the Master of St John's had built a dovecote in this enclosure.

Access to the more private gardens on the other side of the Cam was via a series of bridges beginning with that at St John's and, moving westwards, at Trinity, Trinity Hall, Clare College and King's, as well as two at Queens', one of which was on the site of the later Mathematical Bridge, built by James Essex in 1749-50 to the designs of William Etheridge (*colour 16*). This last, though often referred to as 'Chinese' in style, was derived from Andrea Palladio's third book of his *I Quattro Libri dell'Architettura*.[35] The other bridges are of more conventional design, with three arches springing from breakwaters. In 1697, Christopher Wren suggested that a new bridge be built on axis with Third Court at St John's, but Robert Grumbold eventually built it on the site of the former bridge in 1709-12; the attached gate and piers are of 1711-12 (*colour 17*). The original bridge at Trinity was built in 1613, but rebuilt with two arches in 1651-2.[36] This survived until the mid-eighteenth century, when it was rebuilt in 1764-5 by James Essex. King's bridge was first built in 1472-3, but was frequently rebuilt thereafter in 1595 and again in stone by George Tompson in 1627.[37] However, easily the most beautiful of all the seventeenth-century bridges over the Cam is that at Clare College (*colour 18*), which was built by Thomas Grumbold in 1639-40.[38]

Of all the plates in Loggan's beautifully presented survey of the University, that depicting Trinity College includes the most interesting garden features and certainly the most significant in the form of the Fountain at the centre of the Great Court (*32*). The Fountain was commissioned in 1601-2 by Thomas Nevile, Master of the college, but the steps and paving around it were not completed until 1613. When the whole college was cleaned and decorated for the reception of James I in 1615 it was painted and gilded by John Newton and a craftsman named Thorpe, who had earlier decorated the Great Gate.[39] As well as being an object of display and status, the Fountain provided water via a lead cistern at the bottom with external taps for use by the college community. Water was also available for maintaining the parterres, as shown in a detail of one of the enclosures, where a pump stands ready, next to a garden loggia. Like its

32
Thomas Nevile's 1601-2 Fountain in the Great Court at Trinity College – unquestionably the University's most spectacular garden structure. *Chris Mayer*

neighbour St John's, Trinity had an extensive garden across the Cam, where walks were lined with horse chestnuts, elms and limes, while other areas were planted with holly, juniper, Spanish broom, honeysuckle, philerea, holm oaks and 'an enormous quantity of quick [hawthorn]'.[40] Finally, in the garden of the Master's Lodge at Trinity, there was a parterre centred by a green arbour and, close by, a circular pool dramatised by a statue placed there in 1677-8 (*33*). The building in the wall was the 'Master's Summer House', built in 1684-5.[41] As with almost all of these sylvan enclosures, the walls were liberally covered with espaliered fruit trees.

All the busy horticultural and ornamental detail, together with most of the leisure facilities, in the college enclosures and wider grounds, would be

33 A rare statue and an arbour in the garden of the Master's Lodge at Trinity College.
Reference Library, Bristol Central Library

swept away in the latter part of the eighteenth century, a process of simplification advanced by Lancelot Brown in his, mercifully unrealised, destructive proposals for the Backs. This new aesthetic for open spaces dramatised with exotics would eventually be pushed through in the colleges by the Regency landscape gardeners Humphry Repton and John Claudius Loudon, aided and abetted by the college authorities. One of these was Dr Richard Walker, founder of the University's Botanic Garden, who was Vice-Master of Trinity from 1734 until his death in 1764. He was responsible for ornamenting the ground between the library and the river-bank with 'North-American Poplars, weeping-willows, and other Aquatics, under ye wall next the River' during his tenure.[42] Walker's horticultural contribution to the University was summed up in a contemporary guide-book of 1748:

And tho' there be no public Garden belonging to the University, Cambridge is not destitute of exotic Plants, the Trinity Gardener, Mr Harrison, having, by the Direction of Dr Walker the Vice-Master, introduced several Species of foreign Fruits and Flowers, Natives of the warmest Climates; particularly the Anana or Pine-apple, the Banana, Coffee-shrub, Logwood-tree, and Torch-thistle, the Red Jessamine of the West Indies, &c. which are brought to great Perfection.[43]

16 James Essex was involved in the construction of the Mathematical Bridge across the Cam at Queens' College. Its design was taken from Andrea Palladio's *Four Books of Architecture*

17 St John's Bridge and the adjacent gate piers were built by Robert Grumbold between 1709 and 1712. *University of Bristol Library, Special Collections*

18 Thomas Grumbold's 1639-40 Bridge at Clare College has a typical mid seventeenth-century balustrade decorated with panels of coral-like rustication and a seahorse

19
This view of Balsham Maze from the air reveals the musical inspiration behind its design – a treble clef and two French Horns. *Jim Potter*

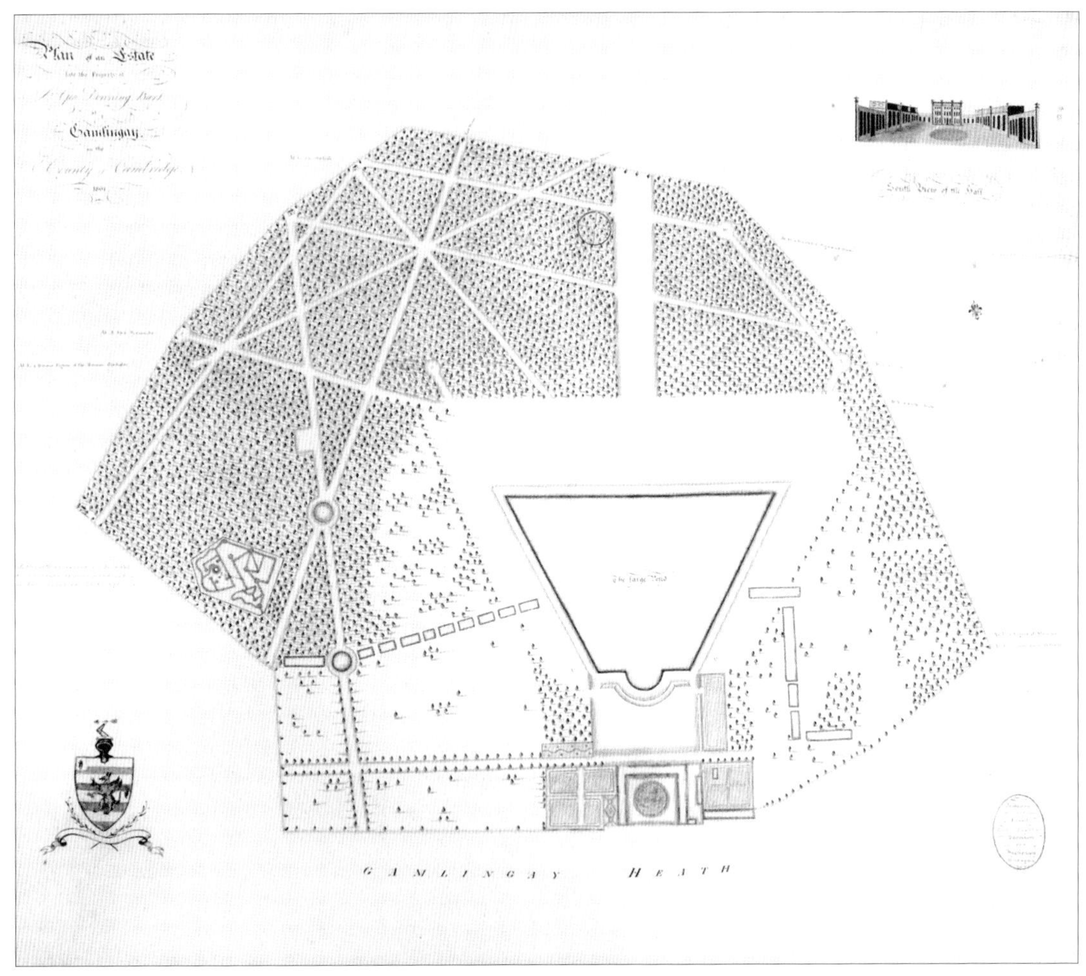

20 Sir George Downing's Gamlingay Park recorded in an 1801 survey. It shows the trapezoidal pool, which survives today, and axial rides, now lost, terminated by statuary. *The Master, Fellows and Scholars of Downing College, Cambridge*

21
A rare painted panel preserved in the late eighteenth-century house at Fordham is the only record of the lost Baroque house built on the site by Admiral Sir Charles Wager in 1711. *By kind permission of John & Jane Lewin Smith*

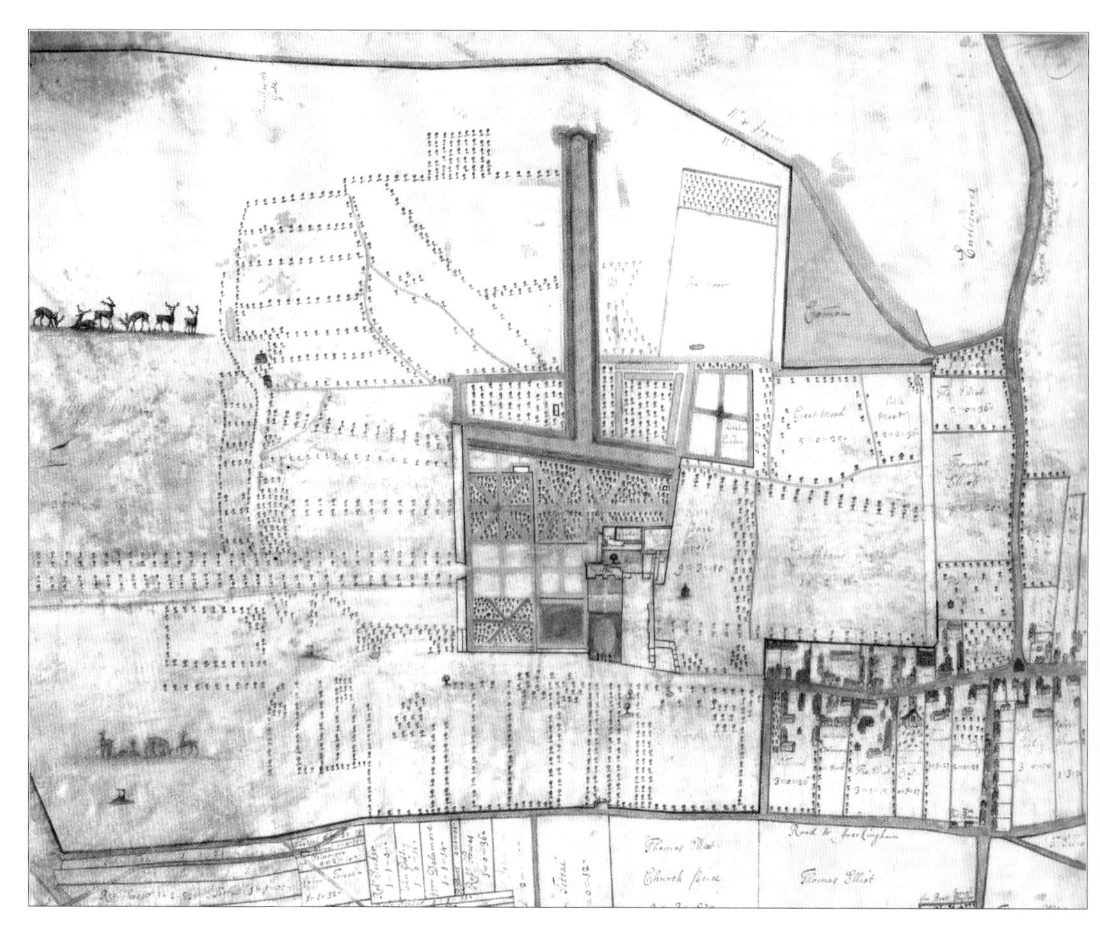

22 Lord Orford's great Water Garden at Chippenham Park, depicted in a 1712 survey.
Cambridgeshire Archives, 71/P3

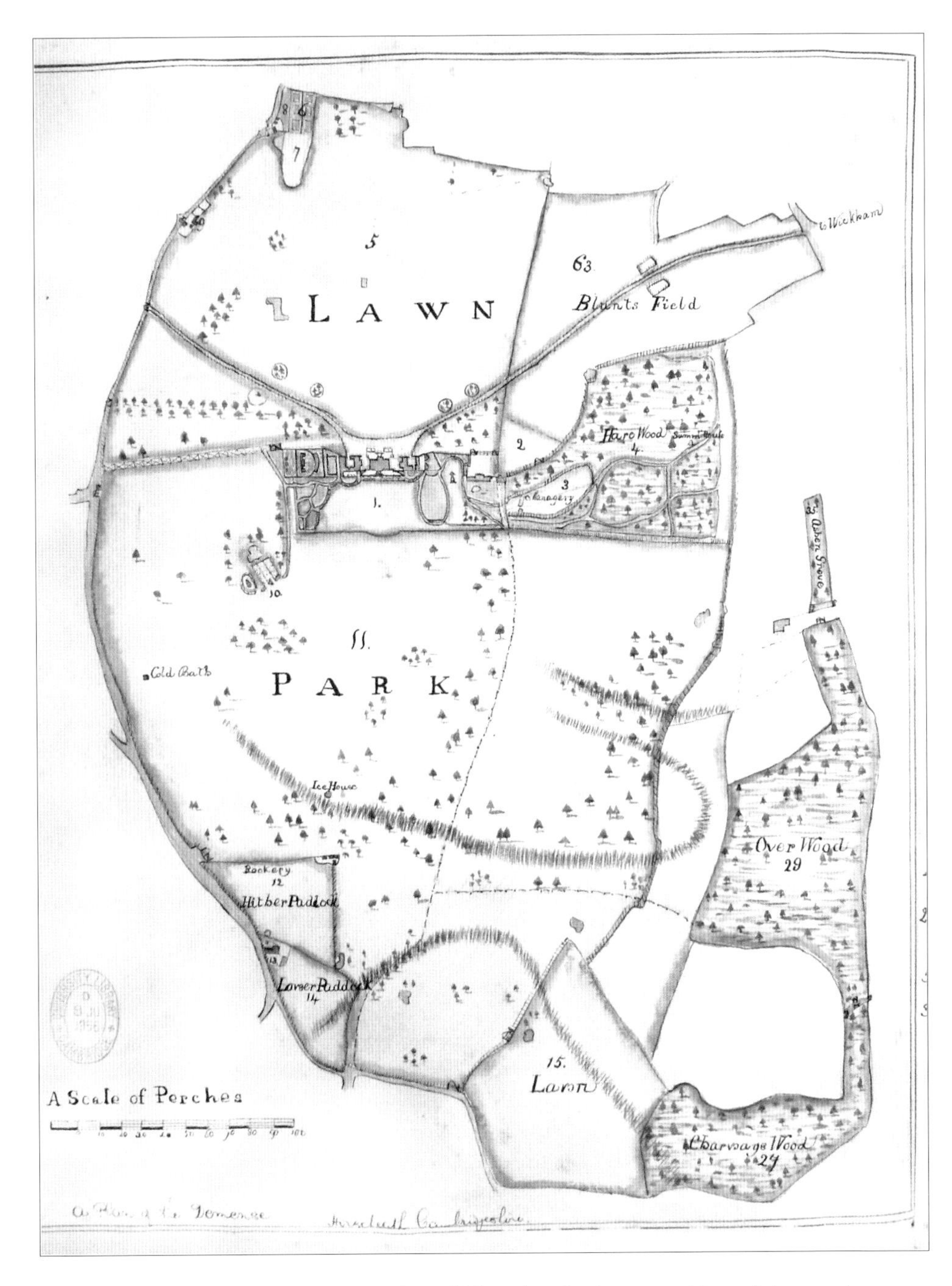

23 The shaded contours on this 1769 plan of Horseheath give some idea of the gently elevated site of Lord Alington's seventeenth-century house, built in accordance with Roger Pratt's aesthetic directions. *Cambridge University Library, Ms. Plans a.5*

24 The pleasure grounds at Horseheath were once studded with ornamental piers like these surviving examples at the Earl of Craven's contemporary house at Hamstead Marshall in Berkshire

25 The idyllic sylvan setting of Madingley Hall, contrived by Lancelot Brown in 1756, required the obliteration of the seventeenth-century formal gardens

26 John Spyers' 1777 plan of Fenstanton, drawn up for Lancelot Brown, records a designed landscape of Brownian character on the common land of Hall Green between Manor Farm and the Manor House on the village street. *Cambridge University Library, Ms. Plans x.I*

27 An undated wooden panel of Ely Cathedral, showing Cherry Hill with James Bentham's planting and the classical column he raised in 1779. *By kind permission of Ely Museum*

28 James Wyatt's lodges and classical Archway form an appropriately grand entrance to Chippenham Park from the south. *Wendy Mayer*

29 Humphry Repton's proposal for a cold bath to take advantage of an existing pool at Waresley Park was sadly unrealised. *RHS, Lindley Library*

4

Canals, avenues and a 'Sweete Prospect' – formal gardens

Wisbech Castle · Hilton Maze · Balsham Manor Maze · Hatley Park
Madingley Hall · Thriplow Manor · King's College · Gamlingay Park
Fordham Abbey · Chippenham Park · Horseheath Hall

UNLIKE MANY ENGLISH COUNTIES, SUCH AS GLOUCESTERSHIRE AND HERTfordshire, both of which have detailed histories of their major country seats illustrated by informative engravings of their parks and gardens, Cambridge is less fortunate. As we have seen, David Loggan's *Cantabrigia Illustrata* is an important source for the form and content of the University college gardens, but there is no equivalent for the country estates. The only Cambridgeshire houses to appear in Leonard Knyff and Jan Kip's 1707 *Britannia Illustrata* are Wimpole Hall, Madingley Hall and Hatley Park, while elevations only for Horseheath Hall feature in the third (1725) volume of *Vitruvius Britannicus.* This is a fair indication that the county lacked major late seventeenth- and early eighteenth-century formal gardens, even if there are some interesting discoveries to be made in the archives, most notably at Gamlingay and Fordham.

As might be expected after the experimental walled gardens of the Commonwealth, some at least of the mid-century houses in the county must have been built within enclosed garden precincts. However, only one significant site survives today, and even then its parent house has disappeared. Fortunately, the layout of the mid-seventeenth-century garden at **Wisbech Castle** (*34*) is shown clearly in an undated survey of the Castle gardens.[1] The Castle was entered, as now, through gates with tall gate piers that led into a walled forecourt leading up to the main door.

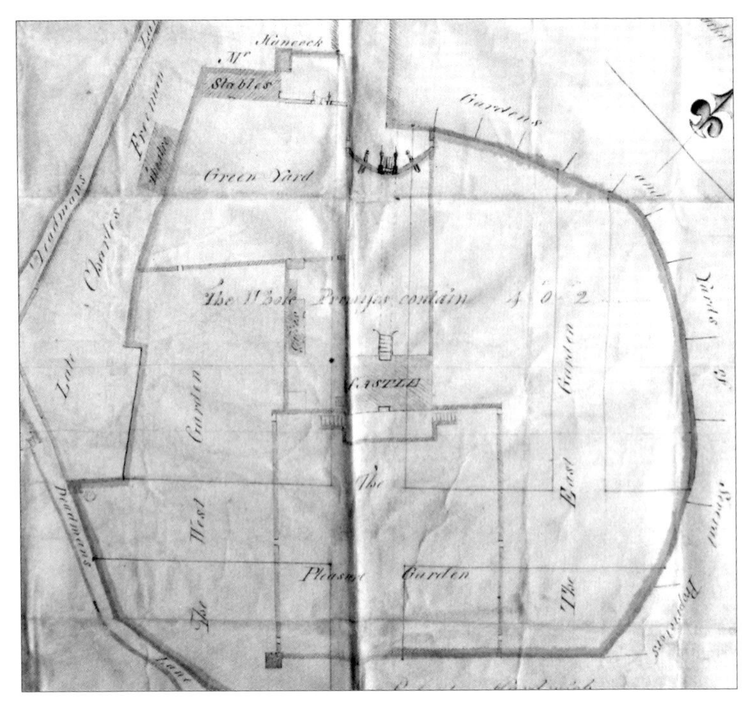

34
This survey of Wisbech Castle shows the typical mid seventeenth-century rectilinear division of the grounds into both ornamental and productive areas. *Cambridgeshire Archives*

To the right was a stable block in its own courtyard, a 'Green Yard' divided by another wall from the 'West Garden', while to the left was the 'East Garden', both bounded by the castle ditch. To the rear of the house a raised perron with a flight of steps either side led down into the 'Pleasure Garden', which was also walled with two entrances to the side gardens and a square building at the south-west corner. Even though the survey is undated, it is likely that it depicts the gardens laid out between 1665 and 1667 by John Thurloe, Oliver Cromwell's Secretary of State and spymaster.[2] The house was demolished in the nineteenth century and replaced in 1816 by a bland Regency block built by a Bermondsey speculative builder, but native of Wisbech, Joseph Medworth.[3] Despite the demolition, stretches of original brick wall survive, as well as the rusticated gate piers.

Sadly, there is no archival record of what the East and West Gardens contained in the 1650s, but a plan of January 1795, although taken over a hundred years later, is close enough in its detail to suggest that many of the original structures survived.[4] Fortunately the plan gives the functions

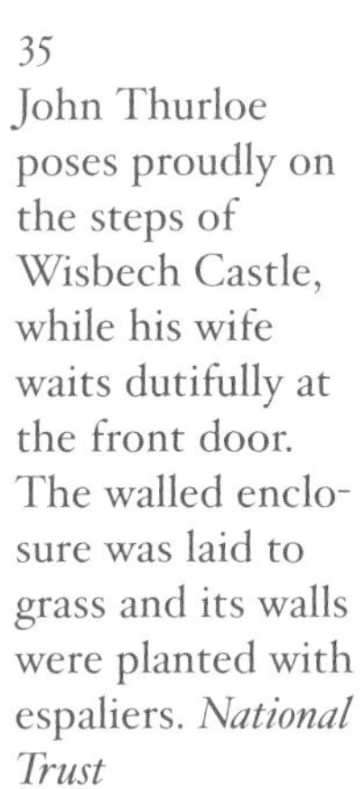

35
John Thurloe poses proudly on the steps of Wisbech Castle, while his wife waits dutifully at the front door. The walled enclosure was laid to grass and its walls were planted with espaliers. *National Trust*

of the various buildings and proves that they followed mid-seventeenth-century practice in combining the ornamental with the productive. The 'Offices' in the right of the forecourt were a brew house and a wash house, while in the corner by the Castle, drawn in faint outline, was the coal house. The East Garden was the kitchen garden and by 1795 the West Garden had become the 'Wilderness'. The 'Pleasure Garden' behind the house would have been a private area for the enjoyment of the family only; in 1795 this was called the 'Blue Gardens', perhaps indicating its specific planting. Although the building in the corner might have been a summerhouse, by 1795 it had become a privy.

There are also no contemporary images of the original garden,[5] but a painting of the main front of the Castle is preserved at Peckover House in Wisbech (35). This shows Thurloe standing proudly at the steps while his wife waits at the doorway; two other women are on the balcony above and a maid looks out from a window. The walls of the forecourt have espaliered trees growing against them and, though the ground is laid to grass with a central gravel path, the roofscape gives a clear indication that there were parterres within the rear garden, for there is a balustraded viewing area on the leads and a further platform above the turret on which a man is looking through a telescope. Such rooftop viewing stations were common in this period and in this part of the country, most notably at Oliver St John's Thorpe Hall, close to Peterborough.[6] Indeed, St John's architect, Peter Mills, also designed Wisbech for Thurloe, who was St John's disciple. With Cromwell's death in 1658, Thurloe gave his support to the Protector's son Richard, but on the latter's resignation of his command in May 1659, Thurloe promised he would promote the Restoration of the Monarchy. However, on King Charles' return in May 1660, Thurloe was accused of high treason and taken into custody. Thereafter, even though he was approached for assistance with the duties of State, he rejected the King's personal request and retired to Lincolns Inn, where he died in 1667.

The Restoration of the Monarchy was little celebrated in such a Protestant county, but there is at least one garden commemorating that dramatic event. At Hilton, to the west of Cambridge on the B1040 from Hemingford Grey to Papworth, William Sparrow laid out a turf maze after the design of another labyrinth, now destroyed, at Comberton, where his brother-in-law, Barron Brittaine lived. The **Hilton Maze** dates from 1660 and is typical of unicursal mazes in that it has a single path with no wrong turnings, coiled into an endless labyrinth. Although present in the classical and medieval periods, most notably at Chartres Cathedral, as horticultural features they derived ultimately from Italian gardens. Designs for them first appeared in the fourth book of Sebastiano Serlio's *Architettura*, which was published in 1537, and, as a result, they were particularly popular in the symbol-laden gardens of Elizabethan England.[7] While almost all have disappeared, another survives at Troy Farm, Somerton in Oxfordshire.[8] If Shakespeare is to be believed, they were once a common feature on village greens, but would disappear if neglected, as in *A Midsummer Night's Dream*: 'And the quaint mazes in the wanton green/For lack of tread are undistinguishable'.[9] Their purpose in private gardens was to provide a path for the walker on which to contemplate life, and in public spaces, like that at Hilton, a path in which to dance and make merry. The Hilton Maze has a central pillar with Sparrow's coat of arms and a Latin inscription recording its date of construction; the pillar was erected at his death in 1729.[10]

This is an appropriate place to mention briefly the county's other delightful labyrinth, even though it dates from 1993. Jim Potter planted his musically themed **Balsham Maze** with green yew and golden yew hedges, the latter forming the shape of a treble clef, which is best seen from the air (*colour 19*). In the centre there are brick-path areas, which form the shape of a French Horn, while in the centre of one horn is a tiered alpine garden with John Robinson's metal spiral, *Joy of Living*, on top. Potter has devised three separate games to play in the maze. The first is merely to enter the maze and explore it; the second is to use the 'Train Rule', in which players must act like trains, approaching each junction like railway points where one must keep going forward rather than doing U-turns. It is vital not to 'play' the French Horns backwards, the air going out from the mouthpiece to the bell. Potter's guide explains, tongue in cheek, that the third game is for professors of mathematics: 'It is possible to get to the centre, always obeying the Train Rule and playing each of the horns once and once only in the correct direction on the way ... and then doing the same on the way out. Don't be discouraged if you don't succeed – it really is very difficult.'[11]

Walled garden enclosures continued to be built long after the Restoration, which had brought with it, in royal gardens and in many of those of the nobility, the formality of French designs, such as those at Versailles and Vaux-le-Vicomte. Even though Charles II had gone French at St James's Palace, commissioning André Mollet in 1661 to produce a bold design with a *patte d'oie* and a central canal, gentlemen in the shires did not necessarily follow suit. Indeed, of the three Cambridgeshire sites that appear in *Britannia Illustrata*, only Wimpole comes close to French design in some of its compartments. The other two layouts at Madingley and

Hatley are clear indicators that the old walled enclosures survived well into the latter part of the century, despite the current trend in more elevated circles for the axial expansiveness of first French and, after the Glorious Revolution of 1688, Dutch design. Yet again the importance of this county-by-county survey is proven by the tendency throughout England of landowners to buck fashionable metropolitan trends.

So it is not surprising that between 1662 and 1674, when Sir Robert Cotton rebuilt the house in its medieval deer park at **Hatley** St George, east of Gamlingay, he set it within a rigidly walled precinct with only a few concessions to the prevailing Franco-Dutch taste (*36*). These were essentially a short reach of canal behind the stable block and an exedral wall where the formal pleasure grounds connected via gates with the regimented orchard beyond. The house and its offices are typical of the early post-Restoration period, with plain façades and high, hipped roofs studded with dormers. The enclosures they commanded were also typical: the usual mix of vegetables, parterres and grass plats centred with statues. What was new, and which might well date from much later in the century, given that the engraved view was published in 1707, is the greenhouse to the side of the main house commanding its own walled enclosure. Such buildings became focus points, particularly after 1688, and are often present in formal gardens where George London was collaborating with the architect William Talman, who made greenhouses an architectural speciality.[12] The accretive appearance of the enclosures at Hatley Park suggests that the greenhouse is a later addition to the existing layout. As we have seen, there was another impressive greenhouse at Wimpole, while the domed cabinets in the grove behind the house there are derived from French design. Similar features were present in the great formal garden at Wilton House, Wiltshire, laid out in the 1630s to a design by Inigo Jones.[13]

Finally, the tree avenues that extend from the canal and form the main approach to Hatley Park are common elements to be found in gardens throughout the seventeenth century, not just in the latter half. Margaret Trefusis, who died in 1734, enlarged the house and there were further extensions and demolitions in the nineteenth and twentieth centuries. Today the avenue in front of the house has disappeared, while the rear garden is not visible from the parish church.[14] The Hatley Road divides two lakes to the east of the house and there is another lake to the south, which may be part of an eighteenth-century naturalising of the landscape.

The last Cambridgeshire garden to appear in Kip and Knyff's *Britannia Illustrata* is curiously undocumented, mainly because almost all vestiges of it were obliterated in a 1756 campaign by Lancelot Brown, whose design, in turn, was altered in the mid-nineteenth century, and again in the early

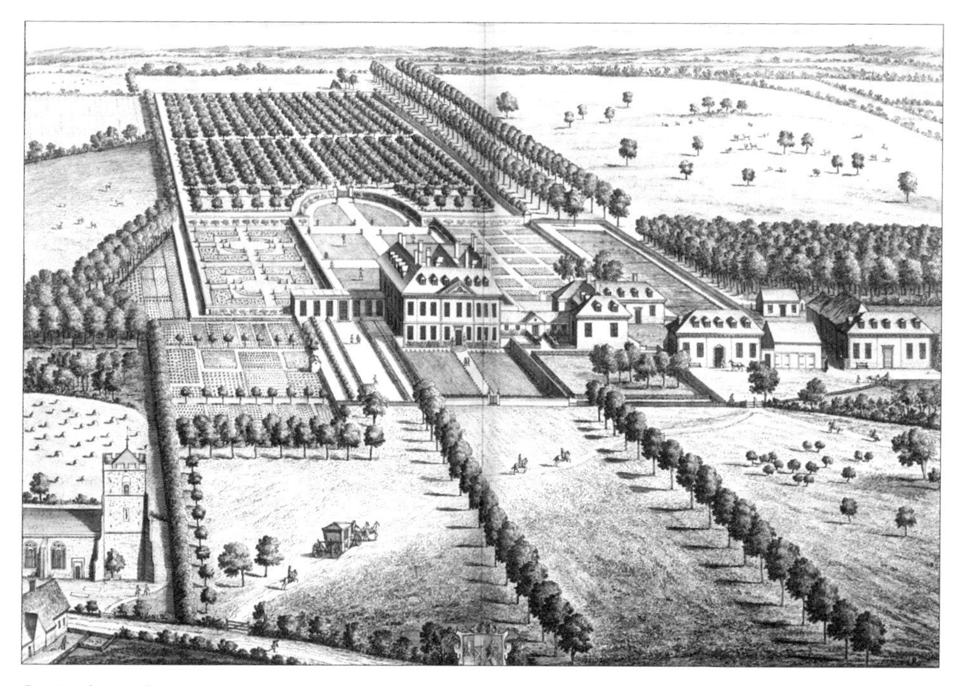

36 Sir Robert Cotton's seventeenth-century Hatley Park from *Britannia Illustrata*. Many of the walled compartments around the house may have survived from an earlier layout. *University of Bristol Library, Special Collections*

twentieth by Colonel Thomas Walter Harding.[15] The key figure appears to be Sir John Cotton, second baronet, whose mother, Jane Hynde, had married in 1647 Sir John Cotton of Landwade. The second baronet, who sided with William and Mary at the Glorious Revolution, inherited **Madingley** on his father's death in 1689.[16] It is not surprising, therefore, that he embarked upon a formal design for the grounds around the house

(37), which must date from between 1689 and 1707, when they were illustrated by Kip and Knyff; Cotton died in 1712. However, there was little attempt to provide fashionable Franco-Dutch features and it is likely, yet again, that many of the walled enclosures dated back to the sixteenth century. There was the ubiquitous bowling green, a rectangular fish tank, a rather desultory parterre to the south of the house and a vast expanse of woodland, cut through with a central gravel walk. While the bones of this design survive, particularly to the south of the house, the only recognisable seventeenth-century features in the gardens today are two gate piers topped with swagged and gadrooned urns either end of a later *clair-voyée* in the north courtyard.

One other seventeenth-century garden that survives is the walled enclosure, built after its purchase in 1672 by Sir Christopher Hatton, at **Thriplow Manor**, due west of Duxford.[17] Beside the fragment of a much larger building there are watery arms of the original moat, while to the rear of the Manor is the enclosure of textured red bricks, which must have been constructed before 1681 when Hatton sold the house to Dr Humphrey Gower, Master of St John's College. That it dates from Hatton's tenure, rather than Gower's, is proven by the stone plinths in the middle of the grass sectors, which have carvings of the golden hind: Sir Christopher Hatton was Queen Elizabeth's Chancellor and funded Drake's famous voyages. Drake's ship was, of course, *The Golden Hind.*

With the turn of the new century the fashion for French axial vistas and canals, combined with the more homely scale of Dutch compartments, continued at many of the more important country estates. However, as we have seen at Madingley, where by 1707 the compartments had mostly reverted to grass, the fussy parterres of Franco-Dutch formality were seen to be both expensive in upkeep and outdated. As a result, the formal layouts of the first two decades of the eighteenth century are characterised by a gradual stripping back of ornamentation, to be replaced by greensward and volumetric landforms, particularly in the designs of Charles Bridgeman, who often worked with Sir John

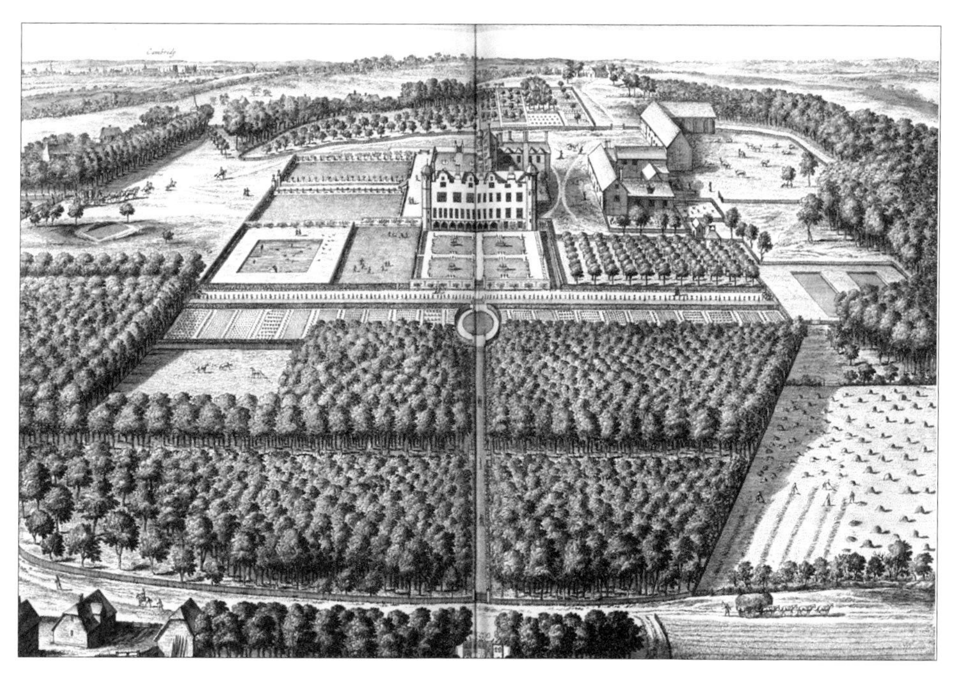

37 While the grounds around seventeenth-century Madingley Hall are of the required scale for a Franco-Dutch layout, they have little of the elaborate horticultural ornamentation of that style. *University of Bristol Library, Special Collections*

Vanbrugh. Between them they developed a distinctive style where a landscape was anchored by a strict geometry, often derived from the form of the Vitruvian Man.[18] Bridgeman favoured particular design features such as canals with apsidal ends; high-banked geometrical theatres like that at the Boboli Gardens in Florence; sentinel garden buildings built on elevated eminences such as earth banks and mounts, often terminating in views or allées; and wooded wilderness areas with both angular and serpentine walks.[19] By the 1720s Bridgeman, soon to be made the sole Royal Gardener to George II, was the foremost exponent of landscape design in the country, and it was to him that the fellows of **King's College** turned when they were planning the re-design of the grounds to the south and west of James Gibbs' New Building.

The fellows had decided to consult Bridgeman on 20 December 1720 'to Lay out the Ground from the West side of the new Building to the Road; and to draw two or three Schemes of different designes for our

Consideration'.[20] The 'Ground' being the land between Gibbs' Building and Queens' Lane, rather than the area behind it towards the river, but there is no record of what he intended. Twenty years were to elapse before a 'Prospect' of the college was published in 1741 (*38*), which shows a formal treatment of the grounds on both sides of the Cam behind James Gibbs' proposed quadrangle.[21] The view gives Gibbs as the architect, James Essex as the artist and P Foudrinier as the engraver. Peter Willis charts Bridgeman's close collaboration with Gibbs at Cambridge and elsewhere, but makes no attempt to ascribe the garden design shown in the engraving firmly to Bridgeman. If it is read in conjunction with the Loggan map of the same area, it can be seen that the designer intended to utilise the walk from the college across the Cam and into the Meadow and the Grove as the axial line, and to obliterate the moated island in the Grove, opting instead for a rectangular basin with an exedral ending. The water feature was to be overlooked by a domed, circular temple. This insistently angular treatment is closer in style to the 1720s than to the 1740s and is reminiscent of the axial alignment of the Queen's Theatre and the Rotunda at Stowe in Buckinghamshire, where Bridgeman worked with John Vanbrugh and where Gibbs was also employed.[22] It may, therefore, represent one of those Bridgeman 'Schemes' of 1720.

Whether by Gibbs or Bridgeman, and whatever the date, the scheme was never executed. Following the publication of the view, between 1749 and 1753, new walks planted with limes were made on the west bank of the river, and another laid out on the south side of the court down to the river. However, if *Cantabrigia Depicta* is to be believed, the Bridgeman plan was still being actively pursued in 1763:

> There are several Gardens and Orchards belonging to this College; and, besides the River that runs thro' them, there are some Moats and Canals, with thick shady Groves of Elms, which render the Avenues to the College exceeding pleasant: and no Place is capable of greater Improvement, by cutting Vista's through the Grove, and

> laying out the waste-Ground about it into regular Walks and Canals; all which is designed to be done (when the remaining Part of the great Square is finished) according to the Plan given by the late ingenious Mr. Bridgman.[23]

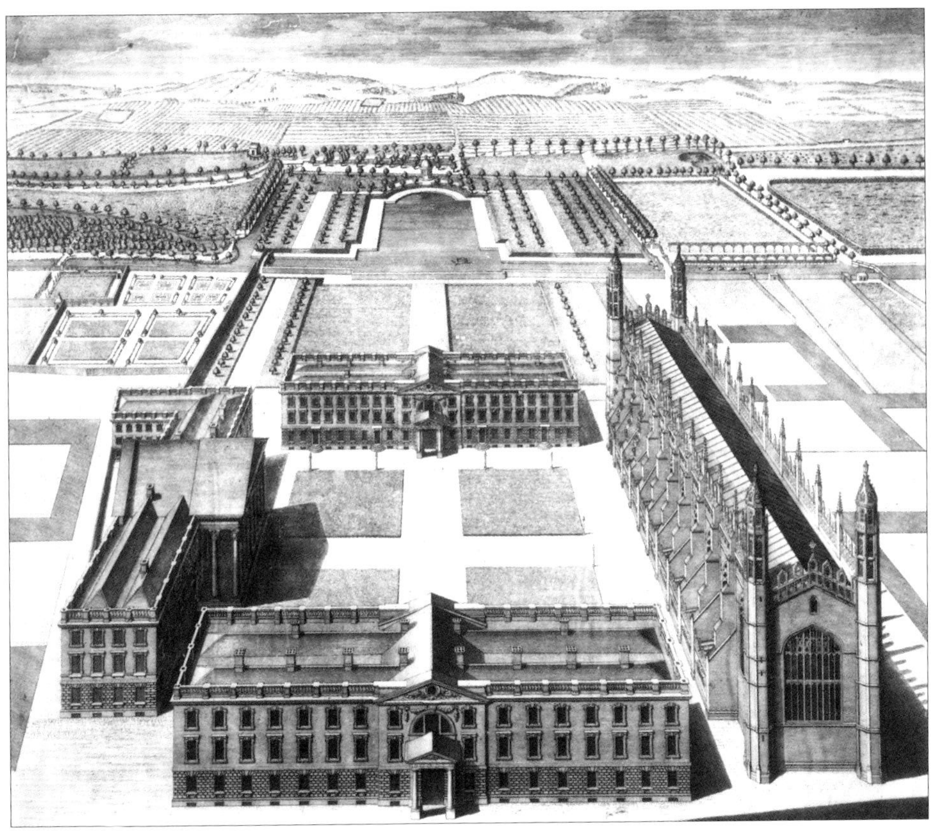

38 James Essex's 1741 engraving of James Gibbs' proposed classical court for King's College depicts a river treatment that may possibly be an unexecuted scheme by Charles Bridgeman. *By permission of the Provost and Fellows of King's College, Cambridge*

It remained a paper plan, with the 'Chapel yard' behind Gibbs' Building surviving unaltered until 1772, when the college voted

> to proceed in the further improvement of the Chapel yard on the West side of the New Building, by laying down the same with grass seeds and afterwards feeding it from time to time with sheep as occasion may require in order to get it into good and ornamental

> condition; to compleat the Gravelling the Walks round the same as now laid out, and not for the future to put any house there.[24]

This effectively opened up the area, which became known as the Back Lawn, to the Cam and provided the focal point for Lancelot Brown's later scheme for the Backs. The garden walls of the original Fellows' Garden on the east bank of the river were demolished at this time under the direction of Essex.[25]

A decidedly Bridgemanic park was laid out at **Gamlingay** by Sir George Downing, who built a house there in 1711-12. This is shown on a much later survey (*colour 20*) made in 1801 by Jenkinson and Lovell, surveyors of Huntingdon.[26] When the survey is viewed in conjunction with aerial views of the site it is apparent that the design was executed and that several features, including the 'large Pond', survive (*39*), though the house itself was abandoned in 1776. Sir George inherited 7,000 acres at Gamlingay in 1711 and spent the considerable sum of £9,000 building his new house, which was nine bays wide and of two storeys and an attic. A vignette of the house is shown on the 1801 survey. The central block was flanked by long wings, which created a U-shaped front courtyard. To either side of the central complex were enclosed gardens, one laid out in quadrants for vegetables, and another as an ornamental parterre.

Sir George's landscape to the north of the house was no less impressive, with semicircular grass ramps – a typical theatrical touch much favoured by Bridgeman – leading down to the trapezoidal pond set within open lawns which merged into dense woodland cut through with rides and walks. The approach to the pond from the house was dramatised on each side by a statue of Mercury and a figure of 'Fame on a Pedestal'. The geometrical axes in the woodland were terminated with further statuary, including an obelisk, an urn, a 'famous figure of the Roman Gladiator', two pyramids, two small buildings that might have been summerhouses and, appropriately for a woodland setting, a 'Beautiful figure of Diana'.

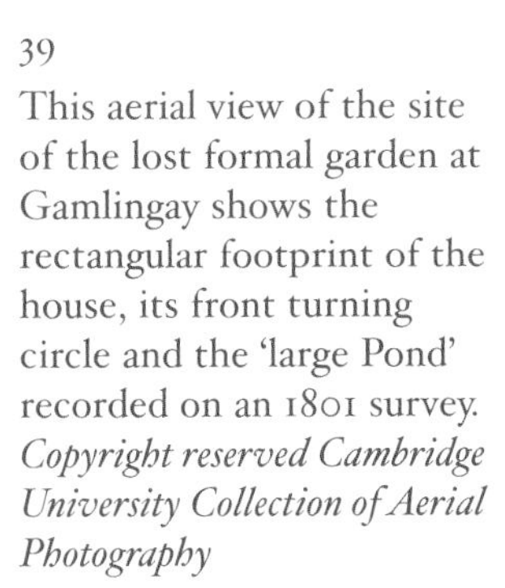

39
This aerial view of the site of the lost formal garden at Gamlingay shows the rectangular footprint of the house, its front turning circle and the 'large Pond' recorded on an 1801 survey.
Copyright reserved Cambridge University Collection of Aerial Photography

Entrances on the outer perimeter were guarded by three gates, one in 'Gothic' style, the other two of 'Half Moon' and 'Full Moon' shape; the latter survives in a hedgerow marking the original northern boundary close to Drove Road. The subjects for the statues are typical of the period and do not suggest any specifically planned iconography. No doubt Sir George saw many such while on his Grand Tour, from which he returned to forsake his young wife, whom he had married before he set out when he was fifteen and she was thirteen. He tried to divorce her but his petition failed and they lived apart.

The most intriguing feature in the woodland was a labyrinth to the west of the house. Visitors would walk across the grass lawn before passing through a gate leading to a tree-lined path that opened out into grassland, where a series of nine rectangular pools switched the axis to the west. These ended in a round pool set within one of the main walks. From this point the intrepid walker would skirt another rectangular pool, find another axial walk heading north and then take a small path off it into the brick-walled enclosure. The labyrinth was laid out with 10-foot-wide gravelled paths and bordered with hornbeam hedges 10 feet high. It is not known whether Bridgeman was responsible for the design, but it has many of his characteristic features and, as we have seen, he had worked in the county at King's College and at Wimpole.

A similar house of English Baroque style, also of nine bays, but with additional quirky blind bays, was built at precisely the same time at Fordham, north of Newmarket. A thirteenth-century Gilbertine priory had stood on the land, hence the name **Fordham Abbey**. It was presumed that the present house of 1790 was built on the footprint of the earlier Baroque building, but an investigation of the site shows it to have been located quite some way off, in an adjacent field, close to a tributary of the river Snail. The clue is the early eighteenth-century Dovecote (*40*), built of brick laid in Flemish bond and with a pyramidal roof, which stands somewhat forlorn in the field. This is present on two rare panel paintings surviving inside the later house, which show both front and rear elevations. The rear elevation is the less impressive as it is dominated by a portrait of a black servant and a St Bernard dog, but it shows the canalised tributary and a hedged compartment alongside a brick boundary wall. The main elevation is far more revealing (*colour 21*). Impressive ironwork gates set within a ramped brick wall give onto a grassed forecourt and turning circle centred by a sundial. In front of the house another walled compartment is decorated with urns and planted up with espaliered trees. Twin pavilions with pyramidal roofs flank the entrance, while the right-hand wing has a loggia set on Corinthian columns. Though the area it commands is laid to lawn, it is likely that the lower building to the right was an orangery that connected with an ornamental garden. As with Gamlingay Park, it is not known who was responsible for the design of the house and garden, but Thomas Archer has been linked with Fordham and also with nearby **Chippenham Park**, north-east of Newmarket.

Admiral Edward Russell, later 1st Earl of Orford, acquired Chippenham Park in 1696 and laid out a park there with a formal garden to the south of the house and two lime avenues.[27] As at Madingley, the early formal landscape at Chippenham has been overshadowed by later interventions, especially after 1795 by William Emes, a follower of Brown, and by Samuel Lapidge, one of Brown's former clerks of works.[28] Chippenham also has a fine modern garden laid out by Anne Crawley within its walled former kitchen garden, which will feature in the last chapter of this book.[29] However, unlike Madingley, most of the Water Garden at Chippenham survives, serving as essential drainage in this watery land on the edge of Chippenham Fen. Celia Fiennes visited in 1698 and saw the house and park before Lord Orford began his campaign. The house had a

40 The early-eighteenth-century Dovecote at Fordham Abbey stands isolated in a field close to the site of the lost Baroque house

distinct architectural emphasis on its roofscape to provide landscape views: 'a flat roofe leaded and railed round full of chimneys'.[30] Significantly, because of its influence on the later planting of the avenues of lime trees, inside the house she saw a painting of the 'battle at La Hogue a large sea piece with an inscription of the Admiralls valour when the great ship the Gunn was burnt, mightily valued by the French King'.[31] Fiennes also mentions 'several good gardens well kept',[32] but not the wider landscape, which suggests that, although Russell was elevated to the earldom in 1697, he did not begin his new Water Garden until 1702; it was completed in 1712.[33] The two lines of limes are thought to represent the positions of the British and French fleets at the battle of La Hogue in Normandy during the Nine Years' War. Interestingly, on the modern OS map to the south-east of the park there are two buildings named La Hogue Hall and La Hogue Farm. They function today as an upmarket delicatessen, farm shop and wine store. Such iconography is typical of a period of military triumphalism, when stands of trees were often referred to as 'platoons'.

Lord Orford's landscape is depicted in a beautifully drawn survey of 1712 by the surveyor Heber Lands,[34] which shows the complex of earlier walled compartments around the E-shaped house and the T-shaped canal of the Water Garden extending out to the north (*colour 22*). Dr Twigs Way has published a definitive account of the Kitchen Garden, particularly after its extension and expansion in the early nineteenth century,[35] so it is the formal enclosures around the house and the outer landscape that require some elucidation here. The former comprise typical yards from the original house, one of which is marked 'Garden', and a series of wooded areas bisected by gravel paths. The main east façade of the house is fronted by a gravelled court and a green court with a turning circle. This has walls and gates and there are further half-moon gates at the end of a tree-lined avenue on the village road. The T-shaped canal on the east is developed from what may once have been a moat system.[36] There is another enclosure with canals, now named the Wilderness, to the north of the main waterway, now known as the Grand Canal (*41*). This last runs parallel to 'The Moor' and terminates in an apsidal-ended bank, while tree avenues march across the park, which is set within its pale. The Lands survey depicts a landscape of status and ownership, if not precisely landed power. The Water Garden was a conscious attempt by Lord Orford to drain a water-logged site for both practical and aesthetic purposes. He continued to work on the landscape long after the survey was drawn, planting hundreds of forest trees and 'quick' to provide hedges in the park. His accounts for 1717-18 reveal the importance he attached to the

41 The Grand Canal at Chippenham Park is the centrepiece of the great Water Garden, laid out before 1712, by Admiral Russell, 1st Earl of Orford

creation and maintenance of his parkland: he paid his 'Master Gardener' £40 per annum, the fisherman £10 and the 'keeper of my park' £25.[37]

Trees featured prominently in the landscape planned in 1663 by the gentleman architect Sir Roger Pratt when he was designing the house and grounds for William, 3rd Lord Alington, on rising land at Horseheath. While it has been taken out of chronological sequence, the park at **Horseheath Hall** makes a fitting end to this chapter of hit-or-miss formality because it demonstrates perfectly the switch from the rigidity of late seventeenth- and early eighteenth-century design to the emergent informality of the 1730s and 1740s. The grounds were originally laid out on an intensely linear plan, but were then naturalised in the 1740s, possibly by William Kent, who was working at that time for the 2nd Lord Montfort.

While there is no contemporary visual source for the seventeenth-century park, Pratt left extensive diaries that discuss his design ethos and detail his several architectural commissions. These comments, taken together with a much later estate plan (*colour 23*) of 1769, give a clear indication of what Pratt hoped to achieve on the windy ridge to the east of the village, parallel to the Roman Road.[38] This green way cuts across the road from West Wickham to Horseheath and heads off east towards Haverhill. The cedars clustering around the site of the house can just be seen from the road, where there is a good parking space and an informative notice board. Once the site is reached, with a roughly triangular area of woodland to the north, two views open up: one due east towards Withersfield of cultivated fields and slight ridges on the horizon; the other to the west more steeply inclined down to Horseheath, with the tower of the parish church rising in the middle distance. The woodland, which is marked Hare Wood on modern OS maps and also on the 1769 plan, is separated from the open fields by a ditch. This is a continuation of the original ha-ha in front of the house. The house site itself is now fenced off, but in amongst the cedars and younger trees the glinting waters of a pond can just be glimpsed.

The ridge-top siting of Horseheath Hall is precisely that which Pratt advocates for all country houses:

> Let the house be placed if not in a park, yet at least in some large pasture, with grounds of that nature round about, for so the surface of the earth always green, will accordingly be pleasant, whereas arable is never so, but whilst corn is upon it. Let it stand at least a furlong distant from the common way out of which you turn up to it, the ground gently rising all along and the level of it both on the one hand, and on the other if not equal, yet at least not remarkably otherwise; the height of the situation will not only render it very pleasant when you come towards it, but will likewise occasion it to stand dry.[39]

Having sited the house correctly, the owner must then consider the immediate environs:

> If the way to the house be not already bounded either with trees or hedges ... let one be laid out by the line, equal at least to the whole front of the house, if not somewhat more, as to that of the court, and so let elms, fir-trees or rather lime-trees ... if they can be had and the ground be fit, be set at 20 foot distance each from other, on both sides of it from one end to the other and the like again cross-ways in a direct line with the front of the court.[40]

This will provide a central walk rather than a way, with ground on either side that might be planted up 'into squares alike', in which something can be placed 'for ornament as statues: trees, little houses or the like, all which cannot but add an exceeding grace to your seat, and will almost with pleasure ravish the beholder'.[41] If the owner were to have 'things thus ordered', Pratt believes that 'when you first come to the house, they will represent as it were a most beautiful scene'.[42]

The earliest entry in Pratt's diary referring to the commission at Horseheath is in November 1662; he went again to meet Lord Alington on 13 December. Thereafter, the entries continue until the work was completed in June 1666, although he was receiving monies in lieu as late as 1668. The foundation stone was laid on 13 June 1663 and the greater part of the building was erected during the following two years. John Evelyn visited on 20 June 1670 and commented that the newly built house was 'seated in a Parke, with a Sweete Prospect & stately avenue, water still defective'.[43] This suggests that Alington had completed the tree planting to Pratt's specifications but that the water by the house had not been sufficiently harnessed into ornamental canals. This raises the question of the siting of the original Horseheath Hall. Catherine Parsons, who has written the most important account of the Hall and its owners, hedges her bets, but ultimately believes that the old Hall was close to the site of the new house and that the chapel mentioned by Pratt might even be that recorded as early as 1580.[44] In 1550 the second Sir Giles Alington enlarged his park by 400 acres, and as the first park lay to the east of Horseheath, 'so the Hall must have stood in the old parkland'.[45] The additional 400 acres near Withersfield became known as the Great, or New Park, as distinct from the Old Park. If the 3rd Lord Alington rebuilt the old Hall then perhaps the 'defective water' was the surviving remnants of a moat, as at nearby Chippenham Park, before Lord Orford made his canal system. One further clue to the possible re-use of the existing site is Evelyn's remark that there was a 'stately avenue', which can hardly have matured in seven years.

What then had Alington and Pratt achieved? Certainly the approach to the house and the view south would have been enlivened with tree avenues, while the close environs of the houses would have been laid out in square grass plats, possibly centred by statues or cypress trees.[46] Houses of this mid-century period tended to have ornamental gate piers, not necessarily with gates hung between them. Pratt himself supervised the construction of Palladian-style stone piers decorated with sculpture busts in niches at Coleshill in Berkshire, while the fields surrounding the site of the contemporary Earl of Craven's lost house at Hamstead Marshall in Berkshire has several sets of elaborate piers (*colour 24*). We know from Pratt's papers that in April 1665 the mason Edward Pearce sent moulds of ornamental scrolls for approval. These were for the stone piers that were to be 'niched on both sides', and would eventually stand 16 feet 4 inches tall.[47] Interestingly, as regards the parkland they commanded, the niches were not intended for busts, but for seats from which to take in the view. With these vantage points and the leaded roof and viewing cupola on the main house, Pratt was making the most of this elevated site.

Parsons believes that the gardens were laid out by Pratt and followed, in their planting at least, the pleasure grounds he devised in 1671 for Ryston Hall in Norfolk. There, the courtyard was on the south side of the house and comprised four grass plats divided by gravel paths. Alongside it the East Garden was planted with fruit trees and there was a flower garden to the north. Gunther gives a list of plants Pratt sourced for Ryston from Captain Leonard Gurle, who had a nursery between Spitalfields and Whitechapel. It is known that Pratt also ordered a great variety of fruit trees from him for Horseheath. Parsons prints a list of fruits for Horseheath, which do not appear in Gunther's book, so she may have obtained it from him via his manuscript notes. They include: plums, grapes, 'pears upon Quince stock', twenty different varieties of peaches, five varieties of nectarines, five of apricots and three types of figs.[48] Gunther notes that Sir Thomas Sclater, who was planting on a larger scale at Little Linton and at Catley Park in 1674-6, also purchased fruit trees from Captain Gurle.[49]

The slow transition from this geometric layout to a more informal Arcadia seems to have been effected by the second John Bromley, son of a Jamaican sugar planter who had bought the Hall from the Alingtons in April 1700, and, thereafter, by his son Henry Bromley.[50] During his eleven-year tenure of Horseheath, the second John Bromley was anxious to improve the estate, but he died in 1718 before the work was completed. His will stated that the gardens were to 'be finished according to plan, unless they could be better contrived with garden walls, iron gates, and all the other things necessary'.[51] If there was insufficient money to carry out the extensive improvements during Henry's minority – he was thirteen when his father died – money was to be used from the Barbados estate. It is clear that, by the time Henry completed his education, first at Eton and then at Clare College, Cambridge, and had married and subsequently lost his wife in childbirth in 1733, there was still much to be done on the estate. Henry remained a widower for the rest of his life and with the help and advice of the antiquary, the Revd William Cole, who since boyhood had been a frequent visitor to the Hall, he embarked upon the creation of a more natural landscape at Horseheath.

Henry Bromley was by far the most cultured and distinguished member of the family, serving as MP and Lord Lieutenant of Cambridgeshire between 1730 and 1741. In the latter year he was created Lord Montfort, Baron of Horseheath, by which time he had spent large sums of money on the Hall and its park. He made new drives across the park, one of which, to the hamlet of Streetley End, was guarded by fine ironwork gates, which are now at the back entrance to Trinity College, Cambridge. In naturalising the landscape he cut down the mile-long elm avenue that extended west from the Hall as far as the main road to Linton, and opened up views south from the house by building a ha-ha, while planting more informal tree clumps in the park. However, his most important contribution to the landscape at Horseheath seems to have been the informal wilderness in Hare Wood, threaded with serpentine paths and enlivened by garden buildings. It is known that Kent was updating the interior decoration of the Hall in the mid-1740s,[52] and it seems likely, therefore, that he was also advising his client upon the landscape. He had already achieved similar enclosed woodlands dotted with garden buildings for Lord Burlington at Chiswick House in Middlesex, at Esher Place in Surrey and at Shotover Park in Oxfordshire.[53] A beautiful drawing by Kent of an octagonal pavilion set over a water-lapped, three-arched grotto (*42*) is inscribed: 'Ld Montfort at Horseheath 1746 WK'.[54] The 1769 plan marks a 'Summer House' in Hare Wood and also a 'Menagery', but Henry's son Thomas Bromley built the menagerie and there is no indication of water by the summerhouse. The archaeologists have found a small mound with brick footings on the south edge of the Acre Pond and surmise that this was the site of Kent's summerhouse-cum-grotto.[55] This seems likely, as does the formation of a second wilderness snaked with wiggly paths to the west of the house within the main gardens. However Twigs Way's interpretation of a building on the 1769 survey as a pagoda is perhaps fanciful.[56] On close inspection it looks more like a memorial column and may date from the next phase of landscaping, during which the grounds were liberally decorated with statuary.[57]

Designing in accord with Kent's advice, Lord Montfort was, no doubt, taking his inspiration from landscape painting. He had amassed an important collection of pictures at the Hall of which, at Horace Walpole's request, Cole made a list. Walpole was a close friend of Cole's and was working on his *Anecdotes of Painting in England*, which was published in

1762. The canvases are typical collectors' paintings of the period and included portraits by Lely and Kneller, Dutch works and Italian religious scenes, but also landscape studies by Claude Lorrain, Nicholas Poussin, Gaspard Dughet and Salvator Rosa. Most significantly, there were over-door landscape pictures by John Wootton in the Grand Salon, which overlooked the park to the east of the house, while in the Grand New Dining Room, which Montfort had converted out of the chapel, there were views of ruins by Arthur Pond and George Knapton, and further

42 William Kent's 1746 design for an octagonal summerhouse set above a triple-arched grotto for the Acre Pond in the pleasure grounds at Horseheath Hall. *Private Collection. Photograph courtesy of the Conway Library, The Courtauld Institute of Art, London*

landscapes by Wootton. Cole mentions a plan of the estate, made in 1746-7 'by Mr. De la Veau, a Prussian engineer', which, if it had survived, would have given a clear indication of what precisely had been achieved.[58] However, under Kent's influence, and that of these continental and native landscape studies, there must have been a softening of the planting and the provision of framed picturesque views across the park.

Lord Montfort was rightly regarded as a connoisseur of art and entertained on a lavish scale at Horseheath. Sadly, he was also an inveterate gambler and his betting and other debts were said to have reduced his estate by about £100,000.[59] In a dramatic gesture, he spent the last evening of 1754 at White's Club, where he gave a party until the New Year was celebrated. The following morning Lord Montfort sent for his lawyer, made his will and promptly shot himself.

5

Brown, Woods, Emes and the Fenstanton mystery

Horseheath Hall · Shudy Camps Park · Madingley Hall
Fenstanton Manor · St John's College
Abbey Park, Ely · Chippenham Park

THAT TRANSITIONAL PHASE OF LANDSCAPING, WHERE THE ECLECTIC, OR so-called 'Rococo' layouts of the second quarter of the eighteenth century gave way to the ideal parkscapes of Lancelot Brown, passed hardly noticed in Cambridgeshire. It is true that when he took over the **Horseheath** estate after his father's suicide in 1755, Thomas Bromley, 2nd Lord Montfort, had inherited a nascent Arcadian landscape, the result of a productive joint collaboration between his father and William Kent. But this layout was confined to the immediate pleasure grounds of the house only, rather than extending across the entire landscape, and in no sense could it be called eclectic or, indeed, Rococo. There were no Gothick rotundas, no Turkish tents, no classical temples, and if Kent had been given any hand in the design, he had been limited to two widely separate wilderness areas and perhaps one, possibly two, garden buildings.

Archaeology on the site has confirmed that Kent's octagonal pavilion above a grotto was built as a focal point on the south edge of the Acre Pond, and that there was a boathouse nearby. The open lawns in front of the house gave uninterrupted views to the tree-clumped parkland beyond, while Hare Wood to the north was threaded with serpentine paths. The summerhouse there might have been by Kent, but the menagerie was added much later, in 1768. As at Badminton on the flat heights of the

Cotswolds, where Kent had worked for the 4th Duke of Beaufort, the extensive landscape at Horseheath was not conducive to a humanly scaled Arcadia like the one at his greatest achievement, Rousham. Kent had attempted to dramatise the level topography at Badminton with isolated garden buildings backed by stands of woodland, or placed sentinel buildings, like the Worcester Lodge, at the end of rides. However, the result was not successful: a mere scatter of classical accents across a vast panorama. Coming to Horseheath at the very end of his career and two years before he died, he must have accepted the limitations of the park and concentrated his picturesque effects on Hare Wood and the wilderness to the south-east of the house.

Kent's designed areas are likely to have included classical statuary, as the 2nd Lord Montfort gave William Cole three lead statues representing Time, Poetry and Painting for his garden at Milton, which had formerly stood at the side of the bowling green at the north end of the Hall.[1] They became surplus to requirements when in 1762 Lord Montfort built a greenhouse on the site, for the colossal sum of £1,300, roughly the equivalent of £78,000 today. The building appears on the 1769 survey (*43*) as a rectangular block with a rear projection, probably containing the heating apparatus. It housed 150 orange trees costing a guinea each. On the lawn next to it was the oddly shaped column, which Twigs Way has suggested was a pagoda. As mentioned earlier, this is more likely to have been a commemorative column, and might well date from Kent's time rather than this later eighteenth-century phase. There are columns raised to the Duke of Marlborough at Blenheim, one to Lord Cobham at Stowe, and another at Hagley Hall in Worcester to Frederick, Prince of Wales. If the structure was, indeed, a Chinoiserie pagoda it would have lent Kent's pleasure grounds at Horseheath an air of eclecticism usually associated with his Arcadian picturesque designs. It is unlikely to have been built after 1755, when the 2nd Lord Montfort took over, as by that time Gothick had generally superseded the Chinese for garden buildings. As well as the greenhouse-cum-orangery, he added the menagerie in Hare

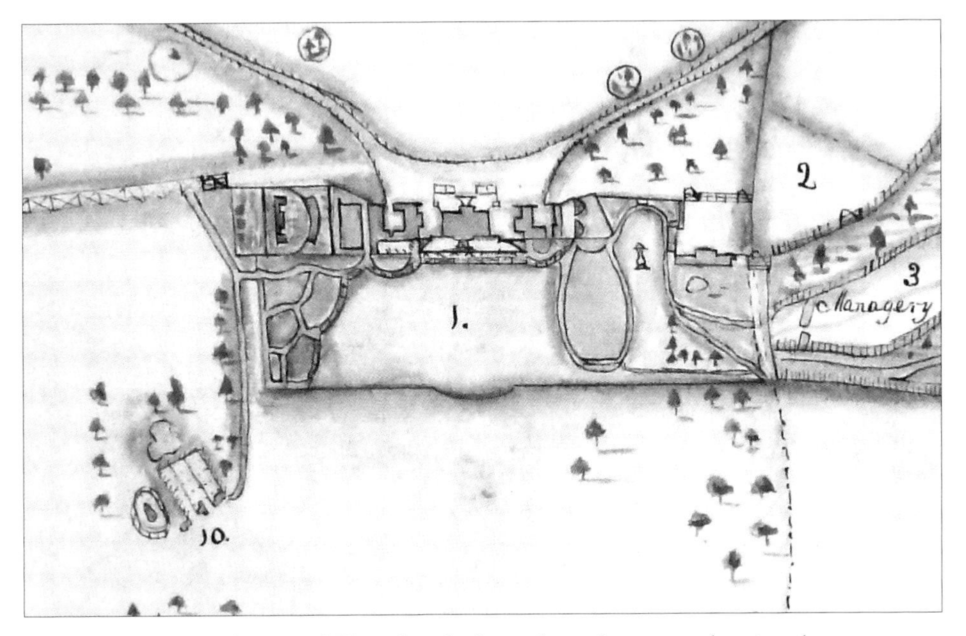

43 The pleasure grounds around Horseheath, from the 1769 survey, showing the greenhouse and the columnar structure sited on an open lawn next to the Acre Pond. *Cambridge University Library, Ms. Plans a.5*

Wood, contained within a fenced enclosure, and an ice house and cold bath, some way off in the park; all these are marked on the 1769 survey.

The 2nd Lord Montfort shared his father's taste for extravagant living and was soon in debt. In order to raise money he sold off his Catley estate in Linton to the Bishop of Ely, who promptly demolished the house and removed some marble chimneypieces and panelling to his palace. However, by 1775 Cole was to write:

> To my great sorrow in the summer of 1775, this noble house [Horseheath] was stripped of its furniture. The owner by an imprudent and unreasonable match three years before, hurrying on what his own extravagant conduct would probably have happened soon after ... His lordship offers the home and estate for £120,000. If he sells it for that he may have £50 or £60,000 to begin again afresh and settle an estate on his son, a fine boy of two years of age.[2]

There followed two sales when 'a large quantity of plants, shrubs, orange and lemon and myrtle trees, exotic plants in pots or tubs, aloes, roses, several garden frames, a large iron roll, [and] a variety of foreign birds with their cages' were auctioned off.[3] The birds had been bought from Joshua Brookes, who had a menagerie in New Road, Tottenham, in London. By August of the same year the mortgaged estate at Horseheath was practically lost to Lord Montfort, and in September the park was let for grazing. Following an abortive attempt to sell the estate in 1777, the Hall was pulled down and the materials sold. These included 'a large quantity of stone steps, pavements, posts, a stone bridge, balustrades, vases, statuary and outside decoration', not to mention the 'greenhouse lately erected'.[4] Today, almost all of the parkland has been ploughed up, most of it during the Second World War.

Little also remains of the mini eighteenth-century landscape created at Park House, in the adjacent parish of **Shudy Camps** to the south.[5] The nine-bay, red-brick façade of 1702, grafted onto an earlier gabled core, stands impressively above a simple grassed enclosure, where there is the ghost of a semicircular ha-ha. To the rear all vestiges of earlier gardens have gone, to be replaced by a striking modern layout. It is difficult, therefore, to ascertain exactly what was achieved on the site between 1763 and 1764 by the landscape gardener Richard Woods, who was working for Marmaduke Dayrell. Woods had a busy and lucrative practice designing landscape parks in the Brownian manner, but enlivened still with evocative garden buildings. He had a predominantly Catholic clientele, and had been introduced to Dayrell by John Spencer of Cannon Hall in Yorkshire.[6] Contemporary correspondence between Woods and Spencer reveals the close interest the latter was taking in his friend's garden at Shudy Camps. A letter of November 1763 from Woods confirms that he had been commissioned: 'I will now according to my promise tell you how Mr Dayrell & I have settled the operations of his plan'.[7] Dayrell's account at Hoare's bank shows a payment to Woods of £20 in June 1763, and a further £80 in March 1764, suggesting that this was a very minor job.[8] After a dispute between Woods and Dayrell, the two men decided 'to make a very small garden behind the house, & to take in the first Lane, & lay it to the Lawn'.[9]

Fiona Cowell, Woods' biographer, believes that he laid out a small pleasure ground behind the house, which extended as far as the oval pond, which still exists to the east of the building. This four-acre area, mostly laid to lawn, but with a patch of woodland masking the service buildings, is shown clearly on the first edition Ordnance Survey map of 1886; so too is the bastion-like ha-ha to the front of the house. The rest of the parkland, whose perimeter is defined by lanes, does not suggest any design input, but a curving drive, tree-lined along its length, snakes in from the west.

There is an intriguing footnote to this commission. A photograph of a country house painting can be found in the parish box for Castle Camps in the National Monuments Record in Swindon. It is a typical mid-century family portrait of a husband and wife and their daughter, with the house prominent in the background (*44*). The building is of seven bays and has a central portico, so it does not match the surviving house at Shudy Camps, which is of nine bays with a rhythm of paired windows, but the ground slopes away from the house as it does at Park House and the service area is in the same position. To the left of the house is a remarkable garden building. It might have been a dovecote that was later converted into a Gothick summerhouse with an ogee-headed loggia, above which is a room lit by ogee-headed windows. This is very much in Woods' style and is almost identical in design to a summerhouse he planned in 1777 for Hengrave in Suffolk.[10] The painting cannot be of the great house at Castle Farm, Castle Camps, set within the grounds of the medieval castle, for that was a sixteenth-century building, which had been demolished by 1738. Might this conceivably be a view of Park House, Shudy Camps, before it was extensively remodelled in the nineteenth century?

Woods was offering a particular brand of designed landscape of shrub and flower-filled pleasure grounds around the house, which edged into the wider parkland where shelter belts, tree clumps and stretches of water were dramatised by eclectic garden buildings such as Gothick seats, grot-

44 A painting of a family group in the grounds of an unidentified house, which may be Park House, Shudy Camps, where the landscape architect Richard Woods worked in the 1760s. The octagonal Gothick summerhouse is close in style to Woods' designs for garden buildings at other estates. *National Monuments Record, Box 0394/2*

toes, cascades, dairies and classical temples. At the same time Lancelot Brown was doing his level best to strip such decorative appurtenances from his parks and render them vacant of habitation, unless by owners riding around in fast carriages or busily shooting birds on the wing. Brown was essentially a minimalist and aimed at a landscape vacancy, one entirely in tune with the wishes of his landowning clients. His parks were first and foremost sporting and leisure arenas and required open spaces rather than enclosures, fussy pleasure grounds and architectural incidents. Hence his determination at **Madingley Hall** to take out trees, sweep away any surviving remains of the formal gardens, including filling in the canal, and 'give the whole a natural corresponding Level'. This was the stated aim of the first of four articles of his agreement with Sir John Cotton for the landscaping work to be carried out between 1756 and 1757.[11] This commission, though on a much smaller scale than his usual undertakings, is interesting in that both correspondence and the articles of agreement survive to give a clear narrative of what was undertaken.

In a rare glimpse of Brown's personal rather than professional life, he writes in November 1756 of his 'indisposition on the Road' due to that of his eldest son, who 'is down of a Scarlet Fever and expect[ed] to fall every day, which renders it next to impossible for me to leave them til it is got over'.[12] Consequently, he was to send down a foreman and would hope to follow soon after to begin the work that had been agreed in the same month. This was standard practice for Brown who, after producing a survey of the estate showing in somewhat sketchy outline what he intended, would then itemise the work to be done in a series of articles. Payments for each of these would have to be met before he would embark on the next article, thereby ensuring that he was paid for all his work. The Madingley commission was to cost £500, inclusive of his usual 80-guinea fee for the initial survey and travel expenses; that equates to almost £30,000 in current monetary values. This was a colossal sum for what was essentially a smoothing out of the existing terrain and the laying of a gravel path around the newly created lawn. To achieve this simple landscape Brown intended to 'fill up the Bason, and all the Pieces of Water', except the lowest reach, which would become the lake, to drain the site, make a 'Fosse', or ha-ha, lay out a new 'Coach Road' and 'to take down such Trees as are thought necessary and to plant others where wanted'. Once this earthmoving and land shaping was done, the lawn was to be turfed to create the desired 'natural and easy Level'. Much of this simple landscape survives today, now browsed by cattle and forming a perfect rural foreground to the house (*colour 25*). Even though Brown aimed to produce a landscape scene devoid of decorative garden buildings, one at least was built, close to the house. This is a beautiful Gothick-arched stone Gateway with matching wooden seats set up as a new entrance to the service court (*45*). Although Brown sometimes offered Gothick designs at this early phase of his career, when owners wanted functional

45 This Gateway, originally at the Schools building in Cambridge, was re-erected at Madingley Hall in 1758 with some new Gothick touches, including the wooden seats, by James Essex

buildings in a decorative dress, the Gateway came originally from the Schools building at Cambridge and was re-erected at Madingley, with new Gothick flourishes, by James Essex in 1758.

Although a relatively minor commission by Brown's standards, the Madingley scheme offers an important insight into Brown's working methods and his family life. Such detail is rare and eagerly seized upon by biographers, particularly as regards his supposed residence in the county. However, by relying on the work of others rather than targeted site investigation, most Brown aficionados have been chasing a hare set running in the 1930s by a Miss Peet, who at that time owned the **Manor House at Fenstanton**, originally in Huntingdonshire, but now part of Cambridgeshire. No doubt impressed and perhaps even excited by their visit, when researchers from the *Victoria County History* came to call, Miss Peet informed them that her small, Dutch-gabled house had been lived in by Brown, who had indeed been lord of the manor of Fenstanton, having purchased the estate from the Earl of Northampton in 1767. Consequently, the *VCH* entry for the Manor House reads:

> There are some 17th-century timber-framed cottages in Chequers Street, towards the east end of which is the Manor House, a good 17th-century brick house with shaped gables at each end and a brick porch of two stories, now the residence of Miss G. M. Peet. Some of the internal fittings are original. This was the house in which Lancelot Brown, generally known as 'Capability Brown', lived after he obtained the manor from the Earl of Northampton in 1768. Brown started life as a working gardener and had a great reputation for laying out gardens after the then new style of landscape gardening, and later practised as an architect. He amassed a considerable fortune, and was sheriff for Huntingdonshire in 1770.[13]

The researchers duly acknowledged Miss Peet in a footnote and Brown's residence in Fenstanton was thus confirmed without further enquiry. Interestingly, the *VCH* parish entry also mentions the **Manor Farm**, due west of the village, 'a good 18th-century brick house with stone dressings and a slate roof. From its design and fittings it was evidently intended for a private residence'.[14] When the relative architectural merits of the two houses are considered in Fenstanton today, the Manor House (*46*), though modestly charming with its shaped gables and tall topiary trees in the front garden, appears insignificant when compared with the now renamed Fenstanton Manor (*47*), formerly Manor Farm, which commands open fields to the east. This is a house of far more consequence, one more fitting for a professional who had, by the time of his arrival in the village, landscaped no fewer than 150 parks and was a wealthy man. However, all Brown's biographers have followed Miss Peet's lead and, until now, no one has disputed her assertion that he lived at the Manor House, close to the parish church of St Peter and St Paul, where in 1783 his Gothick mural monument was raised and where he was buried in the churchyard, north of the chancel.

46 The unassuming Manor House at Fenstanton, on the village street, can hardly have served as the residence of Lancelot Brown, the country's foremost landscape practitioner

47 The polite status and elegant architecture of Fenstanton Manor, formerly Manor Farm, is likely to have encouraged Brown to contrive a designed landscape between it and the main village across the common land in between

It is not surprising, therefore, that when Dorothy Stroud published her pioneering biography in 1950 she wrote that as early as 1766 Brown was thinking of acquiring a 'small estate of his own', and when Lord Northampton, for whom he was working at Castle Ashby, 'contemplated disposing of one of his properties, the Manor of Fenstanton ... Brown got wind of the news' and asked for first refusal.[15] Northampton prevaricated, but the disastrous elections of 1767 'left him no alternative in which the money owing for Castle Ashby could be paid off'.[16] Brown inspected the estate in August 1767 and wrote to Northampton in the September agreeing to take it for £13,000. On the deed of transfer the Earl wrote: 'I take the Manor of Fen Standon to belong to Lawrence Brown Taste Esq., who gave the Lord Northampton Taste in exchange for it'.[17] Stroud concludes:

> So Lancelot Brown became Lord of the manor of Fenstanton, with paramount authority over Elsworth, and here, at such times as he was not at Hampton Court, the foremost exponent of landscape, the devout disciple of Palladio, came to reside in a small, old-fashioned gabled manor house, standing virtually on the edge of the road, with a pair of clipped yew trees growing on either side of a modest front door.[18]

Is this likely? Would the 'foremost exponent of landscape', who had just spent the rough modern equivalent of over £750,000 buying the estate, which he paid in two instalments over just six months,[19] be satisfied with a 'small, old-fashioned gabled manor house, standing virtually on the edge of the road', just because it was styled the Manor House? And would he have thought such a house befitted his status when in 1770 he was appointed High Sheriff of Huntingdonshire? This was a man who, on his death in 1783, left about £35,000 (over £2 million in modern terms), in addition to the estate at Fenstanton, not to mention the sizeable dowry he had given to his daughter Bridget.

Certainly, later writers have thought so, in particular the compilers of the otherwise excellent gazetteer of historic landscape sites in the county, *The Gardens of Cambridgeshire*,[20] and climaxing in the most recent biography by Jane Brown. She writes:

> What had he bought? The estate was the manor of Stanton cum Hilton, two ancient villages, Fenny Stanton and Hilton ... on the edge of the Great Ouse valley ... These were remote places in a watery and gentle countryside in a small quiet county: there were no large houses, no dramatic inequalities of landscape that Lancelot might feel he had to improve, and there was plenty of good fishing in the quiet meadows beside the Ouse.[21]

After such an evocative description of the place, it is strange that Jane Brown did not notice Fenstanton Manor, due west of the village by the A14, which is, without question, the most architecturally significant house in the parish.

It is reasonable to assume that, after his purchase in 1767, Brown took a suitable house on the Fenstanton estate and over time planned to make some improvements to the immediate environs. In the second edition of her biography, Stroud notes that the deed of transfer included 'the Manor Farm and its mid-eighteenth century brick house with stone dressings and a slate roof',[22] but that 'although Brown paid insurance premiums on it, there seems to be no record of his family residing there, and [that] it probably continued to be let to tenant-farmers'.[23] Stroud accepts the received wisdom 'that it was presumably' at the Manor House where 'Brown stayed on his comparatively rare visits to his estate'.[24] However, recent research by Steffie Shields has confirmed that the Manor House was also let, to the yeoman Samuel Clifford.[25] In one respect all the Brown biographers are correct. He could not have made any garden or landscape around the Manor House, which is hemmed in by the village street at the front and by common land to the rear. However Manor Farm, or Fenstanton Manor as it is now known, commands an extensive open prospect across common fields towards the village, with the church spire as a focal point in the view. This land features on a plan of 'Fenstanton Town & the Green &c' drawn up in 1777 by John Spyers (*colour 26)*, ten years after Brown's arrival and under Brown's instruction as lord of the manor.[26] Spyers was a nurseryman and accomplished draughtsman, who, together with Samuel Lapidge, had been engaged by Brown in 1765 to assist with the preparation of garden designs at Hampton Court.

In 1764, the year before he enlisted the help of Spyers and Lapidge, Brown was made 'Surveyor to his Majesty's Gardens and Waters at Hampton Court'[27] and moved his family there, to Wilderness House. This was a late seventeenth-century building, sited a few hundred yards to the west of Lion Gate. Wilderness House remained Crown property throughout Brown's tenure and as a consequence he was keen to possess a house of his own. This would explain his interest in Fenstanton and its surrounding landscape.

An early nineteenth-century plan of Fenstanton survives, which shows the apportionment of land in the village.[28] This confirms that 'T Brown Esqr' owned land to the rear of the Manor House, but also land between Manor Farm and the village, marked as 'Hall Green' on the Spyers plan, together with extensive lands to the rear of Manor Farm. This is likely to refer to the Revd Thomas Brown, Lancelot Brown's grandson, who became lord of the manor in 1808; it therefore denotes family-owned land.[29] Thomas Brown is also given as the owner of two tracts, one 'in Fee', on the other side of the turnpike road on 'West End Green'. The family's specific land holdings are significant, as it is in these areas that the 1777 Spyers plan shows the designed improvements. There might be no 'dramatic inequalities of landscape' here, but the abundance of water and open common must have appealed to Brown's landscape sensibilities, particularly as he owned the estate.

Manor Farm, marked number 112 on the plan, has a U-shaped range of ancillary buildings, while the main rectangular house gives onto a fore-court carved out of the common land. Brown's 1773 indemnity for £1,800, taken out with Sun Insurance, whose plaque numbered 551360 is still on the house, covered a kiln house, dairy, brew house, malting office, corn house, chaff house, cow house, hog stiles, stables and barns, as well as the Manor House and the imposing seven-bay, early-Georgian brick building at Manor Farm.[30] Giant classical pilasters articulate the main elevation to the meadows and there is a prominent plat band between the floors. This must have seemed a far more desirable gentleman's residence to the 'devout disciple of Palladio' than the humble, old-fashioned Manor House on the main village street. It afforded status, privacy and a beautiful prospect, and seen from the village across fields of grazing cattle and sheep must have looked like a small country house waiting to be enhanced by one of Brown's own minimalist parks. Even if the Manor Farm were let out fairly soon after Brown's purchase of the estate because he was, as Stroud suggests, 'never away from Wilderness House for long',[31] its immediate environs could still be remodelled to mark his beneficence as the lord of the manor and to proclaim his status locally as the country's foremost exponent of landscape design.

The land between the house and the village comprised Hall Green, Long Green and Round Green to the north of the turnpike and West End Green to the south. The meandering Hall Green Brook, which survives today, traversed the common land but, as with most fenland waterways, it is now trained to follow a rigidly angular course. The Spyers survey shows the Brook transformed into a serpentine, its banks lined with mature trees clumped at intervals; even the small tributaries were intended to be tree-lined. Most significantly, the Brook has been expanded into a lake at the point where the three northern greens intersected. There is a further pool to the west at the end of a stream, lined again with trees. A series of pathways connects the lower road by the Manor Farm with the lake and a bridge across the Brook gives access to the village; a small footbridge survives at this point today. With its eighteenth-century parent house commanding the extensive prospect, this designed landscape, whether it was eventually realised or not, has many of Brown's hallmark characteristics, as depicted by his trusted employee. It is, perhaps, no coincidence

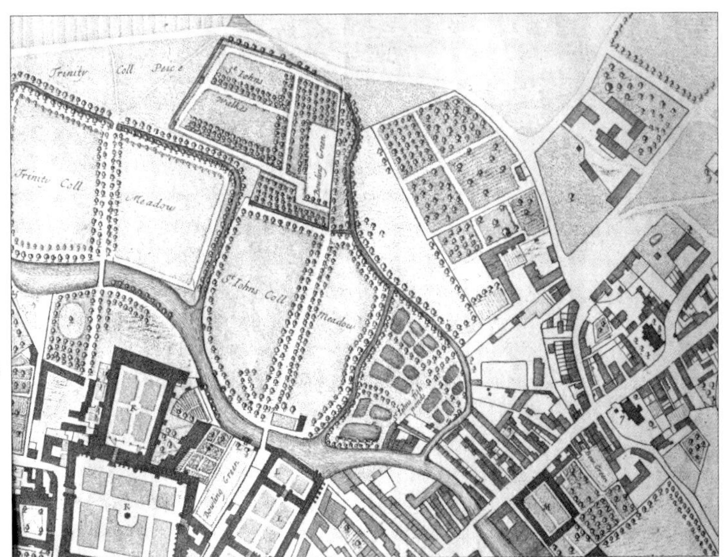

48

The tree-lined walks of the Fellows' Garden at St John's on the west side of the Cam, shown on Loggan's 1688 plan, were swept away by Brown in 1772 and replaced with a spacious lawn edged by trees. *Reference Library, Bristol Central Library*

that Brown was busy at exactly this time, in the summer of 1772, strengthening the banks of the Cam at **St John's College, Cambridge**, a commission which was to prove the catalyst for his later, wildly ambitious and consequently unexecuted, scheme for remodelling the Backs.

Brown had been approached by his good friend, the Revd John Mainwaring, a fellow of St John's who shared Brown's passion for landscape gardening.[32] The College was engaged in encasing the first court in stone and had already called in Charles Miller, first Curator of the Cambridge Botanic Garden and son of the more famous Philip Miller of the *Gardener's Dictionary*, for advice on the grounds. But Miller's two-guinea fee suggests that he did little more than offer some advice, which was not acted upon. Brown's name first appears in the College records for 10 July 1772, when it was 'agreed that the bank of the river should be repaired under his direction'.[33] Brown submitted his plans for the 'Wilderness' or Fellows' Garden on the west side of the Cam a few months later. This area is shown clearly in Loggan's 1688 map (*48*), accessed via a bridge across the river and along a tree-lined walk across the 'Meadow', and, as we have seen, features prominently, marked as the '*Ambulacra*', in his accompanying plate of the college. In true minimalist style, Brown swept this stiff seventeenth-century formality aside in favour of a spacious lawn edged with a thick glade of trees. All this was to cost £800, though Brown did not expect a fee. Instead, the Master, Dr William Powell, and the Fellows presented him with a piece of plate worth £50 for his services.

Fired by his reshaping of St John's area of the Backs and his own proposals for Fenstanton, Brown then turned his thoughts to tidying up the whole sector of the Cam from the rear of Queens' College as far as Magdalene.[34] The 1634 map in Thomas Fuller's 1655 *Church-History of Britain* shows this west bank as a series of enclosed enclaves for the enjoyment of fellows seeking privacy. Little had changed by the time Loggan came to survey the city for his 1688 *Cantabrigia*. Brown presented his ambitious scheme (*49*), entitled 'A Plan presented to the University of

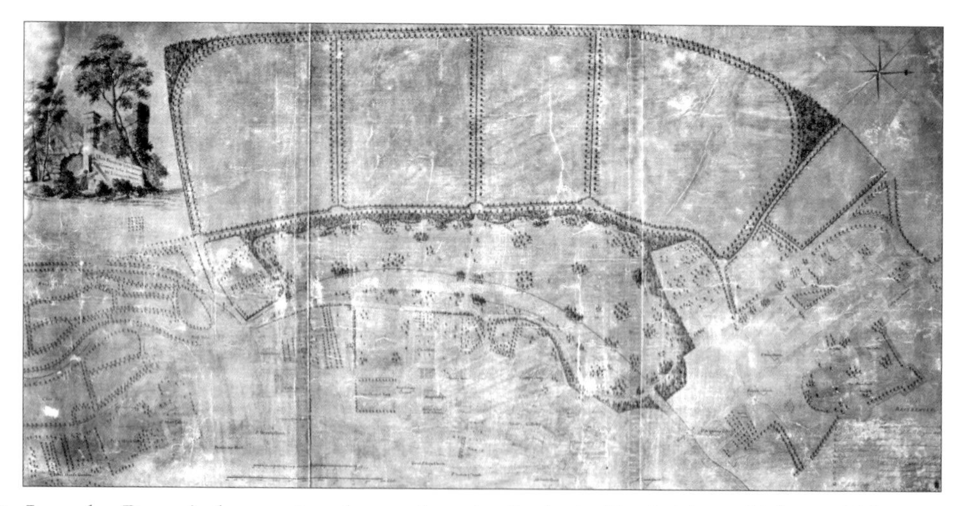

49 Lancelot Brown's destructive plan to alter the Backs in Cambridge, which would have involved the demolition of all the bridges except that at Trinity Hall, was mercifully unrealised. *Cambridge University Library, P.I.3*

Cambridge for some Alterations' in 1779.[35] Marcus Whiffen has interpreted this plan, rightly, as an attempt to restructure the landscape in terms of a parkland setting with Gibbs' Building at King's acting as the focal country house; hence the vast expanse of lawn before it. Brown wanted to widen the Cam into a serpentine lake, with planting along the east bank framing views of the Palladian building, while blocking out all other colleges.[36] George Dyer wrote that 'the eye would certainly have

30 Repton's view, with the slide in place, of the old red-brick house at Waresley, which he hoped might be remodelled under the direction of one of his sons. *RHS, Lindley Library*

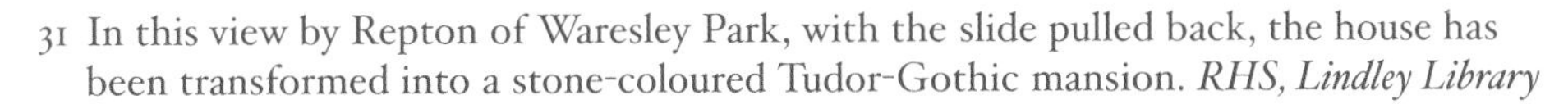

31 In this view by Repton of Waresley Park, with the slide pulled back, the house has been transformed into a stone-coloured Tudor-Gothic mansion. *RHS, Lindley Library*

32 Milton Hall, designed by William Wilkins between 1789 and 1790 to command a designed landscape by Repton

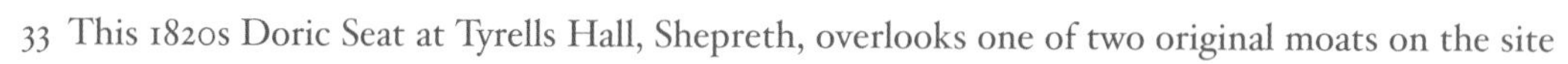

33 This 1820s Doric Seat at Tyrells Hall, Shepreth, overlooks one of two original moats on the site

34 Charles Madryll Cheere's Grand Tour inspired him to commission George Byfield's majestic Greek Revival Papworth Hall and its Italian Garden in the grounds

35 The Summerhouse at Witcham Hall probably dates to the 1840s, when the existing house was remodelled in Tudor-Gothic style

36 The original University Botanic Garden, depicted by Ackermann in 1815, before it moved to its present site. *University of Bristol Library, Special Collections*

37 David Mellor's 1970s Fountain provides a dramatic focal point in the Botanic Garden

38 Some of Sir Michael Foster's irises still flourish at Nine Wells House. *Robin Newman*

39 This majestic black walnut dates from the nineteenth-century planting campaign when the Allix family was resident at Swaffham Prior House

40 The open lawns of Newnham College are surrounded by Basil Champneys' engaging red-brick façades

41 AH Powell's 1906 plan for Newnham College would have transformed the Victorian grounds into an Arts & Crafts linearity with axial walks and a vast pergola. Each College building was to have its own separate garden. *The Principal and Fellows of Newnham College Cambridge*

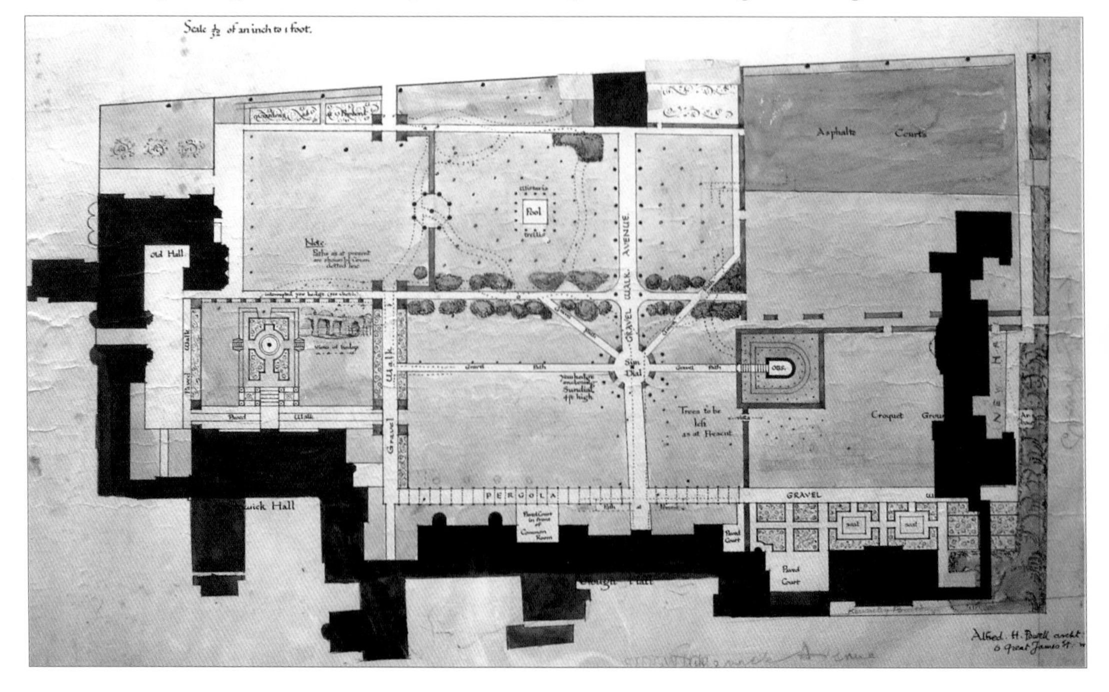

42 The Edwardian-style Croquet Lawn at Madingley Hall was laid out by Colonel Harding just before the outbreak of the First World War

43 The first of a series of graduated garden rooms devised in 1912–13 by MH Baillie Scott at 48 Storey's Way in the suburbs of Cambridge

44 The Arts & Crafts suburban idyll at Church Rate Corner, Cambridge, designed in 1924 by MH Baillie Scott

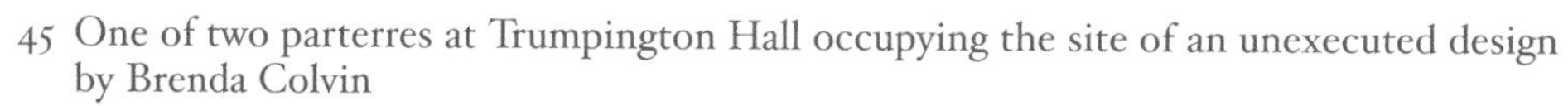

45 One of two parterres at Trumpington Hall occupying the site of an unexecuted design by Brenda Colvin

been pleased with walks more winding, with a greater variety of trees, with something more of a winter garden of evergreens, and of light underwood near the river, and that without affecting to bring the Wye, or Usk, to these haunts, or obstructing the navigation'.[37]

To appreciate quite how radical his scheme would have been if implemented, not only would the private garden areas on the west side of the Cam have been obliterated, replaced by a vast, tree-clumped lawn, but it would also have resulted in the demolition of all the bridges except that at Trinity Hall, which was to be rebuilt on a more appropriately ambitious scale. Not surprisingly, the plan would have been extortionately expensive to carry out, but the main issue must have been the proposed removal of all the historic boundaries between the colleges, which survive today. These fellows' gardens are labelled on the Loggan plates as '*Hortus Sociorum*', horticultural retreats offering collective engagement, whether it was physical, intellectual or aesthetic. These were essential qualities which Brown, whose Ciceronian motto accompanying his coat of arms was, ironically, 'Never less alone than when alone', seems not to have considered important or relevant.[38]

It is not clear whether the **Abbey Park** on the south side of Ely Cathedral offered the same contemplative solace to successive bishops and deans, but it was made to look more like a contemporary Brownian park than a functional deer larder in 1779 by James Bentham, a minor canon of the Cathedral. The park is dominated by Cherry Hill, the remains of a twelfth-century castle, which was originally topped by a windmill. Speed's 1610 map shows the mill, while an engraved print by Samuel and Nathaniel Buck of 1743 marks it as Mill Hill, but at that time surmounted only by a stump. Bentham planted the mound with fruit trees, mainly walnut, pear and cherry, and laid out a spiral path to the top, where he erected a classical column bearing the Latin inscription: 'That these might benefit another age'. His philanthropy was depicted in a wooden panel (*colour 27*), now at the Ely Museum, which shows the stand of trees fenced around and the Ionic column set on its plinth. In 1872 John

Bacon, Clerk of Works to the Dean and Chapter, noted that 'large parties would sit on the grass in circles while they enjoyed the red, the white, and the black heart cherries' on Cherry Sundays, celebrated in Ely in July each year.[39] Today the mound is completely overgrown with trees, including some holm oaks, while at the top is a graffiti-defaced plinth, from which sprouts an armature for a lost column or finial, with one Latin inscription just visible recording Dean Merivale's planting of an oak tree on the summit in 1879.

There was one final flurry of Brownian activity in the county before Humphry Repton breezed into Waresley Park, where he proceeded to pitch for a re-ordering of the deer park, which is what his client William Needham had requested, but also a complete architectural makeover of the house, which he had not. Repton was a chancer and, more often than not, his paper proposals came to nothing. This was not the case with William Emes, another follower of Brown, who worked out of Mackworth, Derbyshire and whose commissions were mainly in the Midlands, particularly in Staffordshire and Cheshire, and North Wales. Emes enjoyed a successful practice, producing brand new landscapes or working at sites where Brown had been previously to modify or complete the original designs, as he had done at Wimpole Hall. Like his contemporary Richard Woods, Emes embraced the design ethos of Brown's ideal parkscapes, but attempted to bring garden architecture back into the mix.

After Lord Orford's death in 1727, the **Chippenham Park** estate was inherited by his niece, changed hands several times and was then bought in 1792 by John Tharp, a Jamaican sugar planter. His first action was to commission a survey from Emes and his assistant, John Webb, for a proposed reshaping of the landscape (*50*). This was essentially a conservation management plan for the difficult watery site, with a few design alterations. The Grand Canal was to be severed from the top stroke of the T-shaped canal and divided from it by dense woodland cut through with a grassy walk ending in a clearing. Further dense planting was to line either side of the Grand Canal and to enclose the Kitchen Garden above it. The top stroke of the canal system was to be widened into a more informal lake and given a pronounced serpentine profile. It was to end in a clump of trees, a typical Emes touch. Interestingly, the smaller water-courses near the Kitchen Garden, which survive today, are not shown on the survey, so perhaps Emes intended to fill them in. The 1843 tithe map marks the wooded area around the Grand Canal as 'Ashwood', suggesting its original planting.[40] In a July 1803 letter from Tharp to his son, also John, who was managing the estate for his father during the latter's absence in Jamaica, he instructed his son how to look after pheasants: 'the pheasants are always fed upon buckwheat from October to the end of winter under the ash wood, which brings most [of] them into the park'.[41] This is yet another instance of the landscaper providing the required environment for rearing birds for sport. In the same letter Tharp asks for news about the tree planting: 'If I am right there are many spruce firs planted in the Fen and more will hereafter be there when I return, but we must have other trees to give beauty and profit to that creation, which when mature will give ample room and cover for all the pheasants Chippenham can support.'[42]

Elsewhere on the estate the Emes-Webb plan advocates the softening of Lord Orford's original regimented lines of trees into more picturesque clumps, while typical Brownian shelter belts were to line the park perimeter. Almost all of this planting is shown on both the 1843 map and the first edition Ordnance Survey map of 1886. Although the survey shows no new garden buildings, James Wyatt was preparing plans for remodelling the house during the same period and, although nothing was done, Wyatt's Lodges and triumphal-arched Gateway (*colour 28*) were built on the approach road from Newmarket. Contemporary commentators, including Arthur Young, writing in his 1805 *Annals of Agriculture*, praised Tharp's successful drainage and cultivation of the landscape, noting the subsequent increase in the value of the land.[43] John Tharp was essentially a gentleman farmer, in the mould of Thomas Coke of Holkham Hall, Norfolk, in Tharp's words, one of the '*GREAT GREAT*

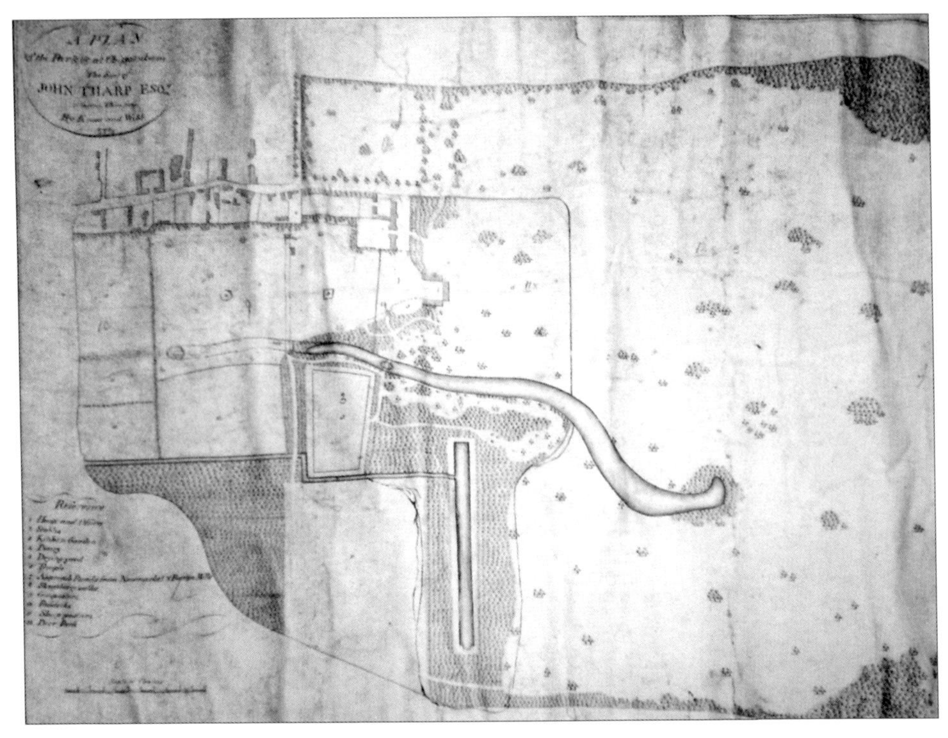

50 A plan for naturalizing some elements of the angular Water Garden at Chippenham Park, commissioned by John Tharp from the landscape architect, William Emes, in collaboration with his assistant, John Webb. *By kind permission of Eustace Crawley*

MEN', with whom he had the honour of dining on a two-day visit to Chippenham in March 1802, just before Tharp left for Jamaica. He died there in 1804 and never came to enjoy fully the landscape that he had done so much to preserve and enhance.

6

'The present taste for cheerfulness & freedom' – Repton in the county

Waresley Park · Island Hall · Milton Hall · Dullingham House
Great Abington Hall · Bourn Hall · Tyrells Hall

ASKED IF HE WOULD RATHER WORK FOR A NOUVEAU-RICHE SUGAR PLANTER like John Tharp of Chippenham Park, or a major landowning aristocrat such as the 3rd Earl of Hardwicke of Wimpole Hall, Repton would have bowed his head most obsequiously and opted unflinchingly for the latter. A love of the aristocracy was his particular passion and a fawning deference his usual attitude when in their presence. So it must have been a great sadness to him that he was constantly in demand by industrialists, bankers and lawyers, the professionals of the middle class. After failing in several professions himself and setting out as a landscape gardener just when the war with France had forced most aristocrats to tighten their belts, Repton could not afford to be choosy. As a result, most of his Cambridgeshire commissions were for middle-class owners like the Cambridge banker, John Mortlock of Great Abington Hall.

Repton's first job in the county was at **Waresley Park**, then in Huntingdonshire, where William Needham asked for his services in May 1792.[1] Repton had completed his Red Book by August of the same year, when it was presented for comments. It is a slim volume of 19 pages, illustrated with a few watercolour sketches, and concentrates mainly on the creation of new approaches to the house across the existing deer park and the removal of barriers protecting the grounds from deer. To 'avoid those lofty and unsightly fences, which deer render necessary', Repton proposed 'to exclude them from all parts where new plantations are to be made'. So that Needham could understand exactly how this was to be achieved, Repton included a monochrome watercolour with 'lines of visibility' from two small figures, one standing on the ground and the other halfway up a ladder. With the slide pulled back the new landscape, unencumbered by barriers, was revealed. Repton's accompanying map of the park (*51*) shows the fences and where, marked with letters, he proposed to take them out entirely by building a 'sunk fence' or a 'line of hurdles', or relocate them, especially on the west side of the estate, in a valley, thereby hiding the park pale from view.

51 Humphry Repton's map of the park at Waresley, from his 1792 Red Book, offers suggestions for the removal of unsightly fences and the creation of new drives with attendant lodges. *RHS, Lindley Library*

Always with an eye to the main chance for more work, Repton also advised upon the approach to the house and proposed new lodges, the possible introduction of two new water features and, in an attempt to get an architectural commission for one of his sons, the complete remodelling of the main house in either Grecian or Gothic style. His delightful sketch of twin classical lodges for the south entrance includes a signpost to give directions. These lodges were intended to give 'an air of attention and property beyond the actual boundary of the park'. Repton was always anxious to aggrandise any estate he encountered in order to flatter the owner. The lodges were never built, but the proposed new drive was intended to pass through that part of the park where there was 'a brook, which holds the possibility of making a piece of water, and tho' it could not be seen from the house, it would be a beautiful circumstance in the approach'. Both the lake and its eastern finger of woodland, planted to obscure views to the water from the house and, therefore, render it a surprise in the landscape, are still in place today. As for the second piece of water, Repton was not so lucky. An existing rectangular pool by the kitchen garden was to have been 'altered to that of a Crescent', commanded by a new cold bath (*colour 29*). Sadly, neither seems to have been implemented, but the main elements of Repton's design survive within the equestrian complex on the site today.

Repton's grand schemes for remodelling the house were never realised. However, his reasons for employing the Gothic rather than the Grecian style in his proposals are pointers to the perceived superiority of the medieval over the classical in achieving a picturesque profile (*colour 30 & 31*). As at Stoke Edith in Herefordshire,[2] Repton was keen to alter the colour of the house from red to cream to produce a 'picturesque harmony', and advised Needham to opt for the Gothic in any new campaign because it consisted of '*perpendicular* lines, breaking up in height with an irregular outline above the roof'. His comments might well have been written by Uvedale Price, whose *Essay on the Picturesque* was to appear two years later. It is not clear whether Repton managed to get any other architectural commissions for his two sons – John Adey and George Stanley – as the estate is privately owned and was not accessible for this study. The present South Lodge looks to be late Victorian in style, while the North Lodge was not visible. However, Repton or one his sons might have been responsible for some semi-detached cottages on the main B1014 Gamlingay Road (52). These have the air of estate buildings, are

52 This pair of semi-detached cottages on the main road at Waresley may have been designed by Repton's son, George Stanley

enlivened with picturesque thatch and ogee-headed archways, and are close in style to cottage designs by George Stanley Repton.

Repton's involvement at **Island Hall** in Godmanchester is far less clear, as the house is of the mid-eighteenth century, and was originally built by John Jackson, of a family of Huntingdonshire merchants, though with strong ties to John Montagu, the 4th Earl of Sandwich.[3] Jackson benefitted from this patronage by becoming bailiff of Godmanchester and Receiver-General for Huntingdonshire. As a result of a lucrative marriage to a local heiress, he was able to commission Island Hall, which was described in the abstracts of title in 1749 as a 'New Built Capital Messuage'.[4] The house has an imposing pedimented front to the main street and a similar elevation to the rear garden, which extends as far as the Great Ouse. The adjacent stable block is topped by a lively Gothick

53 The Chinese Bridge at Island Hall connects the main lawn with the island across the Great Ouse. The original bridge might have been designed by James Essex in the 1750s; or it might date from 1804, when Repton was associated with the then owners

lantern, similar in design to work by the Cambridge architect James Essex, particularly the re-erected Gateway at Madingley Hall mentioned previously. An open lawn edged with trees leads down to the river, where a restored Chinese Bridge (53) gives access to the island beyond. The dating of the Bridge is problematic; it might be Regency to accord with the planting of the grounds, or it could possibly be another mid-century design by Essex. He had constructed William Etheridge's wooden bridge at Queens' College, Cambridge in 1749-50, which has a distinct air of the oriental. There was, no doubt, a bridge at this point across the river, but precisely of which period is hard to ascertain. However, the family connection of a later owner of Island Hall with the Knights of **Milton Hall**, where Repton is known to have worked, is intriguing and suggests that he might have been commissioned by both families.

Jacob Julian Baumgartner, a merchant of Huguenot Swiss extraction, bought Island Hall in 1804. The Baumgartners had married into several local families, including the Tryces and the Knights of Milton Hall. There are two surviving Repton watercolours of a proposed new house for the Revd Samuel Knight, Rector of Milton, one with the inscription: 'W Wilkins the Building, H Repton the Landscape'. John Jacob's son, John Thomas, a doctor, also occupied Milton as his principal residence from time to time in the early nineteenth century. So the connection between the two houses was close and Repton may well have provided design advice for both owners. The Bridge, which has been faithfully restored from old photographs, is very close in style to fretwork fences and other elements of the 'Chinese character' that Repton was currently employing at Woburn Abbey in Bedfordshire.[5] In 1805 he redesigned the pool setting for an existing Chinese pavilion there, provided a new menagerie and connected islands with Chinese-style bridges.[6]

With the two watercolour proposals for Milton Hall we are on much firmer ground. In fact, they comprise three images, as one is a before-and-after treatment of the existing house in its setting with the usual slide, while the other is a view of the new house proposed to be built by the elder William Wilkins, with whom Repton often worked in tandem. The landscape painting is inscribed: 'For Samuel Knight Esq at Milton near Cambridge' and dated September 1789. Knight, who was an old friend of Repton's, had bought the property in 1767 from Jeremiah Pemberton of Trumpington and it is thought that he embarked on its rebuilding in 1790. With the slide in place the watercolour presents a rather desultory scene of pasture grazed by sheep and cattle, which Repton proposed to transform with a new watercourse extending into the existing shrubbery (54). In his 1795 *Sketches and Hints on Landscape Gardening*, Repton remarked that at Milton 'a small river has been made, with great effect, in proportion to its quantity'.[7] Repton was at Milton in 1790 and subsequently noted that he received cash to pay a nurseryman's bill amounting to just over £63, though he was not charging for his own input.[8] The other painting is in the form of an architectural drawing of the new house, which is clearly derived from

54 Repton's before-and-after watercolour sketch for improving the grounds at Milton Hall, with the slide pulled back to reveal a new watercourse extending into the shrubbery. *By kind permission of Christopher Vane Percy*

contemporary designs by Sir John Soane, particularly those published in his 1788 *Plans, Sections and Elevations of Buildings*.

Remarkably, the house survives intact today (*colour 32*), though with the addition of a Doric porch on the entrance front and most sympathetically designed modern wings on either side. The front forecourt is laid to lawn edged with mature trees, while the rear lawn gives on to a ha-ha lost in brambles from which there is a view of Repton's landscape, now bristling with electricity pylons (55). These are all dummy pylons set up to provide operatives with essential practice when the house was used after 1948 by the Eastern Electricity Board as its regional headquarters. Repton's 'river' is now lost somewhere in the scrubby field, though an auction catalogue of 1862 describes it as 'a lake of ornamental water'.[9] The sunken lawn immediately below the windows of the house may have been

55 Repton's landscape at Milton is now overgrown and punctuated with unsightly fake electricity pylons, erected to give prospective engineers essential practice without the shocks

a more formal garden in Repton's time; certainly it was to have been reshaped when Sinclair Research was in ownership. However, Cindi Simon's elegantly angular scheme for Sir Clive Sinclair, which was to have been dramatised by a modern metal sculpture, was only partially carried out.[10] Milton Hall is now the headquarters of Pi Innovo, which with sensitive planting has contrived a new approach to the house from the main road.

In a rare departure from his usual deference to a client's wishes Repton had the temerity to object to Colonel Jeaffreson's desire to have a body of water introduced to the south lawn on his initial visit to **Dullingham House**, south of Newmarket. This important difference of opinion accounts for the long gestation of the Dullingham Red Book, which took over two years to complete, from Repton's first inspection of the site in September 1799 to his delivery of the proposals in February 1802.[11] According to Repton's initial remarks, the site was 'attended with such difficulties as I have never before experienced in the many hundred which have passed under my consideration'. He felt it necessary to acknowledge

56 The front garden of Dullingham House was walled in and fenced off from the village street before Repton arrived in 1799 to survey the site and present a Red Book of proposals in 1802. *Photograph by kind permission of Sir Michael and Lady Nourse*

57 Repton's view of Dullingham, with the slide pulled back to reveal open lawns, artfully placed trees and a new conservatory on the side of the house. *Photograph by kind permission of Sir Michael and Lady Nourse*

that he could not 'fully coincide' with his client's 'wishes, regarding the water in front of the house'. He had no problem with the proposed removal of brick walls to open up the house to the village street and its deer park beyond and gave a before-and-after treatment of the process (*56 & 57*). This would alleviate 'the Gloom & confinement which formerly prevail'd, when every mansion in the County was surrounded by lofty walls', and accord with 'the present taste for cheerfulness & freedom'. By a stroke, the view of walled and fenced confinement from the road is transformed into a scene of contoured lawns dotted with specimen trees and a graciously curving driveway. Always one to gild the lily, Repton also introduces a new greenhouse to the side of the house. Apart from the greenhouse, this is the scene today on approaching the house from the south.

As for the intended water, Repton strengthened his arguments by illustrating two separate layouts: one 'not advisable' and the other 'recommended'. Even with the realignment of the road there was not, in his view, sufficient room to develop the existing watercourse alongside the road into a small lake. If it were to be achieved, then the two areas of lawn by the house and beyond the water by the road would be difficult to maintain, hence his suggestion that the larger grassed area in his preferred scheme be grazed by sheep. His proposal for carrying the existing water under the lawn in a culvert was adopted, as too was the hidden wall to give uninterrupted views over to the deer park. There follows his usual attempt to cover the red-brick house, not with stone-coloured stucco, but with 'such a wash as may resemble the Colour of grey Suffolk bricks, as more in harmony with the surrounding greens of nature'. Repton also advocated 'white washing & painting' the nearby cottages and fixing 'trellis ornaments' to them, or training plants against their walls, so that 'the whole village should appear part of the place'. In everything, Repton was aiming for a harmony of parts and the 'view of uninterrupted Lawns & plantations' around the house. The Red Book does not focus on the rear of the house, where Sir Martin and Lady Lavinia Nourse have laid out a rill garden and a walled parterre with a pergola by the house. There are sumptuously planted borders against the walls, while further out, beyond the enclosure, there is an octagonal bowling green surrounded by old yews.

Much less survives of Repton's work at **Great Abington Hall**, which is now surrounded by the modern structures of the Granta Park Estate near Linton. The red-brick house is set in a dip below a utilitarian canteen block with a small reach of the Granta snaking to the rear. This is the site of the medieval manor house of the Earls of Oxford, which was rebuilt in about 1712 by Maximillian Western, son of a wealthy ironmonger. Western built new stables to the north-west of the Hall and canalised the Granta to the rear. The present house is late eighteenth century in date, probably built around the core of the 1712 structure. This campaign may have been

58 The verandah at Great Abington Hall is a Regency feature that was probably built during Repton's remodelling of the pleasure grounds around the house for the Cambridge banker, John Mortlock. Nothing of Repton's design survives on the site today

carried out by James Pierson, a London merchant, who bought the house from the Revd Charles Western in 1784. It was later given a beautiful Regency ironwork verandah along the whole length of the south façade (*58*). This must be coeval with Repton's landscaping of the immediate park around the house for the Cambridge banker, John Mortlock, who had bought the house from Pierson in 1800. The tall French windows giving onto the verandah, opening up the house to the pleasure grounds beyond, suggest that any flowery formality would have been concentrated on this front. Unfortunately, the whereabouts of the Red Book, if one was ever produced, is unknown, and Repton's precise input must remain conjectural. Dorothy Stroud wrote in 1962 that 'some good planting survives', but that was when the British Welding Research Association was in residence and long before the creation of Granta Park.[12] The only reference to Repton's involvement at the site is given in his *Observations on the Theory and Practice of Landscape Gardening*, where he cites Abington Hall when discussing diverting the course of roads from the close environs of country houses.[13] Stroud refers to payments to Repton between 1799 and 1812 in the Leigh Papers at Shakespeare's Birthplace Trust in Stratford-on-Avon, so he had a long association with the place.[14] What is clear today is that much of his planting has disappeared, but also that this is an old site, with an ancient pollarded oak standing as a boundary marker by a silted-up ditch, which leads to the church of St Mary, marooned in the fields beyond.

If the present approach to Great Abington Hall, via faceless modern blocks and car-parks set in a new, as yet immature, landscape of scientific research, is unexpected, that to **Bourn Hall**, south of Cambourne, is refreshingly predictable: a short drive through a small landscape park commanded by a 1602 gabled brick house with Tudor-Gothic embellishments of 1817-19.[15] As befits the site of an original eleventh-century castle, the house sits on an elevated position, close to the remains of an embankment overlooking the surrounding countryside. It is thought that a formal-style garden was laid out to the south of the Hall in the seventeenth century,[16] but it is Repton's work for George John Sackville-West, great-grandfather of Vita Sackville-West, that is the most important garden campaign on the estate. Here, at least, Repton was to work for an aristocrat, for George John had inherited the earldom of De La Warr at his father's death in 1795, when he was only five years old. After graduating from Oxford in 1812, the 5th Earl married in 1813 Elizabeth Sackville, daughter of the 3rd Duke of Dorset, and later acquired a special licence to put his wife's surname before his own. The Bourn connection was through his mother, Catherine Lyell, whose family lived in the village.

The Bourn commission was one of those rare occasions when Repton managed to get some architectural work for his son, John Adey. In fact, the Tudor Revival interior decoration is one of the earliest examples in the country, particularly in the entrance hall with its ribbed plaster ceiling. Elsewhere in the house John Adey re-used wooden panelling and inserted a seventeenth-century staircase and a fireplace in the drawing room, dated 1555, both of which he brought from Haslingfield Hall. On the exterior he added the ornamental brick chimneystacks and the five-arched loggia flanked by canted bays giving onto the sunken lawn to the south-west, which is contained within the inner bailey of Picot de Cambridge's castle of 'Brune'. Richard Norman Shaw, who was working for John James Briscoe between 1884 and 1885, filled this loggia in. Today

59 An archival photograph of the elaborate parterre garden on the south-west front of Bourn Hall. It is likely to have been an original Repton design, but renewed and remodelled in the 1880s. *By kind permission of Bourn Hall Clinic*

the lawn is devoid of horticultural ornament, but early photographs (59) at the house show a complex three-tier parterre of scalloped flowerbeds threaded with gravel paths. It is likely that Humphry Repton laid out the original design, even if it had been replanted by the late Victorian period, as a formal garden appropriate to a house of this age. He had done the same at Beaudesert in Staffordshire, where his elaborate parterres, contemporary with his similarly historicist work at Ashridge in Hertfordshire, were based on his knowledge of the Tudor ruins of Oxnead Hall in Norfolk. John Adey had drawn a reconstruction of the Tudor gardens at Oxnead for John Britton's 1809 *Architectural Antiquities of Great Britain*, which is close in style to the lost parterres at Bourn.[17] While all trace of Repton's formal garden has gone, a brick bridge crossing the remains of the moat survives and may be a Reptonian addition. As for the approach drive to the house, which Repton might have thought needed adjusting, that was altered to its present configuration after 1826.

The final garden of this pre-Victorian period has earlier antecedents in the form of another multi-moated site, but it retains miniature garden buildings of the kind that Repton would have introduced, if he had been allowed, into his Cambridgeshire landscapes, particularly at Waresley. On our visit, **Tyrells Hall** at Shepreth was buzzing with horsey activity in the stable yard by the main house. This last had been built after 1759 by William Woodham, who commissioned the surveyor, Jeremiah Slade, to prepare a map of the estate, which is dated 1764.[18] The map shows the original moat by the house enclosing an orchard, two arms of which survive, and a further rectangular moated orchard in the fields to the west, which survives in its entirety, planted up now as a wild wood; a small enclosed garden abuts the house at the western end. Following a land enclosure in 1823, the orchards by the house, the 'Roundabouts' field to the west and 'Lammas Mead' and the 'Old Mead' across the southern reach of the moat were made into a small park. At least three ornamental garden buildings were introduced at this time: a canopied Doric Seat with slender columns (*colour 33*) for views over the southern arm of the moat by the house, a miniature mock Castle of flint and render overlooking a pond to the north (*60*) and, close by, a plunge pool, of which only the bath remains. These last two features are in another originally moated area of the park known as Hallyards; the Castle is thought to have been built on the site of an oratory, connected with William de la Haye's manor house, a licence for which was granted in about 1280. One further building, an

60 A late Regency folly Castle of the 1820s overlooking a pool, which was originally part of a moated area of the estate, at Tyrells Hall, Shepreth

elaborate cottage at the entrance, has been turned into a thatched motel. The present owners have done much to restore the two surviving garden buildings, maintain and re-plant the woodland and create a new garden around the swimming pool within the Walled Garden to the west. This enclosure must also date from the 1820s, when the land was emparked and the main house given a makeover. The modern planting has been designed and supervised by the Kendricks' gardener and horticulturalist, Rachel Macintyre. Her plant expertise leads us seamlessly to the late Regency period, with its increasing emphasis on horticultural experimentation, and then inexorably to the Victorian excesses of regimented bedding and overblown garden rhetoric.

7

Nineteenth-century diversity and a question of stylistic identity

Papworth Hall · Babraham Hall · Cherry Hinton Hall · Witcham Hall
Windmill Folly · University Botanic Garden · Pampisford Hall
Harston Park House · Little Shelford Priesthouse · Elterholm
Nine Wells House · Swaffham Prior House

UNWITTINGLY OR NOT, IN THE REGENCY PERIOD HUMPHRY REPTON HAD ushered in that fussy, surburban style that J C Loudon was to term 'Gardenesque', with its emphasis on horticultural experimentation and the cultivation of exotics in increasingly more sophisticated greenhouses. Pleasure grounds close to the house became awash with flowerbeds and shrubberies threaded with gravel paths while, where they were indulged, parterres were tricked out with garish bedding plants. Cambridge had a sprinkling of such gardens that cohere only by their chronology, for there is no connecting theme in this free-for-all of stylistic diversity. This chapter must, therefore, feature several layouts at surviving late Regency and Victorian houses in order to provide some coverage, but it should be stated at the outset that the most significant site of this century in Cambridgeshire is undoubtedly the University's Botanic Garden. It quite literally puts all other nineteenth-century gardens in the county into the shade and is a model of intellectual endeavour and inspired benefaction. It must be treated in its chronological place; however, other earlier gardens will not detain us too long.

One curious and, unfortunately, ill-documented garden was laid out by Charles Madryll Cheere, who built **Papworth Hall**, at Papworth Everard, between 1810 and 1813 to designs by George Byfield. He then set about creating a park around it, which was completed by 1824 and incorporated a circular moat. Cheere linked this feature to the house by a central, tree-lined walk, one of three forming a *patte d'oie* radiating out into the park. The northernmost of these passed a circular pool and cut through Papworth Wood, both of which survive on the site today (*61*). To the rear of the moat was a walled kitchen garden, divided into quadrants, in which there were bothies and glasshouses. The first edition Ordnance

61 The circular pool and wooded area of the moat, around which Charles Madryll Cheere contrived his Italian Garden, are clearly visible in this aerial view of Papworth Hall. The crescent of buildings relates to the Tuberculosis Colony that was established at Papworth in 1918. *Cambridgeshire Archives, 1140/5/13/173*

Survey map of 1887 shows all this in place, as well as marking a statue on the south side of the moat. The *CGT Gazetteer* states that this was the centrepiece of Cheere's 'Italian garden', that there were once 'cages for rare birds between the Italian and kitchen garden', and that 'a breed of exotic pheasant was named after Cheere'.[1] Quite what was Italian about the layout is unclear as Cheere, who had been on the Grand Tour, was more interested in Greece, encouraging his architect to incorporate Greek details at the house. These included on the outside a semicircular porch with unfluted Doric columns and a portico with four giant unfluted Ionic columns (*colour 34*). In addition, the entrance hall was given red scagliola columns and pilasters. However, it is likely that while he was abroad Cheere collected sculpture and statuary for the grounds at Papworth and their classical style gave rise to the epithet 'Italian'.

Almost all formal layouts of this pre-Victorian period, which deployed statuary and urns, often displayed on terraces, were invariably called Italian. The most significant early examples were Thomas Hope's Deepdene in Surrey of 1818-23, and Lady Pembroke's 1826 terraced garden at Wilton House, Wiltshire, laid out with the help of the sculptor Richard Westmacott.[2] The architect Charles Barry contrived more archaeologically informed layouts at Trentham in Staffordshire and Shrublands in Suffolk.[3] Charles M'Intosh listed the different nationalities of gardens and their character, including the Italian, in his *Flower Garden* of 1837-8:

> ITALIAN: characterized by one or more terraces, sometimes supported by parapet walls, on the coping of which vases of different forms are occasionally placed, either as ornaments, or for the purpose of containing plants.[4]

Although the lead statue is thought to survive at Papworth, most of Cheere's garden was lost when the Hall became the Cambridgeshire Tuberculosis Colony in 1918 and its grounds were built over for the sanatorium. Early photographs of the poolside area show the hexagonal cubicles in which patients could enjoy the benefits of fresh air. The Papworth National Health Service Hospital Trust now owns the site.

Two houses – Babraham Hall (1833-7) and Cherry Hinton Hall (1834) in the suburbs of Cambridge – represent the stylistic confusion of the 1830s and 1840s, when Tudor vied with Elizabethan and Jacobean, the styles being yoked together in the portmanteau terms 'Jacobethan' and 'Tudorbethan'.

Witcham Hall, west of Ely, was remodelled in Gothic style slightly later, in 1840. All have gardens of no discernible character surviving in fragments around them. An early photograph of the garden front of Jacobethan **Babraham** (*62*) shows a low-lying parterre with urns by the loggia and a single sundial further out in the lawns. Just visible are small statues by the house, which still cower underneath the arcaded basement floor. These are

62 This archival photograph of the garden front of Babraham Hall shows the original fussy parterre enlivened with urns and naked putti. *Cambridgeshire Collection, Cambridge Central Library, Y.BAB.K03*

the epitome of naked putti kitsch, their nether regions covered ostentatiously by strips of carved drapery. One listens intently to a conch shell (*63*), the hand of another rests on a cornucopia, while others have lost their hands and whatever they held. Further out in the lawns is another urn with the backdrop of new research facilities on the other side of a yew hedge.

Of more consequence is a yew and holly-shadowed raised walk, whose sloping bank facing the house has been made into a Rockery. At one end of this feature are the brick, pebble and clinker footings of a lost summer-house, while similar materials mixed with knapped flint decorate the

63 One of the putti surviving from the Victorian formal garden at Babraham Hall

bank. This is a typical early Victorian feature, which first emerged in the 1820s and reached its height in the 1840s; these rock gardens were usually planted up with alpines. Parallel to the bank is a canalised reach of the Granta, which might have been part of a late seventeenth-century scheme created by one of the Bennets who owned Babraham at that time.[5]

Almost every garden feature has gone from **Cherry Hinton Hall**, a dull version of the Tudorbethan, except its lake. The grounds are now a public park which was playing host to the annual Cambridge Folk Festival on our visit. The house was built in 1834 for John Okes, a surgeon at Addenbrooke's Hospital, and stood in a 35-acre park. It was originally surrounded by lawns, flower parterres, shrubberies and a fernery; there was also a kitchen garden, as well as two orchards. Sale particulars of 1870 list a fine collection of trees: Ailanthus, walnut, maple, elm, ash, pine and birch.[6] Some of these have survived the tree surgery carried out in 1963, while the parterre garden south of the Hall dates from 1983. The former Kitchen Garden is now a plant propagation centre, which contains a

64 A charming confection of flint and brick at the Windmill Folly on Bungalow Hill

National Collection of hardy geranium and bergenia cultivars.

Witcham Hall is a more interesting site, due mainly to its private nature and the presence in the grounds of features that combine well with the 1840 additions. From the earlier house there are fine ironwork gates and brick gate piers topped with gadrooned urns on the perimeter wall to the road. The lawns are enlivened with two topiary yews and generous herbaceous borders, but the real interest of the grounds is in the garden buildings. There is a gabled, brick Earth Closet attached to the garden wall and a delightful thatched and arcaded Summerhouse backed by a tall Scots pine (*colour 35*). The charming **Windmill Folly**, in the east of the county, to the south of the A1304 on Bungalow Hill, must also be of this period. This single-storey building (*64*), built of flint and brick dressings with pointed-arched windows and sweeping Chinese-style roofs, sits next to an old windmill, hence the name. It has recently been most sensitively extended to provide suitable accommodation for modern living. In a county almost devoid of eighteenth- or nineteenth-century garden buildings the Folly, which was probably used as a hunting lodge, is a rare survival.[7]

Although the original 1762 **University Botanic Garden** was along Downing Street at the junction of Free School Lane, it was relocated to its present site along Trumpington Road in 1831. An act to effect an exchange of land between the University colleges authorised 'the Removal of the present Botanic Garden of the said University to a new and more eligible Site'.[8] It was opened to the public in 1846. As we have seen, the inspiration behind the venture was Dr Richard Walker, whose generosity was recorded in *Cantabrigia Depicta*:

> The Botanic Garden is a very commodious Piece of Ground, containing near five Acres, and a large House for the Use of the Governors and Officers of the Garden: It was lately purchased at the Expence of 1600l. by the present Vice-master of Trinity College, Dr. Richard Walker, and by him given to the University for ever: In trust nevertheless that the Premises so given should be employed for the sole Use and Purpose of a Botanic-Garden, and with this View he has appointed the Chancellor; the Master of Trinity College; the Provost of King's College; the Master of St. John's College, and the Professor of Physic and their Successors for the Time being; particular Inspectors and Governors of the said Garden. And as the Design which the Garden is intended to promote, will constantly require two Officers, a Reader on Plants, and a Curator, or Superintendant of the Works of the Garden; the said Vice-Master has appointed the Rev. Mr. Martyn, (Professor of Botany) to be the first reader; and Mr. Charles Miller, the first Curator. – A very large and elegant Greenhouse and Stoves are now near finished; and the Whole will be completed as fast as Contributions come in.[9]

This is the garden in Rudolph Ackermann's 1815 print from his *History of Cambridge*, where the greenhouse is prominent and two young ladies fresh from a Jane Austen novel inspect the plants (*colour 36*). These appear to be planted informally, with only a few serried ranks, but another contemporary source maintained that 'the whole garden is accurately arranged according to the system of the celebrated Linnaeus, and a catalogue of all the plants has been published'.[10] An intriguing letter of 24 August 1799, written by his daughter Philadelphia to Sir Charles Cotton from Madingley, mentions an exotic plant in the collection: 'There was some time ago, at the botanic garden, a beautiful Mexican plant, called Ferraria Pavonia [*Tigridia pavonia*], Ferraria, from that being the supposed name of the person who first discovered it & Pavonia from the bloom resembling peacock's feathers, when Mama went to see it, it was out of bloom.'[11]

In its new incarnation the layout for the Garden was based on an idea put forward by the first Garden Curator, Andrew Murray. This design is shown in an 1856 plan.[12] The Garden is bordered by a serpentine walk, devised by Murray and Professor John Stevens Henslow, Professor of Botany, whose most famous student was Charles Darwin. It leads from the old entrance by Hobson's Conduit to where there is now a circular Fountain (*colour 37*) designed by David Mellor in the mid-1970s. While the earlier Botanic Garden was laid out on Linnean principles, the beds of the current Garden are arranged according to De Candole's classification. Henslow was responsible for the first rock garden and glasshouse range along the north boundary, as well as the bog and water garden, which was redesigned in 1882. The first ornamental bamboo collection was planted a year later. The layout begins with a woodland area planted with hellebores and anemones, beyond which is a lake with the water garden and moisture-loving plants, and then comes the Rock Garden constructed out of weathered limestone (*65*). On the other side of the path are beds containing some of the National Collections of alchemilla, bergenia, fritillaria, geraniums and tulips. There is also a Winter Garden, the restored glasshouses and a Scented Garden.

Cory Lodge, re-named after Reginald Cory, who left the Botanic garden a major legacy in 1934, had been designed ten years earlier by Baillie Scott, for the Director. Brookside, a fine Regency house, was not integrated into the complex until 2008, when a new main entrance was created at the corner of Trumpington Road and Bateman Street. Brookside was adapted for offices and an education suite. At the other end of

65 The Rock Garden at the University Botanic Garden was devised by Prof James Henslow

the Garden, near Cory Lodge, the Sainsbury Laboratory has now been completed.[13] This is a research facility for the study of plant development. The area by the new building has been landscaped to include a café and a wide terrace facing Cory Lodge lawn (*66*). Bradley-Hole Schoenaich Landscape Architects have laid out the lawn with 'rectangular bluffs of yew, clipped at different heights into interlocking geometric shapes' as a formal counterpoint to the herbaceous plantings.[14] These are 'designed as a basal matrix of grasses, ferns and ground-covering foliage and flowers from the grasses'.[15] Two mixes are used: one for shade and one for sun. In seasonal sequence the plants deployed are: snowdrops, tulips, irises, salvias, asters and late-flowering red hot pokers. The Laboratory is accessed through a grove of 27 Ginko trees, while the central courtyard is enriched with olives. Although in its horticultural infancy, this Cory Lawn Landscape may prove to be one of the county's most significant modern gardens.

66 The new Cory Lodge Garden at the Botanic Garden was designed by Bradley-Hole Schoenaich Landscape Architects to complement the award-winning Sainsbury Laboratory

The remaining roll-call of Victorian gardens is meagre, for the county has no great *nouveau riche* palaces built by be-whiskered industrialists, but it does have an important arboretum of conifers and the remains of a formal garden designed by Robert Marnock at **Pampisford Hall**. This is an intensely private house, its decorative gate piers supporting a deer and what looks to be a snarling boar at the main entrance from the A505 near Granta Park. The driveway is hemmed in on both sides by tall evergreens until the house is reached, its plain stock brick façade enlivened by a banded brick porch to match the gate piers. Although there were additions to the house in the 1860s by the architectural partnership of Goldie and Child, this feature is dated 1893. On the side elevation there is a spectacular wooden conservatory,[16] which is undergoing restoration, and around the back is Marnock's sunken box-edged parterre surrounded by fastigiate conifers. William Parker Hammond began laying out the pleasure grounds and arboretum after 1820, but did not commission Marnock until after 1840. He had already designed the Sheffield Botanic Garden, becoming its first curator in 1834, and, in conjunction with the architect Decimus Burton, had masterminded the layout of the Royal Botanic Society's gardens at Regent's Park in London. He was curator there from 1841 to 1869. Sadly, many of the decorative ornaments have gone and there is little original planting left, but the bones of Marnock's garden survive and the owner is attempting a brave restoration.

The extent of the arboretum is well conveyed in a plan (*67*) taken from sale particulars of 1893.[17] This shows the entrance drive from the north-west, the open lawns around the house, the great south-eastern walk and the walled Kitchen Garden to the north, which was constructed by Goldie and Child in 1861. The Parker Hammonds are said to have imported 1,000 trees to the park, their achievement being recorded in an article of 3 May 1884 in the *Gardeners' Chronicle*, which confirms that 'the grounds were improved some years since under the direction of Mr. R Marnock, who besides other alterations, laid out a new carriage-drive from the Whittlesford station side of the Newmarket road, leading past the mansion into the same road about a mile further on'. The correspondent then describes the collection of conifers, 'extending over an area of 150 acres, and comprising over 400 species and varieties'. The trees lining each walk and surrounding each open lawn are given in detail, including not only their Latin names, but the most suitable growing habitats for them and their cutting regimes for the best timber.

Having made the tour of the plantations to the north and east of the house the writer then moves to the remaining sectors to the south-west and south-east, where there are a terrace walk, lawns and the pleasure grounds. 'A sunken Italian garden adjoins the terrace on the south-western side, in which are fine examples of Cupressus Lawsoniana erecta viridis, the lawn beyond and on the south-east having grand examples of Cedar of Lebanon planted fifty years ago [1834], and now 50 to 60 feet high; magnificent trees, furnished with branches to their base'. These

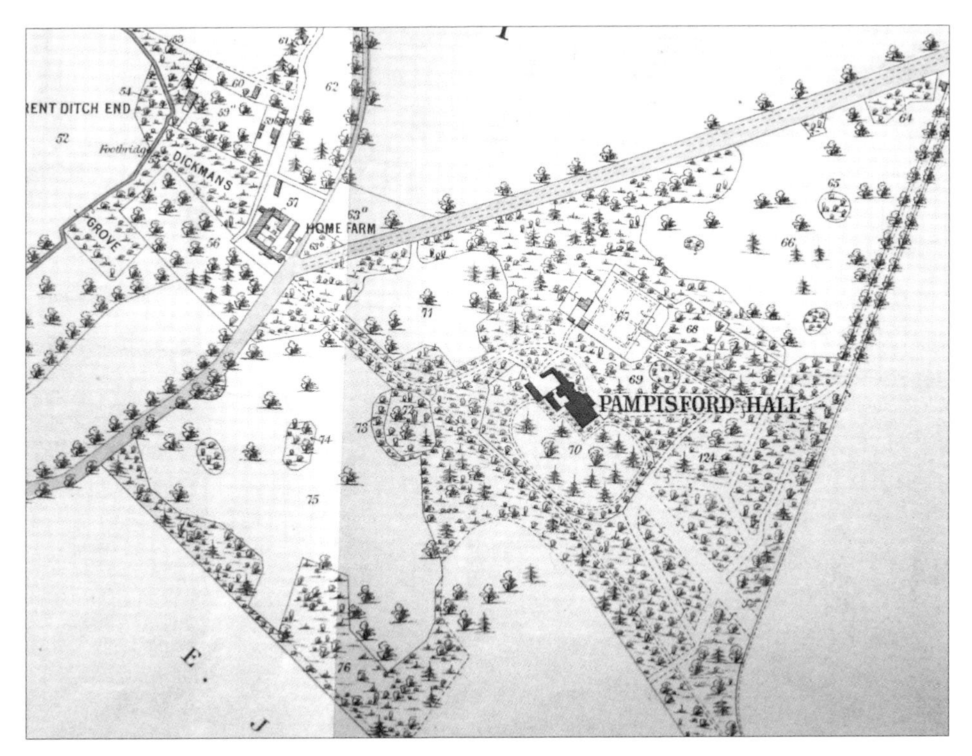

67 This 1893 plan shows the vast range and often claustrophobic extent of the arboretum at Pampisford. *Cambridgeshire Archives, 296 SP945*

evergreen specimens were mixed with deciduous trees 'to diversify and outline and colour the more formal shapes and sombre hues of the Conifers'; these included birches, 'a magnificent Turkey Oak, Copper Beech, and other equally pictorial trees amongst them'.

The correspondent ends his piece with a considered judgement of the importance of this wooded parkland:

> The lines upon which the planting of this large area has been carried out are grand in conception and complete in their unity, whilst the arrangement and disposition of various groups and specimens has been effected with great judgement and good taste. A few years hence, when the representatives of the foreign Conifers can dispense with the shelter now necessary for their protection, and when they themselves approach the majestic size to which it is possible for them to grow, then will the woods around Pampisford Hall be ranked

amongst the grandest and most beautiful in this country.

Over a hundred years on, and even allowing for a period of neglect between the 1960s and the 1980s, the arboretum at Pampisford has reached a striking maturity of scale and intensity. All it needs now is for Marnock's 'Italian garden' to be restored and to act again as a formal foil to the picturesque outlines of the surrounding woodland.

Similar formal gardens may once have been laid out at **Harston Park House** (dated 1854 on a cartouche) and **The Priesthouse at Little Shelford**, which is dated 1858 in Gothic script by the front porch. Both are elegant buildings of their period and represent that transition from the Tudor Gothic of the first half of the century to the more full-blooded Gothic Revival of the 1850s and beyond. The grounds in front of Harston Park House have been completely remodelled with box-edged parterres, while an original yew walk has been retained to the rear. The first edition Ordnance Survey map of 1886 shows the small park to have been threaded with winding paths through the trees, while to the rear, beyond the walled gardens with their glasshouses, the field was planted as an orchard. A fountain is marked close to a pool to the south-west and there may well have been a small summerhouse at the end of a walk looking out to the fields. The pool survives, but the fountain has been built over by a modern house and the summerhouse has gone. At The Priesthouse the front lawn is still open, but topiary yews enliven a raised area by the boundary wall and there are specimen conifers in other parts of the garden. Apparently, the garden was laid out for the Revd E J Law, a natural scientist who housed his telescope in a thatched summerhouse, which has long since disappeared. There is no sign of it on the 1886 OS map, though ranges of glasshouses are shown on the boundary of the rear garden.

In other counties, gardens were laid out in urban centres in the mid-nineteenth century for the professional classes to rent. These were often called 'Guinea Gardens', because leases on the plots cost a guinea a year, the most well known being Edgbaston Guinea Gardens in Birmingham.

Another complex survives in Warwick, close to the racecourse at Hill Close Gardens.[18] Cambridge had such a group of pleasure gardens, just outside the town along the Madingley Road. These date from about 1860 and are clearly shown on the 1886 OS map next to Mount Pleasant Nursery (*68*). The fifteen separate gardens were all individually designed, with summerhouses, greenhouses, winding walks and ornamental shrubberies. They have all been built over, but there are some mature trees from the original plots in the grounds of '**Elterholm**', 12 Madingley Road, which is

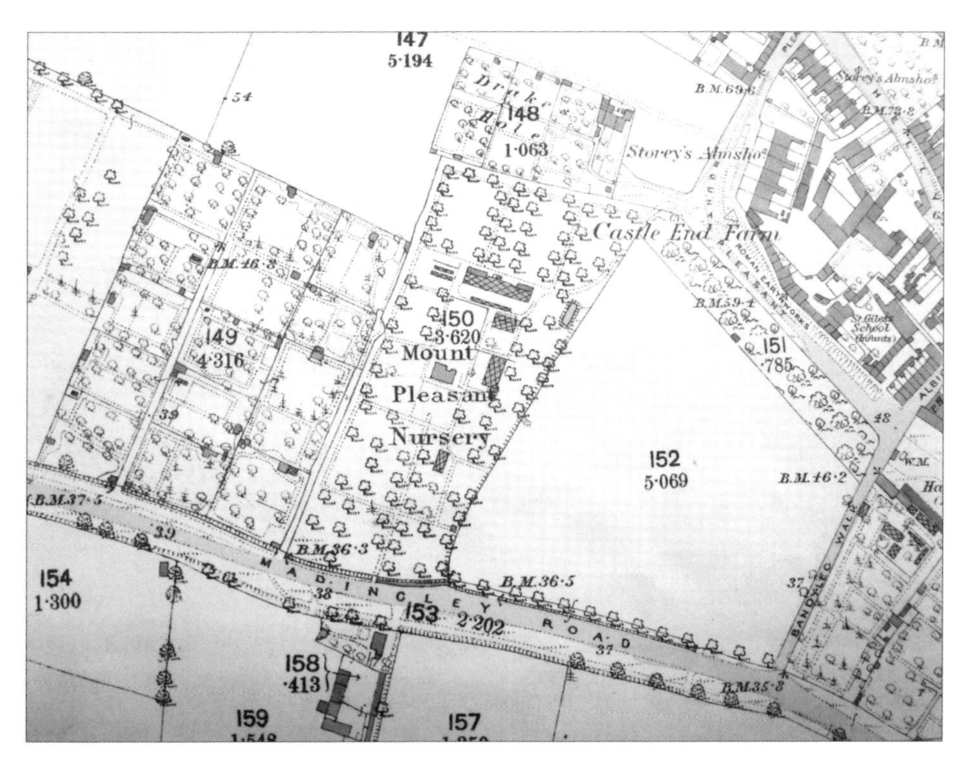

68 The lost Mount Pleasant Nursery along the Madingley Road in Cambridge was laid out in rental plots for the professional classes of the town. *Cambridge University Library*

a half-timbered Edwardian house now owned by St John's College.

Thomas Hobson is rightly celebrated in Cambridge for bringing fresh water to the town from a series of springs in the chalk at Nine Wells near Great Shelford. Together with Dr Andrew Perne, Master of Peterhouse, he devised a channel for the water to flow to Hobson's Conduit, which was originally sited in the Market Place. In woodland at Nine Wells an

Obelisk was erected in 1861 to commemorate all 'benefactors to the watercourse and conduit'. Nearby is the eponymous **Nine Wells House**, the home from 1878 of Sir Michael Foster, distinguished physiologist, eminent horticulturalist, University professor and Secretary of the Royal Society. Around the grounds of his house he grew no fewer than 200 species of iris, including the famous bearded iris, on which he wrote a monograph that was posthumously published in 1913. Some of his original plants, including *Iris* 'Katarina', still flourish in the garden today (*colour 38*). The 1885 OS map reveals little of his planting, but does mark the long glasshouse, since demolished, where he cultivated his plants and the open nursery planting area close by, which is now a wood.[19] Foster's obituary in *The Gardeners' Chronicle* of 2 February 1907 is illustrated by an engraving of his house with a rockery in the foreground, planted up with alpines and irises.

The grounds at **Swaffham Prior House**, south-west of Burwell, make a fitting end to this overview of nineteenth-century garden history in the county, as they represent a fascinating departure from conventional contemporary design. Many landowners were anticipating a return to formalism around their houses, encouraged by the architectural lobby and the advocacy of Elizabethan and Jacobean-style gardens of old England by the Arts and Crafts practitioners. However, one member of the Allix family was opting for a version of the Scottish picturesque. Dr John Allix, Dean of Gloucester and later of Ely, built the house in 1750, but it was not until the early nineteenth century that a small park was laid out to the west. There was a further enlargement to the park in 1880, when the road to the south-east was diverted. This provided new terrain for a water garden, which had been laid out before 1887; it was recorded on the first-edition OS map of that date. The map shows a mature parkland with circular and rectangular clumps of trees, a tree-lined drive leading into the park from a lodge at the south-east corner and another at the north-east. A long avenue of trees extends from the rear of the house across a field to the newly built Swaffham Railway station. Next to the house there is an extensive walled kitchen garden, while the water garden is marked as

69 A touch of Scottish picturesque in the flatlands of Cambridgeshire – the Water Garden at Swaffham Prior House

two elongated serpentine pools fed by a springhead, bordered by walks and shrub planting.

When Sir Michael and Lady Marshall bought the property in 1982 this area was overgrown and the water garden was completely obscured by brambles. At first they found a small bridge and then uncovered the rest of the feature which, together with the lower, canal-like reach, they have restored most sensitively. The story goes that the water garden (*69*) was created by an Allix who had married a Scottish girl and wanted her to feel at home in the new surroundings. Water cascades noisily down from a restored springhead at the top of the course into the first pool, which is crossed by an arched stone bridge, then via another cascade into the lower pool and on to the canal section, heavily shadowed by dark yews. As well as rescuing the water garden, the Marshalls have added a formal parterre close to a new wing of the house and created a refreshingly modern space of angular paved pathways set in grass between the house and a timber-framed service range. In the park new planting has enhanced the original nineteenth-century trees, of which the towering black walnut (*colour 39*) is a spectacular survivor. But it is the wonderfully atmospheric water garden that remains in the memory. It is a rare topographical marvel, more akin to a scene from a Walter Scott novel, or a painting by Sir Edwin Landseer, than the flat wastes of the Swaffham Bulbeck fenland.

8

'A solace for the varying moods' – Edwardian gardens

Newnham College · Middlefield · 80 Chesterton Road · Madingley Hall
48 Storey's Way · Church Rate Corner · Trumpington Hall
Anglesey Abbey · Impington Village College

TWO EDUCATIONAL ESTABLISHMENTS BEGIN AND END THIS SHORT SURVEY of gardens and landscapes created in the period between 1892 and 1939: Newnham College for women, masterminded by Henry Sidgwick and his wife Eleanor, and Impington Village College, the brainchild of Henry Morris, who served as Cambridgeshire Education Secretary from 1922 until 1954. The grounds of Newnham include the design input of no fewer than four landscape practices in Edwardian imperial mood, including Edwin Lutyens and Gertrude Jekyll, while Impington represents the first flush of International Modernism in this country and was to have incorporated in its precincts works by major artists. The intervening years in the county saw Arts and Crafts gardens laid out by Lutyens and Mackay Hugh Baillie Scott, an Art Deco-inspired parterre garden by Brenda Colvin and a late formal landscape of audacious pomposity at Anglesey Abbey, on a scale to rival the axial layouts of the late seventeenth century.

Newnham's garden history is a complex story that centres on open lawns enclosed by a series of beautiful Renaissance Revival brick ranges (*colour 40*), designed by Basil Champneys between 1874 and 1893.[1] In 1870, due mainly to the encouragement of the Sidgwicks, lectures for women started at Cambridge. Anne Jemima Clough was appointed Principal of Newnham, whose first home was at 74 Regent Street. Thereafter, the college moved to Merton Hall, where the girls played croquet on the lawn and held debates under an old medlar tree. After land had been found at Newnham, Champney's Old Hall was ready for students in 1875. Clough laid out the garden in typical mid-Victorian style, with serpentine paths threaded through shrubberies and orchard trees; a medlar was planted in memory of Merton Hall. Croquet was again played on the lawn, there was a gravel tennis court and pigs were kept on land behind the Laboratory. A contemporary student wrote in 1876: 'it is just like the country here. We are completely private in our garden, and quite surrounded with country sights and sounds'.[2]

The new building was North Hall (now Sidgwick), completed by 1880 on the other side of the public road. Clough Hall followed in 1888, when the college appointed a head gardener, Fred Blows. In June 1889 *The Builder* published an illustration of the grounds that made them look like parkland with shrubs and young trees, particularly featuring an oak next to Sidgwick that had been planted by Mr Gladstone in 1887. After Clough's death in February 1892 her niece, Blanche Athena Clough, took over the supervision of the garden and wrote her first Garden Committee Report for the Council. As early as September 1892 she commissioned the York firm of James Backhouse & Son to prepare a garden design. This was a fairly simple affair of shrubberies flanking a central walk extending from Old Hall, which was crossed by another path linking Clough Hall with the Laboratory on the other side of the lawns. Serpentine paths were to be laid out on the north-east lawn. At this point Newnham Lane was still a right of way and the college authorities were negotiating to build Sidgwick Avenue to the north of Newnham's land to ensure the college's future privacy. Work began on the garden, Sidgwick Avenue was opened in 1893 and the Pfeiffer Arch and Buildings were completed, the line of the old Newnham Lane being retained as a gravel path flanked by the existing limes and hawthorns. Backhouse's garden was finished in May 1894, including the installation of an observatory on a mound, built to house a telescope given to the College in 1891 by Mrs Bateson, wife of the

Master of St John's.

The Backhouse garden was left to mature until 1900 when, following the death of Professor Sidgwick, the College decided to erect a memorial to him in the garden. Instead of commissioning Lutyens, who was known to Miss Mary Ann Ewart, a member of Council and benefactress, a less celebrated architect, Alfred Hoare Powell, who had been building a cottage next door to Ewart's house in Surrey, was appointed. Powell's watercolour plan (*colour 41*) of the garden conversion probably dates to 1906.[3] This was to transform the somewhat jejune Victorian layout into Arts and Crafts regularity, with each College building dramatised by its own garden feature. Clough Hall was to have a pergola along its entire length, while the windows of Kennedy would look out onto an elaborate flower garden. The existing serpentine paths are rendered in dotted lines to show their present position and how they would be eradicated in favour of geometrical pathways aligned on a sundial in the centre. The Observatory was to have been enclosed in a rectangular yew-hedged compartment, as too was the sundial. The most significant feature was a sunken rose garden with a central pool in front of Old Hall, which was realised with an inscription around the rim, carved by Eric Gill. It read: 'The daughters of this house to those that shall come after them commend the filial remembrance of Henry Sidgwick.'[4] The path from Clough Hall to the sundial was also introduced, its borders planted by Blanche Athena with lilies, irises, peonies, lupins, achilleas, eryngiums and sweet-smelling herbs.

Mrs Sidgwick retired as Principal in 1910 and the College decided to commemorate her tenure with more garden improvements. The aim was to move the Observatory to more open ground south of Old Hall and lay out a new garden around the recently built Peile Hall. This time Blanche Athena approached Gertrude Jekyll, whose 1911 plan (*70*) is inscribed: 'Proposed treatment of Sidgwick Memorial'. Jekyll concentrated on the south-west corner of the grounds, proposing a hexagonal pavilion on the mound with a matching pavilion further south linked by a gravel path.

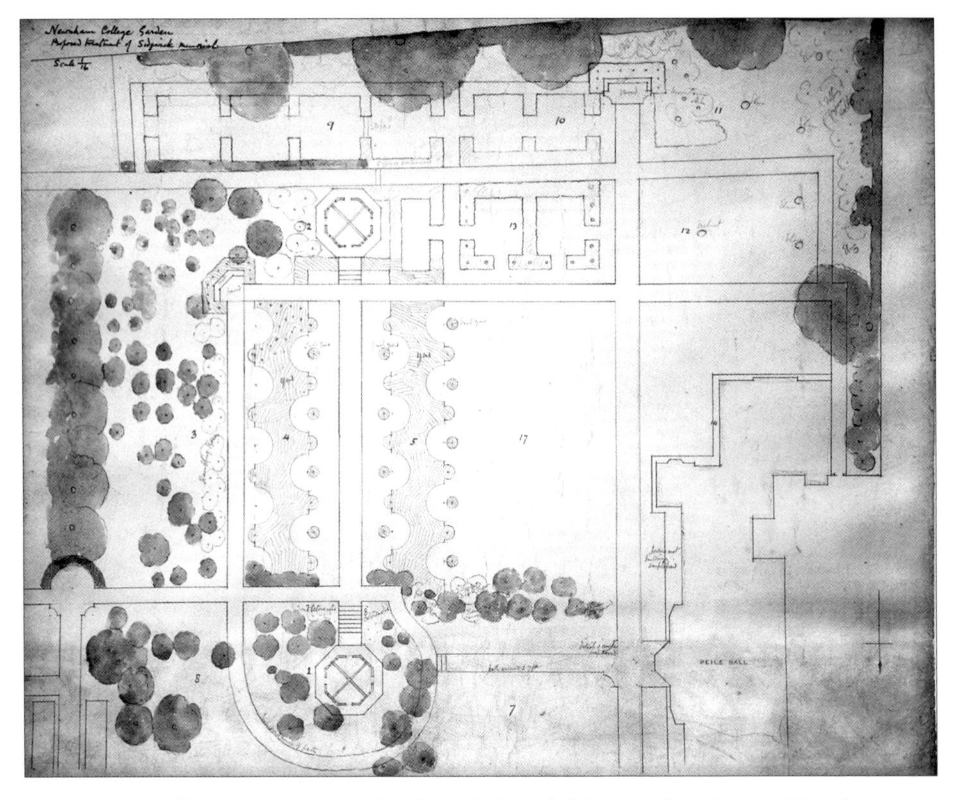

70 Gertrude Jekyll's ambitious 1911 plan for a Sidgwick Memorial garden at Newnham included twin pavilions on an axis to be designed by Edwin Lutyens. *The Principal and Fellows of Newnham College Cambridge*

Scalloped yew hedges creating sitting areas and squares walled in cypress continued Powell's earlier geometry. Sadly, Jekyll's plan never materialised, even though Lutyens had already sketched out some Mogul-style designs for the pavilions; he was busily working on the New Delhi commission at this point. In November 1912 a design by Walter Crum Watson of Edinburgh was accepted instead. Watson's memorial to Mrs Sidgwick was an Obelisk with a sundial on top (*71*), while the ghost of Jekyll's scheme is evident in the rather desultory Summerhouse to the south of the mound. Fortunately, the more extravagant floral excesses of Watson's scheme were omitted. The College finally achieved, in September 1914, a garden of good intentions and worthy commemoration dominated by the effortlessly picturesque and warmly embracing ranges of Champneys' buildings.

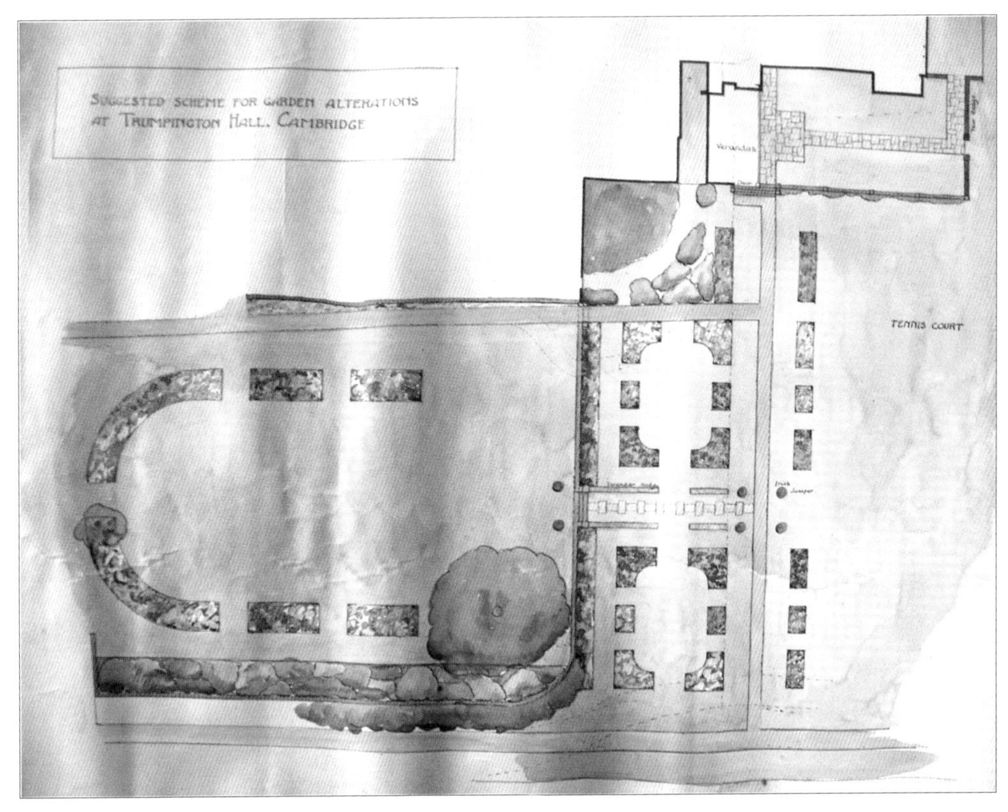

46 In Brenda Colvin's 1924 scheme of garden alterations at Trumpington angular blocks of dramatic colour combine with open lawns and gravel paths. *By kind permission of Richard Pemberton*

47

The Pagoda, a piece of architectural salvage sited in one of the vast walks at Anglesey Abbey, strikes an incongruous note among the classical statuary

48 Professor Willmer's double-sided herbaceous borders in the Fellows' Garden at Clare College were consciously planned to reflect his theories on colour

49 The green theatre in the Fellows' Garden at Girton College was designed in 1992 by Penelope Hobhouse. It is approached from the Croquet Lawn via a pergola planted with summer scented flowers

50 A garden treated as a road – Green Lane at Trinity Hall's Wychfield Site

51 Docwra's Manor, Shepreth, where the Ravens have created one of the county's most lusciously planted gardens

52 The planting in the Walled Garden at Docwra's Manor is almost overwhelming in its profuse beauty

53 The owners and their cat Bramble in the Cider Press Garden at the Crossing House, Shepreth, open free of charge to all plant lovers

54 A stunning garden of low walls, box balls and pergolas smothered with hops, clematis and roses has been created by Pam Thornhill on the up railway platform to Cambridge at Barnwell Junction

55 Trellis towers based on tombs in eastern Turkey rise up from verdant growth in the wild garden at Hardwicke House

56 Wooden structures of Regency, Chinese and Gothick style have enriched the grounds at Abbots Ripton Hall, making it one of the best contemporary gardens in the county

57

In grounds once walked by the poet Rupert Brooke, Lord and Dame Mary Archer have created an exceptional garden of modern figurative sculpture at The Old Vicarage, Grantchester. *The Salmon and the Otter* is by Laurence Broderick

58 As well as contemporary sculpture, the Archers have added earlier works by Eric Gill and Maurice Lambert. Lambert's *Oceanides*, a goddess nymph who presided over the source of the earth's fresh water, was once in the main hall of the SS *Queen Elizabeth*

59 The Great Mall of the American Cemetery at Madingley – the county's one garden of truly international significance

71 The lawns at Newnham are centred by this Obelisk, designed by Walter Crum Watson as a memorial to Eleanor Sidgwick, who retired as Principal in 1910

It is not surprising, given the benefactions and cultured intellect of a Cambridge college, that such a garden was created at Newnham, and that Clare College also approached Lutyens at this time for a proposed new court and garden.[5] However, outside the confines of the University, gardens of this period are few and far between. The main reason must be that Cambridgeshire failed to produce a strong vernacular tradition of building, especially in the seventeenth century. This may be due, in part, to the paucity of good building stone and the reliance on brick, but also to the lack of yeomen and merchant wealth. Counties like Northamptonshire, Gloucestershire, Somerset and Dorset, sited favourably on the limestone belt and with revenue from wool, experienced a wave of building in that period with small gabled manor houses that were the perfect accompaniment to later Arts and Crafts gardens of an architectural nature. In other counties it was the local presence of major landscape architects and gardeners that encouraged owners to commission new layouts. Many of Thomas Mawson's gardens are to be found in his native Lancashire and in adjacent Cheshire, while Surrey, with its own tile-hung vernacular, has a plethora of innovative gardens by Lutyens and Jekyll, who lived locally. Consequently, Cambridgeshire has a sporadic coverage with M H Baillie Scott, who worked out of nearby Bedford, featuring, but few other landscape gardeners of note. Lutyens did at least build one house in Cambridgeshire at Stapleford, where Jekyll was invited to lay out a garden, but her design never materialised.

Middlefield, originally known as Mount Blow, was designed by Lutyens in a volumetric classical style between 1908 and 1909 for the legal scholar, Henry Bond. It is featured in Lawrence Weaver's 1913 study of Lutyens' houses and gardens, where the photographs taken on Weaver's visit earlier in 1910 show the house set in a bald landscape. They were taken when 'the gardens were on paper only ... the house sits starkly on the ground, but pergolas will be built from the loggia and from the other end of the south front to enclose a garden'.[6] Weaver was not sure whether they had been constructed prior to the publication of his book, but a note sent from Lutyens to Jekyll promised her that the garden was ready for her attention.[7] Sadly, Jekyll's garden was never realised, though Jane Brown states that volume 1 of the Lutyens *Memorial* shows the house with a formal garden laid out.[8] However, the *Memorial* photograph is the one taken in 1910, where there are only vestiges of gravel paths and some spindly bushes. It is presumed that this garden is the one that was restored and elaborated in the 1990s.[9] Unfortunately, access for this study was denied, so no considered assessment of the restoration could be made.

Jekyll did achieve a small garden at **80 Chesterton Road** in Cambridge, which she designed for the Revd Charles Macan Rice, Chaplain of King's College, when he was living at the house in 1916. While there is nothing left in the back garden, which has been truncated by an Anderson shelter and garaging, her planting plans for it are preserved in the Surrey Record Office. They reveal a central path with a narrow lawn to one side and wide herbaceous borders. The borders were to be planted with roses, spireas and lupins along the walls and santolinas, dicentras, pinks and stachys along the front edges. The Revd Rice has written on his plan, 'where someday we shall have an arbour for garden seat as in your former plan'.[10]

A more publicly accessible Edwardian garden, now owned by the University, was laid out at this time around **Madingley Hall**, which had been bought by Colonel Walter Harding in 1905. He embarked upon a wholesale restoration of the house with the intensely scholarly architect, J A Gotch, rebuilding the north-east wing and creating a terrace on the site of the sixteenth-century long gallery. He also developed the area immediately around the house, providing a further terrace at the west end of the north façade.[11] The arched balustrade and steps leading down to the Croquet Lawn with its octagonal pond (*colour 42*) are entirely appropriate for the house and add that touch of imperial swagger that characterises the years before the Great War. The Croquet Lawn does not feature in a *Country Life* article on the house of October 1912, so it must be of about 1913-14. Ambrose Harding inherited in 1927; he added the angular yew hedges, which divide the upper from the lower terrace, and also the Yew Topiary Garden. The yews appear to have been transplanted from his previous home, Histon Manor; at the centre is an astrolabe commemorating a family pet.

Lutyens' mention of pergolas at Middlefield to bridge the gap between the house and its grounds brings to mind Baillie Scott's preference for these axial features. Fortunately, Baillie Scott left a design manifesto in his 1906 *Houses and Gardens*, which was the culmination of a lifetime's work in architecture. It sets forward his vision of how a house and garden might interact to produce 'the most important as well as the most human expression of the Art of man'.[12] In this quest he had been influenced by the progressive socialist ideas of William Morris, Philip Webb and Richard Norman Shaw and, latterly, the Garden City movement. At this time Baillie Scott was employed in the Pyghtle workshops on the outskirts of Bedford, where metalwork, stonework and joinery were being created for Raymond Unwin and Barry Parker's Letchworth Garden Suburb. This immersion in crafts provided Baillie Scott with an intensely practical approach to constructing a house and garden, while contemporary books such as John D Sedding's *Garden-craft Old and New* of 1890 and Reginald Blomfield's *The Formal Garden in England* (1892) suggested ways in which gardens could be contrived to extend the living environment. As Baillie Scott was to put it: 'the function of a garden is to grow fruit and vegetables for the household, and also to provide outdoor apartments for the use of the family in fine weather'.[13] These 'outdoor apartments' were the 'rooms' that became such an important design component of Edwardian gardens.

Baillie Scott was careful to avoid the pitfall of taking sides in the current battle of styles between the William Robinson-inspired wild garden and Blomfield's architectural layouts, which contained more formal areas: 'I can do no more than indicate a few general principles. Neither have I any wish to pose as a partisan in the quarrel between the naturalists and formalists on design. In the large garden each should have free scope, and natural garden and formal garden will enter into no rivalry there, but each will only enhance the peculiar charm of the other, and afford a solace for the varying moods.'[14] Baillie Scott's book was illustrated with his own delicate watercolours and with many line drawings of house and garden plans. His views are expressed in a simple, forthright manner. Where possible, and depending upon the size of the plot, he believed that gardens should comprise a wild garden and an orchard, as well as being threaded with paths, though 'as few as possible, and should follow the lines of natural traffic'.[15] There should be lawns for tennis, bowls or croquet, a rose garden and a flower garden where 'delphinium, phlox, hollyhocks, day lilies &c ... instead of being repeated at regular intervals, like the geranium and calceolaria formula of the villa garden, will be massed in single clumps'.[16] In the suburban plots, where there was little scope for a wild scheme, 'a more formal kind of garden is suggested by the rectangular enclosure of the site and the somewhat artificial character of the surroundings'.[17] All these features are present in the garden he laid out around Everdene (72), which was allotted three watercolours

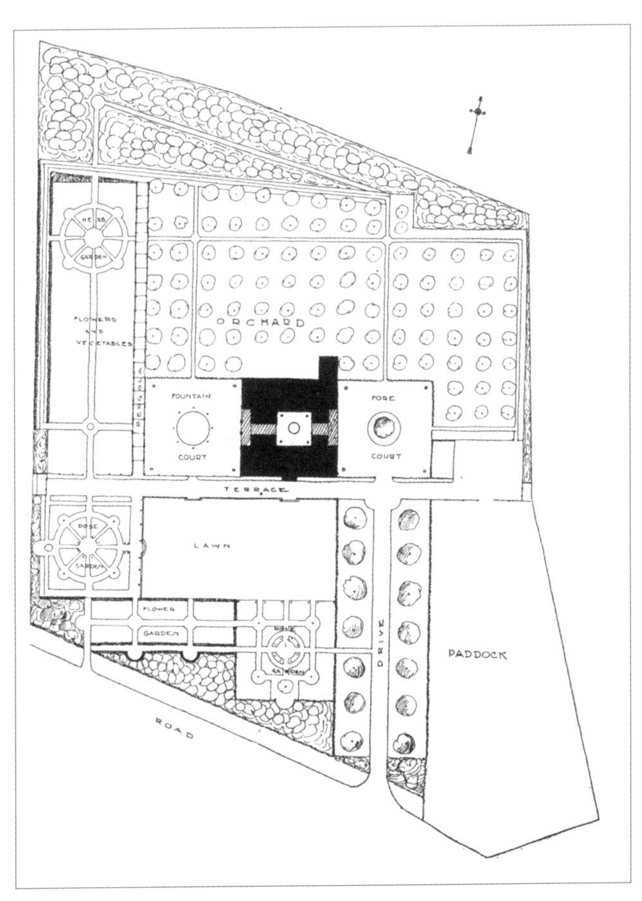

72
A typical garden plan by Mackay Hugh Baillie Scott, which includes formal and wilder areas, an orchard, a rose garden and a pergola, all elements favoured by the architect and found at 48 Storey's Way. *University of Bristol Library, Special Collections*

and two line drawings, as well as plans. In addition, Everdene utilised a pergola to extend the axis from the terrace out into the orchard and provide a scented and sheltered walk with views out to the flowers and vegetables alongside. Baillie Scott sums up this emphasis on shade and surprise views:

> The garden should not, moreover, be too open and exposed to the sun, but should be full of mystery, surprises, and light and shade. One of its most attractive features will thus be the pergola, with its paved walk checkered by the shadows of the climbing plants which form its walls and roof. It matters little what the structure of the pergola is. It may be rough poles with the bark on, roofed with branches, or it may be piers of stone or brick, with an open timber roofing. It should at any rate be rude and simple, and look as if it

> is meant for an outdoor life in rough weather. Other effects of shade may be gained by walks bordered with, perhaps, hazel or willow, and through these shadowed vistas we may look beyond to an open sunlit space bright with flowers. Actual size has little to do with the effect of such a garden, and a variety of effects may be achieved in a comparatively small area by careful planning.[18]

These central principles underpin Baillie Scott's design for the garden at **48 Storey's Way**, Cambridge, which was designed in 1912-13 for H A Roberts. Dianne Haigh, an expert on Baillie Scott whose seminal book, *Baillie Scott: The Artistic House*, was published in 1995, restored the garden in the early 1990s.[19] The front garden with its shaped yews, hedged enclosure and central path is reminiscent of the frontispiece of William Morris' *News from Nowhere* depicting Kelmscott Manor; all that is missing are the standard roses lining the path. To the rear the garden is long and narrow and, according to Haigh, its layout is likely to have been inspired by a series of articles by E S Prior, published in *The Studio* in 1901, one of which contained a plan of an 'Oblong Garden'.[20] At 48 Storey's Way the compartments are graduated from ornamental formality to productive informality. The sequence begins with lawns flanked by twin pergolas by the house (*colour 43*); then comes a rectilinear garden divided from the wild garden by a hedge (*73*), which in turn is separated from the vegetable garden by a circular arbour crossed by a nut walk. The last sector is an orchard by the southern boundary with land owned by Churchill College. All these elements survive today, though less rigorously maintained, producing a more seamless route from the formal to the rustic.

Baillie Scott's garden at **Church Rate Corner**, also in the suburbs of Cambridge, is much less extensive, though it harmonises perfectly with its parent house.[21] The garden is completely secret, accessed via a gate in the wall alongside Church Rate Walk.[22] A short, tree-lined drive leads to the north-west angle of the garden, with the house still out of view to the left. Then the garden opens out into a spacious lawn, with the double-gabled façade set within generous clay-tiled sweeps of roof (*colour 44*). Scott built the house in the orchard of Plâs Dinas, on the south side of Malting Lane, for Marjorie Watson Duckett. It was subsequently lived in by Mrs Sewell, a Cornish tin mining heiress, and after 1928 by the Bennetts, who were academics. As a result, the site has mature trees, including horse chestnuts, a beech, yews and an acacia, around which Scott introduced his signature elements. On the back of the deeds for the property a sketch plan shows how the L-shaped garden locks neatly around the L-shaped house.

73 The sequence of garden rooms at 48 Storey's Way. The former Rose Garden is now dramatised by a modern sculpture, *Canis and the Archer*, by Tom Lomax

Indeed, the sunken lawn is the footprint of the house in reverse. The main garden is laid to lawn, but a raised area with rectangular planting beds has steps leading down to the grass, while further rectangular beds border the perimeter walk. A very narrow path beneath the main windows of the house is indicated on the plan, but this has now been extended into a more serviceable terrace planted with drifts of lavender. The perimeter pathway was laid out as a hazel walk and has now been dramatised by a striking pleached yew hedge. Most of the planting has been carried out by Michael

Nedo, who bought the house in 1986 when the garden was in a state of neglect. Assisted by Gillian Moore, he has brought the grounds back to horticultural life and complimented Baillie Scott's original design most sympathetically.

Access to **Trumpington Hall** is via a long, tree-lined drive, just opposite the parish church, which takes the visitor either to the curving walls and entrance gates of the front forecourt, or through a service entrance, past a weather-boarded barn with the date 1772 painted on its end wall, to the back door of the house. Sir Francis Pemberton bought the estate and its Tudor mansion from the Pytcher family in 1675 and the present Hall was built in 1710. It is not known what the estate comprised before the park was established in the 1820s, but there were certainly fishponds in the grounds in 1760 and the kitchen garden has a remarkable crinkle-crankle wall, which may predate the emparkment. From here the turrets of King's College Chapel rise on the horizon, while to the west there are views across the park to Grantchester Meadows. A late nineteenth-century estate map shows a simple landscape of open fields, plantations and walks threaded around the fishponds, which have now been canalised and given a Gothick Seat derived from William Kent's bowling green seats at Rousham. However, it is the two box-edged parterres below the west front of the house that must be considered here (*colour 45*). These were planted in the twentieth century by Richard Pemberton's parents, but a plan for the area exists in the Hall archives for a similarly formal garden by Brenda Colvin (*colour 46*). Her 'suggested scheme for garden alterations' is dated 31 October 1924 and has Colvin's signature planting of blocks of colour.[23] This geometric approach of vibrant colour is typical of the period and relates closely to Art Deco design. Irish junipers were to give vertical accents to the top parterre, while lavender hedges lined the path down to the open lawn, which had further block planting and a counterpoint of billowing shrubs along the border. What is most significant about the plan, and marks a change in design approach from the Edwardian to the interwar period, is the lack of connection between house and garden. There might have been an opportunity to link the garden with the existing verandah, something Arts and Crafts landscape gardeners would not have missed. Colvin's garden stands alone, almost turning its back on the house, demanding attention in its own right.

In a similar way the vast formal landscape at **Anglesey Abbey**, created after 1926 by the 1st Lord Fairhaven, was also laid out with scant reference to the parent house; it creates its own spaces, unencumbered by existing landscape features. These included some specimen trees, an enclosed formal garden and an orchard, all probably the work of the Revd John Hailstone, Vicar of Bottisham, who altered the house in 1861. Lord Fairhaven's 100-acre garden began with little or no plan; the vistas, walks and avenues created almost upon a whim in collaboration with his head gardener, Noel Ayres, and with advice from his close friend, Major Vernon Daniels.[24] The site is divided roughly into three separate areas: the East Lawn with its flanking Arboretum and Bishop's Walk, the more open lawned area to the south of the house, and the vast western sector with its Temple Lawn, Coronation Avenue and myriad cross avenues. During the Depression in the 1930s Lord Fairhaven was able to buy garden ornaments – statues, urns, columns and vases – at bargain basement prices, which were used to terminate and dramatise the existing avenues. They include figures from the Temple of Concord and Victory purchased at the Stowe sale (*74*), casts of which have been made for the Fairhavens' garden at Kirtling Tower. The result is a landscape of sinister oppression that owes little to contemporary trends or, indeed, to the recent Edwardian garden. It is much closer in style and conception to the great forest gardens of the late seventeenth and early eighteenth centuries. There are few intimate spaces at Anglesey, merely high-hedged walks of Brobdingnagian scale.

When the gardens had reached their maturity they were visited in 1954 and subsequently written up by Christopher Hussey for *Country Life*. As an advocate of the Picturesque, having published the seminal work on the aesthetic in 1927, Hussey viewed Anglesey in intensely pictorial terms:

74 Fugitives from the Stowe sale – statues from the Temple of Concord and Victory, bought by Lord Fairhaven, now enrich the vistas of Anglesey Abbey

> The sense of space, the playground of sweeping shadows and the infinite gradations of light exhilarate one, giving the fen landscape a poetry of its own. And these are the elements that must principally be used in the making of a landscape garden in so otherwise unhelpful a terrain: space, broad shadows, Impressionist appreciation of light, with the addition of that essential element of height which is needed as much for shelter as by the eye.[25]

On such a flat site only trees could produce those effects and, as Hussey continues, 'the prevailing memory of Anglesey is of trees, rarely of special note or size in themselves, but most admirably handled'.[26] That almost sycophantic deference to the owner is a rarity in Hussey's otherwise objective writing, but it is evident throughout the text of his two articles and also in some of the captions. 'Splendid urns well placed before a yew hedge', is enriched in the narrative by: 'They are superbly placed and transform into a work of art what would otherwise be a competent but conventional boundary planting.'[27] It may seem a harsh criticism, but these urns, admittedly by Scheemakers and Delvaux, merely stand proud of the hedge; they do nothing more. Similarly, the statue groups that litter the grounds are beautiful in themselves but add nothing of value to the landscape; they are often arbitrarily placed and seldom offer an iconographic programme, although the Emperor's Walk, an avenue of Norway spruce and larch, has 12 marble busts of Roman emperors. But this sense of classical dignity is then wrecked by the ungainly Pagoda (*colour 47*), purchased from an architectural salvage company, on a cross path between the Emperors' and Warriors' Walks, even if it does shelter an ancient Roman bowl.

The grounds of Anglesey Abbey are close in conception, though not of course in scale, to the contemporary garden that Harold Acton was creating at La Pietra, outside Florence. They are both essentially repositories of garden ornament laid out by wealthy opportunists with none of the intellectual subtleties of, for example, Harold Peto's Iford Manor in Wiltshire, with its found classical objects, or Frederick Gibberd's garden at Harlow in Essex, brilliantly enlivened with architectural salvage and modern sculpture.

Modern sculpture must end this chapter at that exciting point in art and architecture when the émigrés of the International Modern movement began to influence contemporary design in this country. Allied to this new aesthetic approach to the applied and decorative arts was a fresh outlook on the education of the village folk of Cambridgeshire pioneered by Henry Morris. The two came together at **Impington Village College** to produce an educational complex of brilliant innovation, one that would have been enhanced, had there been funds enough, by a bronze statue group by Henry Moore and an external mural by Graham Sutherland. So, while the venture is only peripherally relevant to garden history, though the site was originally part of the Impington Hall estate, offered to the Council by the Chivers family, it presaged a modern way forward for design in gardens. Sadly, that modernist trend found little favour in a country hidebound by conservatism and insularity, but at least the Impington project offered hope for a bright future during the gloomy austerity of the interwar years.

Henry Morris became Secretary for Education in Cambridgeshire in 1922 and by 1924 his ideal educational system had been thought through, written up in report form and then published a year later as *The Village College*.[28] The idea was simple: to provide good education for the rural community while offering a cultural focus for the activities of neighbourhood groups. This would be delivered and facilitated in a complex which would contribute both socially and aesthetically to the quality of life of these villages, hence Morris' desire for 'fine architecture, good furniture, and carefully chosen pictures' and, of course, sculpture to enliven the grounds.[29] The first two colleges were at Sawston and Bourn; Impington opened in 1939. Its architects were Maxwell Fry and Walter Gropius, whom Morris had met in 1934, in his friend Jack Pritchard's flat in Belsize Park. Even though there were difficulties over the architects' fees, money was raised, Pritchard and Morris guaranteed the remainder and the County Council accepted the designs. Sadly, there was no money for the Family Group by the up-and-coming sculptor Henry Moore, nor any funds for an external mural by Graham Sutherland for the main promenade of the College. However, the designs for both are held within a private collection in the county and reveal the intentions of the two artists. Moore's sculpture was to be of a family seated on a square bench; one child embraced by his father, the other quietly read to by the mother. Moore was to write: 'In my own case, the Family Group in its differing forms sprang from my absorbing his [Morris'] idea of the village college – that it should be an institution which could provide for the family at all its stages.'[30] Moore went so far as to produce a maquette similar to his initial watercolour design, although with only one child, but the price asked and the shocking nature of the representation was too much for the councillors and they refused to commission the bronze. After the war Hertfordshire County Council bought the maquette of the Family Group

75 The desultory scene at the entrance to Impington Village College, where once there might have been an uncompromisingly modern bronze of a family group by Henry Moore

to stand outside the Barclay Secondary School in Stevenage.[31] Sutherland's two watercolour schemes for the mural were never to progress beyond the design stage, yet with their bull and bare-breasted female figures clearly referenced the most monumental mural ever produced, Picasso's *Guernica*, created for the 1937 World Fair. Sutherland's College mural would have been a reincarnation in colour of Picasso's iconographic statement for peace within communities. Today, at Impington, there is only a rather desultory patch of grass outside the Assembly Hall, with a single tree and bulbous stone bowl (75) where Moore's great sculpture would have signalled the importance of family and learning within the community. Progressive educational ideas had triumphed at Impington, but modernist art remained an anathema to this rural county.

9

Railways, sculpture and a flourish of plants – the twentieth century

Peckover House · Elgood's Brewery · Sibald's Holme · Clare College
197 Huntingdon Road · Girton College · Trinity Hall Wychfield Site
Docwra's Manor · Shepreth Crossing House
Station House, Barnwell Junction · Hardwicke House
Chippenham Park · Wilbraham Temple · Abbots Ripton Hall
Chilford Hall · The Old Vicarage, Grantchester
American Cemetery, Madingley

In a county of few gardens regularly open to the public, and only three run by the National Trust, it is refreshing to cross the fenlands and reach Wisbech, a textured market town of brick Georgian houses with the River Nene flowing through the middle. Here there are two gardens of historic worth: the grounds surrounding Elgood's Brewery, which incorporate the nineteenth-century gardens of adjacent Sibald's Holme, and the walled enclosure behind Peckover House. Both sites have nineteenth-century origins, but each has been overlaid with mid- to late twentieth-century elements and planting schemes, hence their place here in the last chapter of this book. These begin a somewhat arbitrary sequence of twentieth-century gardens, roughly chronological in order, but linked by connecting themes: the University, plantsmen's and plantswomen's gardens, two of which encompass railways, sites where modern sculpture invigorates the grounds, and a cemetery landscape of heartbreaking brilliance.

Overlooking the North Brink, **Peckover House** was built before 1727 and was given to the National Trust by Alexandrina Peckover in 1948. The walled garden to the north of the house is essentially a Victorian pleasure ground with a wilderness, lawns, shrubberies, a croquet lawn, an orangery, two summerhouses and mature specimen trees. It was begun in the early nineteenth century and developed by the Peckovers, who were Quaker bankers, over the next two centuries. Internal walls and green barriers divide the garden into four distinct sections. Directly behind the house is the Wilderness Walk and the Croquet Lawn; next moving west are Alexa's Rose Garden and the Palm Lawn; then come the linear Cut-Flower Border and the Graham Stuart Thomas Borders, terminated by the Orangery to the north and the Pool Garden with its Victorian Summerhouse to the south; and finally the Orchard Lawn, bordered on the east by the Centenary Border and on the north by the Red Border, while the open lawn is shadowed by a mulberry and a quince. In a shrubbery to the south is that ubiquitous late nineteenth-century feature, a Fernery, with a thatched Summerhouse.

Since the Trust acquired the house it has instigated campaigns of re-planting and of scholarly re-creations, beginning in the 1960s with Graham Stuart Thomas' deep double borders in four colour-themed sections. In spring, each quadrant of the Pool Garden in this sector contains a different narcissus, which were originally bred by another Quaker banking family, the Backhouses. The four varieties at Peckover are: *N.* 'Magnet', *N.* 'Texas', *N.* 'W P Milner', and *N.* 'Mrs R O Backhouse'.[1] Alexa's Rose Garden (*76*) is named after Alexandrina, who gave the estate to the Trust. In the nineteenth century, flowerbeds, roses and ironwork dominated the Palm Lawn, the Croquet Lawn and this area. With the aid of early photographs the Rose Garden and its pool were recreated in 1999. The roses are highly scented varieties, some of which were popular in the Victorian and Edwardian periods. They include: *R.* 'Phyllis Bide', *R.* 'Aimée Vibert', *R.* 'Madame Grégoire Staechelin', *R.* 'Honorine de Brabant', and *R.* 'Céline Forrestier'.[2] Between the Pool Garden, which is commanded by the Victorian Summerhouse (*77*), and the Stuart Thomas Borders is a clipped yew hedge with peacock topiary of Edwardian style introduced by the Trust. Oddly, for

76 In the sheltered grounds behind Peckover House, Wisbech, Alexandrina Peckover planted this Victorian Rose Garden, which was recreated by the National Trust in 1999

77 The Pool Garden at Peckover is commanded by the Victorian Summerhouse, which provides an axial view through an Edwardian-style topiary hedge to the greenhouse beyond

grounds that have hints of Loudon's Gardenesque and fussy high Victorian taste, the Trust has avoided a kitsch suburban atmosphere.[3] The various garden rooms merge seamlessly into one another and offer a palpable sense of restful quietude.

Just along the Brink, the off-river breezes bring wafts of richly caramelised hops, emanating from **Elgood**'s, the first brewery to be built outside London in 1795. The Elgoods mashed their first brew in 1878 and the firm continues to be run as an independent family brewery. In an inspired gesture, the Brewery opens the four-acre gardens to the rear on three weekdays between April and September every year. They were originally developed in the late nineteenth century and incorporate part of the grounds of **Sibald's Holme**, laid out by Algernon Peckover behind his Italianate house on the Brink. Photographs in an album on display at Peckover House show these to have had crescent-shaped flowerbeds, rose beds and gravel paths, while a watercolour hanging at Peckover shows a latticed wooden bridge over a stream. That busy, exuberant feeling is present in the gardens at Elgood's, which have been restored in the last 20 years under the direction of Claire Simpson, Nigel and Anne Elgood's middle daughter. Much of what has been achieved at Elgood's has been based on pre-war photographs, the grounds having been dug up for vegetables during 'Dig for Victory'. The result is a brilliant combination of mature specimen trees and open lawns with feature elements including a Japanese Garden, a Herb Garden with arbours of hops – Fuggles and Challenger – that are used in the beers, a Rose Garden, a Maze and a small lake developed from the original factory reservoir, shown on an 1836 sale particulars map.[4] Although these would appear to be stylistically disparate, they are integrated skilfully in and around the lawns and the barrier hedges to produce a garden of rewarding surprise vistas and enclosed views, while all the time the tall brick ranges of the factory buildings loom up on the south boundary (*78*).

In the main, the University's college gardens remained resolutely suburban in style throughout the century. However, in 1947 Professor

78 The gardens at Elgood's Brewery in Wisbech are wrapped around the original house and factory buildings. The ornamental lake is marked on an 1836 map as the 'Reservoir'

Nevill Willmer, a distinguished physiologist with a keen interest in colour vision, was commissioned by **Clare College** to redesign the Fellows' Garden. Willmer was an amateur painter and garden designer and this riverside oasis is now his best-known work and certainly the University's greatest twentieth-century garden. It is sited directly across the Cam from the Old Court and Master's Lodge, occupying a low-lying area sheltered by tall trees and bounded by dykes on three sides and the river on the other. Willmer was a fellow of Clare, and his fascination with colour greatly influenced his flamboyant choice of planting, while a knowledge of painting led him to divide the garden up into a series of carefully framed views.[5] These vistas include the west range of Old Court across the river, fringed by scarlet island beds, and the elegant Clare Bridge, which links the seventeenth-century buildings with Sir Giles Gilbert Scott's twentieth-century Memorial Court on the garden side. Willmer was acutely aware of the different uses to which the Fellows' Garden would be put, especially as Scott's additions had destroyed any recreational areas on that side of Queens Road.[6] His approach was, therefore, to divide the garden into as many different areas as possible, giving each one 'a special character with respect to such things as season, colour, scents, privacy and use'.[7] The garden includes informal swathes of lawn open to the riverbank, at the west end of which is Barbara Hepworth's *Two Forms (Divided Circle)*. Along the garden's western boundary is a gloomy tunnel-walk of overhanging trees, using illusionary perspective and visual trickery to exaggerate its length when viewed from the southern end. To the left of this tunnel are the remains of Willmer's scented area, now replanted in the style of a Victorian sub-tropical garden. Perhaps the most striking feature of the Fellows' Garden is the double-sided herbaceous border (*colour 48*). This is planted in shades of violet-blue and golden yellow, and leads up from the water garden to the banks of the river. Incorporating ligularia, delphiniums and aconites, it is rumoured that Willmer created these borders in order to bring to life his theories on colour and to turn the heads of visiting academics. Yet in his quest for scientific accuracy he was constantly frustrated by the dictates of nature, writing of the red borders that 'in the planting of these the sense of distance has been increased by putting the more orange reds at one end and the more crimson reds at the other. However, unlike artists' pigments, plants tend to have wills of their own'.[8]

In the middle of the Fellows' Garden and sunk into the lawn is the fully enclosed Water Garden (79), still used by the College's theatrical societies for open-air productions. A solemn and tranquil mood pervades this formal area, which is completely cut off from the rest of the garden by a clipped yew hedge, and discovered almost by accident. The formal pool at its centre is flanked by two ancient apple trees at the north end, relics of the original Kitchen Garden, and two new yews either side of the north gate entrance. As well as the apple trees, Willmer also salvaged part of the old stone wall, an ancient Judas tree and a swamp cypress from the previous layout.

79 The formal pool in the Fellows' Garden at Clare College adds an Edwardian touch to Professor Willmer's 1947 design

This idea of a garden 'room', sited on a different level to the rest of the garden and screened by high hedges of yew, formed the basis of many of Willmer's landscaping schemes. Indeed, they can be found again at number **197 Huntingdon Road**, a major arterial route linking central Cambridge with Junction 14 of the M11. Here, as in the Fellows' Garden, beds of iris and dahlia were deliberately planted to display dramatic graduations of colour, set off against a dark backdrop of yew hedging. Sold to a developer and rebuilt into nine flats and a townhouse in 2006, access to what remains of Huntingdon Road's Willmer garden was not possible during this study.[9] The original house was built in 1938 in a neo-Georgian style by Harold Taylor, another fellow of Clare College, and stood on a rectangular plot augmented by a narrow strip of garden filched from the adjacent number 195. This ribbon of land now belongs to the new townhouse, but was originally separated from the landscaped part of the garden by hedging and blackberry bushes, and contained a wilder, grassy area, apple orchard and vegetable plots. Willmer landscaped the main garden for his colleague and friend Taylor in the Jekyll-Lutyens tradition, with high hedges denoting a progression of enclosures.

Victor Whittaker, who lived at the property with his family between 1961 and 2006 and greatly restored the garden, describes this progression of garden rooms as a paved terrace leading from the house onto a lawn, enclosed by a semicircular raised bed on which a tall yew hedge was planted.[10] A central gap in this hedge leads down to a sunken rose garden enclosed on three sides by a rectangular beech hedge and on the fourth by the curved wall of yew. Beyond, an opening in the beech stepped up to a raised orchard of plum, pear and apple trees, with a central grass path flanked by kidney-shaped flowerbeds. Whittaker replanted these wildly overgrown beds as herbaceous borders, with pink lupins, blue delphiniums and red peonies. This third and final enclosure was originally sheltered by a semicircular yew hedge with a topiary cock flanked by spheres and cones. Willmer's book on garden design was never published, and Whittaker believes 'his views about colour vision and the evolution of vertebrates from an invertebrate precursor were somewhat heterodox and, although he was a successful scientist and an FRS, this may have denied his later work the recognition he hoped for'.[11] Nevertheless, there is now a ten-year plan in place to restore the Fellows' Garden at Clare College to Willmer's original 1947 design, fully re-instating his colourways and intended views.

The educational and garden history of **Girton College** reads rather like that of Newnham, with a mid-Victorian foundation for women, through new planting schemes for the grounds by Gertrude Jekyll and, most recently, a 1992 green theatre designed by Penelope Hobhouse for the Fellows' Garden.[12] Unlike Newnham, however, whose open lawns are lined by cheerful brick façades that are humanly scaled and welcoming, Girton's enclosures are bordered by brooding ranges of doleful, pointed-arched windows. Happily, its gardens alleviate this somewhat institutional character, particularly the sunken pool in the Eliza Baker Court (*80*), which was gifted to the College in 1932 by Oswald Lewis in memory of his mother, who had been a student at Girton.[13] Cloister Court, now an area of somewhat indiscriminate planting, its borders encroaching too heavily in places upon the brick ranges, was given a new planting scheme, designed by Jekyll, in 1921. The cloister wall had long drifts of cotton lavender, catmint, white pinks, stachys, rock pinks and helianthemums, backed by lavenders, eryngiums, echinops, olearias and Pink China roses.[14] A restoration of the border to this original conception is well overdue. Jane Swindale, who was appointed Garden Steward in 1921, supervised the planting of Cloister Court, as well as Jekyll's additional plan for Emily Davies Court, which was to have borders 'in keeping with the William Robinson ideal'.[15] The planting comprised: ceanothus, *Jasminum nudiflorum*, pyracantha, escallonia and *Vitis coignetiae,* with drifts of bergenia, hyssop, godetia, stachys, dwarf French marigolds, snapdragons, peonies, erigeron, mallow and *Chrysanthemum* 'Morning Star'.[16] Much of this has also been lost, as has the rose garden planted in front of Woodlands Wing in 1926, designed by a Thomas Henslow, who appears to have been the grandson of the Revd JS Henslow of the University Botanic Garden. Only shadows in the grass remain to indicate that his garden was achieved. The rose garden was removed by Chrystabel Proctor, who became Garden Steward in 1933. A new one was planted outside the Hyphen Gates between the Chapel and the Library, which has been expertly restored and replanted by the present Head Gardener, Robert Bramley.

To the north-east of the College buildings, open countryside connects with the more formal areas via the Old Orchard, where 60 varieties of apples were grown in the 1870s. The women fellows all had their own garden plots close by, while adjacent to the pond by the Orchard Wing, dug in case of fire, is the Fellows' Garden. This is divided from the Croquet Lawn within the enclosure by a pergola, planted with scented summer flowers flanked by 'John Downie' crab apple trees, and beyond is Hobhouse's green theatre, its yew hedges staggered like theatre flats, a

80 The Eliza Baker Court at Girton College is Edwardian in its architectural character, even though it was a 1932 gift to the College from Oswald Lewis in memory of his mother, a Girton student

Lutyens bench placed centre stage (*colour 49*).

Trinity Hall, the fifth-oldest surviving college of the University of Cambridge, is divided between two main sites: the central medieval complex and the stunningly contemporary **Wychfield site** on Storey's Way, a short distance to the west.[17] Here the whitewashed balcony of Wychfield House provides a romantic foil to the modern accommodation blocks, which house the majority of Trinity Hall's students. These blocks, including Greenhouse Court, the adjacent Round Court and the remainder of the modern complex, were built in 2006 on the site of the House's former 'Cabbage Patch', winning a David Unwin architectural award in 2010.

Wychfield House was built at the end of the nineteenth century by Sir Francis Darwin, son of Charles Darwin, and acquired by the College in the 1920s. Today much of its Edwardian pleasure grounds survives, including the Cedar Tree Lawn, flowering borders and mature specimen trees. In front of the building is the Sunken Garden, with pleached lime hedging, and on the south side, just outside the back door, is a small parterre made up of box hedging. This is riotously planted with foxgloves, calendula and nasturtium, and lovingly described by Head Gardener Andrew Myson as 'a bit bonkers'.[18] Sandwiched between prettified Wychfield House and the airy courtyards of the bright modern accommodation blocks is Herrick House, a bleak 1960s cube, cunningly softened by trees and cottage garden- style planting, where there is a sculpture, *Twelve*, by Jonathan Clarke.

The design of both Greenhouse Court, with its formal topiary pieces, and Round Court, with its circular lawn, is deliberately in keeping with the distinctive Arts and Crafts houses of Storey's Way, including Baillie Scott's number 48, discussed in Chapter Eight of this study. At the heart of Greenhouse Court there is mixed planting, as well as a communal space with grass surrounds. The working buildings, including the Greenhouse that gives the complex its name, are made deliberately visible on the south-east side of the courtyard. Round Court's enclosure has an unusually warm microclimate, allowing heat-loving plants to thrive. To the east of these two residential courts is Green Lane, a long grass 'road' flanked by two terraced buildings with a *clair-voyée* onto Storey's Way, designed to represent a residential street and invite access (*colour 50*), unlike forbidding Fitzwilliam College next door. Henry James praised Trinity Hall's historic city-centre buildings and traditional garden layout,[19] but it is Wychfield's inventiveness that remains in the memory, successfully uniting old and new in peaceful domesticity.

There are two fascinating gardens in Shepreth, south-west of Cambridge, where the main King's Cross to Cambridge railway line loops around the back of one – Docwra's Manor – and actually passes right alongside the other by a level crossing. This last is appropriately named the Crossing House.

Docwra's Manor is a beautiful early eighteenth-century house of blue and red patterned bricks, clay-tiled roofs and gleaming white fenes-

81 The Gravel Courtyard at Docwra's Manor takes advantage of the local dry climate and signals a distinct change in mood between the pleasure grounds and the Walled Garden

tration, centred on the first floor by a Venetian window (*colour 51*). Its front railings to the street are draped in May with luscious white roses, while further ramblers climb up the façade. Entry is not through the front gates, guarded by tall brick piers topped with ball finials, but to the side of the house, where there is an honesty box for entrance fees, postcards and John Raven's *A Botanist's Garden*, first published in 1971. If one is fortunate, the present owner, John's wife Faith Raven, is on hand to take the money and direct the visitor into the garden. This has two distinct moods: a Victorian-type pleasure ground behind the house with an open lawn, a modern Temple, a sun-dappled Wild Garden and, divided from it by writhing yew topiary shapes, a Spring Garden, while to the side there is an original Walled Garden of flowery profusion. The link between the two areas is the Gravel Courtyard (*81*), a dry Mediterranean-style garden of gravel, pebbles and ornamental pots with spiky plants. Finally, after the heady experience of the Walled Garden, there is a calm Kitchen Lawn reaching back towards the house and the front driveway. Any visit should be rounded off with refreshment at Christine and Maurice Prové's excellent Teacake café next door.

In addition to John Raven's book, Faith has written an informative guide to the garden and has continued to develop it since her husband's death in 1980.[20] They started in 1954 when there was little on the site except some fine trees. The idea was to work outwards from the house, introducing plants given to them by friends or sourced from expeditions abroad. 'Species were preferred to hybrids, and the old-fashioned to modern novelties.' This gives the place a cottage garden feel, where plants intertwine ebulliently in a calculated wildness. Apart from the Temple, which looks somewhat incongruous in amongst all this growth, there are no other formal or non-plant forms, such as sculptures or garden buildings. In the various sectors the plants alone are allowed to define the spaces and enliven the views, even though the main gardener, David Aitchison, was trained in drawing and sculpture. As Docwra's has evolved since John Raven's death, before which the plants tended to be grouped botanically, it has become more 'in tune with modern fashion, flower colours have become more dramatic, although vivid colours are used as focal points rather than as large eye-catching medleys'. The aim is to 'grow plants in their natural form', which encourages wildlife, and also to select those which will respond to the local dry climate; hence the creation of the Mediterranean area. The effect is one of sure-footed professionalism and breathtaking beauty, especially in the Walled Garden (*colour 52*) with its crescendo of colour from cynara, *Geranium asphodeloides*, *Iris sibirica* and *Iris pallida* 'Dalmatica'.[21]

The **Crossing House** is another case entirely. While Docwra's oozes horticultural erudition, the small triangle of land around the 1850 level crossing manager's house just up the road towards Meldreth is easy-going and relaxed, a cheerful mix of plants and structures, all cowering in the lee of thunderous trains heading for the capital. The garden is so unfettered that drifts of geraniums and irises seep out onto the pavement edge where there is a gate with a typically hospitable sign: 'Plant lovers are welcome to walk around this garden. Children welcome with an adult.' There is no charge and Margaret and Doug Fuller, who have lived here since 1959, are usually around to answer questions, accompanied by John Marlar (*colour 53*). On our visit we were welcomed by John, who had a tubby British cream cat, Bramble, on a lead and was deep in a book. The front garden has a cider press at its heart, which is circled by box hedging, and on our late May visit there were swathes of nodding aquilegia. Behind the house the plot expands into a lawned area, with a small pool with a waterfall overlooked by a beautiful tree peony, and then funnels down alongside the

82 The Crossing House garden at Shepreth is full of surprises like this fairground horse, which peeps out of the narrow walk alongside the main railway line from Cambridge to King's Cross

railway into a narrow walk terminated by a silver sphere. Along this walk a fairground horse peeks out (*82*) and an iron sleigh bristles with flowers. Walking back to skirt the lawn the visitor passes topiary sheep, all named to chime with their bleating: Barnabus, Bartholomew and Barbara. Margaret, who started by exchanging plants with Lord de Ramsey and the Ravens at Docwra's Manor, aims to have plants flowering throughout the seasons to take the place of others as they fade. The garden has a delightful homespun feel to it and shows how an unpromising plot can be coaxed into vibrant life with the right plant knowledge and a light touch when it comes to design.

The trains flashing by at Shepreth add to the garden experience, while at **Barnwell Junction**, in the northern suburbs of Cambridge where the A1134 crosses over the main line, a disused branch offers only railway nostalgia. It is as if Dr Beeching had just wielded his axe, and one half expects John Betjeman's cheeky face to peek out in mischievous delight from the timber-framed Ladies' Waiting Room (*83*) across the line from the stationmaster's house. This is on the down platform to Mildenhall, its bank terraced and spiked with conifers and herbaceous plants, while the main garden, which extends out from the station house, is on the up platform to Cambridge. The house itself is just one element of a whole complex of whitewashed, timber-gabled buildings, alongside which there was once a Pullman Montana coach, since restored and removed to Petworth in Sussex. The garden has been made by Pam Thornhill who, like Margaret Fuller at Shepreth, came to Barnwell with her husband, who worked on the railways, in the 1950s. The narrow plot is laid out in a linear pattern, with low brick walls providing planting areas and a double pergola reaching out to the entrance and running parallel with the line. In late July the garden was verdant with sweet peas, fading rose climbers, hops and clematis, while lower down, the views towards the formal herb garden were punctuated with box balls and terracotta pots (*colour 54*). The layout is compressed within its small compass, but there are internal views down the pergolas and out across the railway line. It is a remarkable survival, kept going by a tenacious woman, who on our visit was dressed from tip to toe in dashing vermillion.

Our visit to **Hardwicke House** at Fen Ditton, on the parallel road to the Fleam Dyke, was nostalgic for other reasons. It was where John Drake welcomed us just before he died, so our tour of his garden was both poignant and never to be repeated. Even though he was very ill, recuperating from major heart surgery, his quiet enthusiasm for the garden he had created over the last 40 years at the back of a house his parents had built was infectious. Foundations for the house were laid in 1937, but the war stopped progress and it was not finished until 1948. It was also tragic to hear of his plans for a new area around the septic tank, which he will never realise. It was a real privilege to walk the grounds and scribble frantically as Drake rattled off the names of plants and trees that he had chosen carefully for the odd conditions – fenland soil and chalk – which

83 The Ladies Waiting Room is on the Mildenhall platform, across the line from the Station House garden at Barnwell Junction

had to be taken into account as he planned the layout.

The garden is divided into three sectors: two intensely planted areas to east and west, with a calm lawn directly behind the house in between. The first to the west is dense woodland lined with silver birch avenues underplanted with narcissus, and other areas populated with Turkish hazel, oaks from Crete, syringa, viburnum and black poplars. It is crossed by a vista that works both ways, in which there are two wooden sculptures by Richard Bray: a column tapered and ribbed like an animal's vertebra (*84*), and a 1968 ash wedge sculpture surrounded by low box quadrants. Further

84 Two wooden sculptures by Richard Bray in visual axis within the woodland garden at John Drake's Hardwicke House

out in the woodland there is another Bray piece made of six shafts of wood, carved to represent asparagus spears, rising up directly from the earth. At the ash wedge the axis switches to the north and leads into an open area dramatised by two wooden trellis towers shaped like tombs in eastern Turkey. These are surrounded by Turkish plants: philarea alternating with box, while the towers were writhing in late July with sweet pea (*colour* 55). The other area to the east is enclosed by high yew hedges, which provide shelter for plants that were available in John Tradescant's time. Drake worked on this section in collaboration with Lady Salisbury, although his overall philosophy was to see what would grow and thrive in the conditions. It was adjacent to this Tradescant garden that Drake was devising a mount to command a formal area of diagonal beds planted with hepatica. Like its maker, the garden was in a charmingly careworn state on our visit, so it is our hope that a new owner will take it in hand, but tend it gently.

A mount was achieved in the walled garden at **Chippenham Park** by Anne Crawley, who died just before we visited her husband Eustace, who now lives in the former gardener's house. This has been re-named Hare Hall after the hare sculpture on the cross axis by Stanley Dove. Other sectors of the enclosure have hedged compartments with standing stones enlivened by pencil-thin conifers; round-arched arcaded hedges produce a theatrical effect, while the Mount itself, which is topped by a viewing seat, is ringed with quince trees. Another quadrant has a Mediterranean-style gravel area planted with grasses in between huge clay pots lying on their sides. While all these disparate elements would appear to have little connection, the ambitious scale of the design succeeds admirably in unifying a vast area laid to grass. The same could be said for the new interventions at **Wilbraham Temple** where, since 1980, Richard Wright has commissioned new yew-hedged enclosures to the south and east of the lawns of the house. These have enlivened a rather staid landscape and provided visual links across the new ha-has between the pleasure grounds and the wider parkland. He has also sited a circular Doric Temple on the edge of Star & Garter Wood, across the stream which flows through the estate, and installed a new north terrace with planting, designed in 1982 by Anthony du Gard Pasley. But his most significant achievement at Wilbraham has been the ongoing campaign of tree planting – well over 1,000 trees have been introduced – which began with a new shelterbelt in 1981.

One further garden where knowledgeable owners have combined beautiful planting schemes with delightfully whimsical garden buildings is sited four miles north-east of Huntingdon. **Abbots Ripton Hall** is just outside the boundaries of this book, but is still close enough to the old county border to be included in this survey as one of Cambridgeshire's greatest modern gardens.[22] Here a combination of eclectic features, careful planting and fine specimen trees succeeds in bringing a topographically unpromising site to life. There are stretches of managed park and farmland to the north and east of the Hall, while to the south the Abbots Ripton Brook runs parallel to the garden façade of the house, curving to embrace the main sweep of lawn and forming the garden's south-eastern boundary. Originally an outpost for the monks of Ramsey

85 A touch of Rococo exoticism in the county at Abbots Ripton Hall – Peter Foster's Chinese Fishing Pavilion

Abbey, with a productive medieval garden, the Hall dates from the eighteenth century and was extensively remodelled in 1856 by Anthony Salvin. Today, an ancient London plane at the southernmost corner overshadows the lawn and threatens to dwarf the house entirely.

The present Lord De Ramsey's father moved into the Hall in 1937, carrying out major restorations and changes to the garden throughout the 1950s under the instruction of Humphrey Waterfield. Work on the pleasure grounds then continued well into the next two decades with the advice of Lanning Roper. Finally, an extensive lake was dug to the east of the garden in 1971-2; this is commanded by a brightly painted Chinese Fishing Pavilion (*85*) on the far side designed by Peter Foster, Surveyor of Westminster Abbey, who was also responsible for the garden's other Chinese and Gothick timber follies. Foster copied the design for the pavilion from one admired by Lord De Ramsey in John Constable's painting of Wivenhoe Hall Park, Essex.[23] The present Lord and Lady De Ramsey are continuing to improve and maintain the grounds, re-planting the borders and maintaining the garden buildings. They have also initiated a new arboretum with a collection of unusual oak trees. The brook essentially divides the garden in two, but can be crossed in three places: via a bright white Chinese-style bridge in front of the house (*colour 56*), a second, Gothick wooden footbridge leading to the octagonal Gothick Summerhouse, and an eighteenth-century triple-arched brick bridge. The route across the main lawn from the house towards the lake leads to a pair of flowering White Borders and a Rose Circle. These White Borders are planted with forget-me-nots, creamy roses, white irises, peonies and philadelphus, while the Rose Circle contains only old specimens, including *R.* 'Cardinal Richelieu' and *R.* 'Boule de Neige'.[24] Aside from the majestic plane, the extensive pleasure grounds and ornamental gardens also contain many other fine trees, including two oaks dated to 1600, limes, white willows and sycamores.

Our visit having taken place during the last days of autumn, perhaps the garden's most striking feature was the broad grass walk, flanked by fading herbaceous borders, which forms a key axis from the house on the opposite side of the brook. This walkway is a staggering 150 yards long, the flower borders backed by alternating yew cylinders and *Philadelphus coronarius* 'Aureus', the whole bisected at its mid-point by Foster's Gothick Trellis (*86*). These deep borders are informally planted with a profusion of cottage garden perennials, providing a sharp contrast with the crisp, formal outline of the vista. Beyond the Gothick rondel is a pair of wrought iron gates, leading to an avenue of horse chestnuts. The urns on the gateposts are fibreglass copies of the Ramsey incense burner, the fourteenth-century original of which is in the Victoria and Albert Museum.[25] Ultimately this is a modern Arcadia, an intensely personal garden that has turned its back on evolving fashions and triumphed accordingly. Therefore, Abbots Ripton's contemporary garden goes some way to make up for the county's conspicuous lack of intimate eighteenth-century Rococo layouts with their exotic follies.

Recycled history, like the Georgian-style follies of Abbots Ripton Hall,

86 The Rococo-Gothick trellis screens on the grass walk at Abbots Ripton Hall add a hint of Batty Langley frivolity to the profusely planted borders

but in the form of architectural salvage, enlivens the grounds of **Chilford Hall**, just outside Linton. These reclaimed fragments jostle happily with modern sculpture to make a visit to the winery and its café a rewarding experience. The complex has been built up by Sam Alper, who moved into the nineteenth-century farmhouse on the site in the mid-1960s. To this he added a shuttered concrete extension of unmitigated brutality around which he has sited the sculpture, some of which is his own (*87*). Other ornamental and structural stonework was rescued from Hyde Park Barracks, Nonsuch Park and the Long Bar in Waterloo Station. The Chilford Hundred Vineyard was planted between 1972 and 1976 and, despite a recent fire at the Victorian house, continues to thrive.

While much of the sculpture at Chilford is either abstract or only semi-figurative, the sculptures that dramatise the gardens at **The Old Vicarage, Grantchester**, are unashamedly figurative, signalled in the entrance driveway by the imposing Paul Day bronze of Rupert Brooke

87 An unlikely venue for a modern sculpture park – the Chilford Hundred Vineyard and Winery just outside Linton was set up by Sam Alper, an amateur sculptor

88
Paul Day's bronze of the poet Rupert Brooke is the first sculpture in a varied collection that enriches the grounds of The Old Vicarage, Grantchester

(*88*), whose mother bought the house in 1916. Brooke had initially lodged with the Stevensons at The Orchard next door while he was working on a postgraduate dissertation on the dramatist John Webster, but moved into The Old Vicarage in 1911 as the Neeves' lodger.[26] Brooke has left his impressions of the house and garden at this time: 'This is a deserted, lonely, dank, ruined, overgrown, gloomy, lovely house: with a garden to match. It is all five hundred years old, and fusty with the ghosts of generations of mouldering clergymen. It is a fit place to write my kind of poetry in.'[27] It was, indeed, a clergy house until 1850, when the then incumbent refused to live there and it was bought by Samuel Page Widnall, the son of a successful Grantchester nurseryman. Widnall was responsible for building the Castle Ruin at the end of the garden by the Mill Stream, which has been sensitively restored by Lord and Dame Mary Archer and extended, between 1989 and 1990, by a spectacular conservatory. Its cloister houses a beautiful Eric Gill bas-relief *Female and Serpent*, together with Gill's *St Andrew Casting His Net* and *The Good Samaritan*; these were restored and installed in 2008. Widnall added other, typically Victorian, structures to the grounds, including a conservatory, Swiss cottage, bathing house and pigeon-cote, but these have all gone.

Today the grounds are essentially the Victorian gardens remodelled by Dudley and Annemarie Ward, who passed the house on Dudley's death in 1957 to her son Peter Ward. Peter and Lona Ward sold the house in 1979 to Jeffrey and Mary Archer. While the Archers have done much to the house itself, the grounds have been retained in their nineteenth-century maturity with advice on new planting from Professor Willmer, but are now enlivened with a series of sculptures. There are too many to mention in detail, but a few catch the eye, particularly the *Salmon and the Otter* in the lake (*colour 57*) by Laurence Broderick and *Oceanides*, a green patinated bronze statue of 1936-7 by Maurice Lambert (*colour 58*), which originally formed the centrepiece of the main hall of the SS *Queen Elizabeth*. As Mary Archer writes, apart from the modern sculptures, 'much in the garden and beyond remains as Mrs Brooke would have wished to see it. The chestnuts still make a tunnel of green gloom by the river and the immortal river [as in Rupert Brooke's poem] still laughs under the nearby Mill House into the Mill Pool'.[28] And, no doubt, given the Archers' celebrated hospitality, there is still honey for tea. On a ferociously hot afternoon in late July we were treated to homemade lemonade, which we gulped under the shelter of the thatched Summerhouse.

On another hot afternoon, this time in late September, we made a pilgrimage to the **American Cemetery at Madingley**, not expecting to be so overwhelmingly moved by the stark simplicity of the angular Memorial Chapel and the seven arcs of serried white crosses marking the graves of servicemen killed in the Second World War (*89*). The 30-acre plot was established in 1944 on land donated by the University and was dedicated on 16 July 1956. The stele-like stone at the top of the steps leading down to the Canal gives the architects as Perry, Shaw, Hepburn

89 Pristine white against verdant green – the graves and Memorial Chapel of the American Cemetery, Madingley. The landscape plan was designed by the Olmstead brothers from Brookline, Massachusetts

and Dean of Boston, while the landscape architects were the Olmstead brothers from Brookline. Madingley is the only American World War Two cemetery in the British Isles. It is framed by woodland to the south and west, but there are open views to the north across the back road to Madingley and out to the fields beyond. This north entrance is the best one to take, avoiding the main entry point on the A1303, which is a little pompous and dominated by a towering 72-foot flagstaff in the centre of a platform of yellow roses. The lower entry point leads up West Mall, which is lined with Japanese pagoda trees and bordered by beds of pachysandra in which are planted flowering shrubs and perennials, including peonies, day-lilies, evergreen barberry and viburnum.

The axis shifts to the east at the flagpole platform and down the Great Mall, its reflecting pool bordered appropriately by blood-red polyantha roses, the north side lined with pink hawthorns (*colour 59*). At the far end

90 American servicemen stand vigil by the Wall of the Missing at Madingley Cemetery

is the Memorial Chapel, while along the cemetery's southern edge stretches the Portland stone Wall of the Missing, supported at intervals by four statues representing a soldier, a sailor, an airman and a coast guardsman (*90*). Out in the field, in meticulously maintained grass, are the 3,812 graves, set in seven ranks fanning out from the two malls. It is shattering to think of all those buried here, yet their country could have devised no finer monument to their bravery and Cambridgeshire is fortunate to have at least one historic garden of international significance.

Chapter Notes Introduction and Chapter 1

Introduction, pages 9-20: Fenlands, horses, literary figures and a university

1 For the original Bishop's Garden see Christopher Hussey, 'Ely Palace, Cambridgeshire', *Country Life*, 9 June 1928; see also Robert Hallmann, 'A Garden Blessed', *Cambridgeshire Life*, August 2003. On our visit the garden was a building site for the new Sue Ryder Home.

2 The menu was kindly supplied at Kirtling by Anna Markwell.

3 *A History of the County of Cambridge and the Isle of Ely* (hereafter *VCH*), vol.8 (1982), pp.227-30.

4 Christopher Morris (ed.), *The Illustrated Journeys of Celia Fiennes c.1682-c.1712* (1982), p.78.

5 Information from another of the excellent display boards at Wandlebury.

6 Cambridge University Library (hereafter CUL), Views Relhan 1 No.10.

7 *VCH*, 8, p.227.

8 Amanda Chapman has made a new sunken terrace garden to the rear of the house and she is currently (March 2012) restoring the walled kitchen garden.

9 Extract at the house taken from Theo Taunton's *Famous Horses*.

10 Norman Sherry, *The Life of Graham Greene*, 3 vols., 1989, 1, p.52.

11 Ibid.

12 Richard Greene (ed.), *Graham Greene: A Life in Letters*, 2007, p.261.

13 William Heinemann first edition, 1943, p.127.

14 Faber & Faber first edition, 1958, p.12.

15 AN Wilson, Introduction to Virago's 1983 edition of her *Told by an Idiot*, p.xiii.

16 We are grateful to Nicholas Browne for showing us this map at The Grange.

17 Puffin Books edition, 1976, p.42.

Chapter 1, pages 21-39: Wimpole Hall – 'a flower in the desert'

1 Gervase Jackson-Stops, *Wimpole Hall* (National Trust, Hatfield, 1984), p.40.

2 Cambridgeshire Gardens Trust, *The Gardens of Cambridgeshire: A Gazetteer* (The Cambridgeshire Gardens Trust, Huntingdon, 2000), hereafter *CGT Gazetteer*, p.114.

3 David Souden, *Wimpole Hall, Cambridgeshire* (National Trust, Swindon, 2009), p.6.

4 David Adshead, *Wimpole: Architectural Drawings and Topographical Views* (National Trust, Cambridge, 2007), p.29.

5 An aerial photograph of 1949 in Jackson-Stops, *Wimpole Hall* shows them (p.6).

6 Cambridgeshire Archives (hereafter CA): R77/1.

7 WM Palmer (ed.), *John Layer of Shepreth* (Cambridgeshire Antiquarian Society, Cambridge, 1935), p.111.

8 Souden, *Wimpole Hall*, p.80.

9 RC Latham & W Mathews (eds), *The Diary of Samuel Pepys*, 10 vols. (2010) 2, pp.418-19.

10 Quoted in Jackson-Stops, *Wimpole Hall*, p.50.

11 Ibid., p.52.

12 Daniel Defoe, *A Tour through the Whole Island of Great Britain 1724-6* (1971), p.10.

13 British Library (hereafter BL), Add. MS 5834, fol.162.

14 Adshead, *Wimpole*, p.30.

15 This plan, 'Survey and final proposals for the gardens to the south of the house', of about 1721-5: National Trust (hereafter NT), WIM/D/464, shows the great avenue and subsidiary vistas.

16 Quoted in Adshead, *Wimpole*, p.33.

17 Souden, *Wimpole Hall*, p.17.

18 Lady Llanover (ed.), *The Autobiography and Correspondence of Mrs. Delany*, 6 vols. (1861-2), 2, p.156.

19 R Halsband (ed.), *The Complete Letters of Lady Mary Wortley Montagu*, 3 vols. (Oxford, 1966), 2, pp.246-7.

20 Souden, *Wimpole Hall*, p.18.

21 PC Yorke (ed.), *The Life and Correspondence of Philip Yorke, Earl of Hardwicke, Lord High Chancellor of Great*

Britain, 3 vols. (Cambridge, 1913), 2, p.558.

22 BL, Add. MS 5823, fol.135.

23 This is Robert Greening's 'Proposal for the gardens to the north of the house' of about 1752: NT, WIM/D/456. He also submitted a 'Proposal for the gardens and park to the north and west of the house' of the same date: NT, WIM/D/459.

24 BL, Add. MS 35679, fol.24.

25 Souden, *Wimpole Hall*, p.88.

26 Bedfordshire Record Office (hereafter BRO), L39/9a/6, p.117.

27 Letter from Walpole to Richard Bentley dated 1753, W S Lewis (ed.), *The Yale Edition of Horace Walpole's Correspondence*, 48 vols. (New Haven & Oxford, 1937-83), 35, p.148.

28 Warwick Record Office, CR 125B/348: letter from Sir George Lyttelton to Sanderson Miller, dated 1 June 1749.

29 Quoted in David Adshead, 'The Design and Building of the Gothic Folly at Wimpole, Cambridgeshire', *The Burlington Magazine*, vol.140 (1998), pp.76-84; p.76.

30 'Perspective drawing for the folly at Wimpole', of 1749-51: NT, WIM/D/455, attributed to Sanderson Miller.

31 Michael McCarthy argues for the sole attribution of the Gothick Folly to Essex in *The Origins of the Gothic Revival* (New Haven & London, 1987), p.53. *CGT Gazetteer* also states that 'in 1774 James Essex reworked Sanderson Miller's proposals for a Gothic tower on Johnson's Hill' (p.115).

32 BRO, Lucas MSS, L30/21/2/7: letter from Annabel Yorke, later Polwarth, to Miss Catherine Talbot.

33 BRO, L/30/11/122/26: letter from Marchioness Grey to her daughter Lady Annabel, 1 October 1772.

34 Adshead, 'The Design and Building of the Gothic Folly', pp.76-84; p.76. For a controversial study of the Gothic style as a considered political statement when applied to garden buildings, see David Stewart, 'Political Ruins: Gothic Sham Ruins and the "45"', *Journal of the Society of Architectural Historians*, vol.55 (1996), pp.400-411.

35 Michael Hall (ed.), *Gothic Architecture and its Meanings 1550-1830* (Spire Books, Reading, 2002). Hall defines the Gothic as being a 'forum for the struggle over Hanoverian legitimacy', which broke into open revolt in 1715 and 1745 (p.19).

36 Dorothy Stroud, 'The Charms of Natural Landscape: The Park and Gardens at Wimpole – II', *Country Life*, 3 September 1979.

37 BL, Add. MS 69795, fol.20.

38 Lancelot Brown, 'Design for the lakes and the northern extension of the Park', of about 1767: NT, WIM/D/448.

39 Stroud, 'The Charms of Natural Landscape', p.759.

40 BRO, 9a/9, p.125.

41 James Stuart, Elevation for the south front of the Hill House; after 1766, before 1774: Royal Institute of British Architects Library, Drawings Collection SD 62/7(1).

42 BL, Add. MS 35378, fol.305v.

43 BL, Add. MS 36278 G.

44 Souden, *Wimpole Hall*, p.35.

45 Ibid., p.33.

46 Jackson-Stops, *Wimpole Hall*, p.42.

47 Wimpole Red Book, 1801, held at the Hall: NT, WIM/D/485a.

48 The first plate in the Red Book, 'View from the north of the house, without slide', 1801: NT, WIM/D/485a.

49 Wimpole Red Book.

Chapter 2, pages 40-62: Watery enclosures and the progresses of a queen

1 *An Inventory of Historical Monuments in the County of Cambridge* (hereafter *RCHM*), vol. 1 (West Cambridgeshire), 1968, pp.lxi-lxv.

2 CUL, Ms. Plans 273.

3 The plan is illustrated in *RCHM*, vol.1, plate 29b; the original is in CA.

4 CUL, Map.bb.53(1).93.83-86.

5 We are grateful to Peter Johnson for information on the house.

6 Information from Peter Johnson.

7 CUL, Maps.bb.53(1).95.25-33.

8 See A E Brown & C C Taylor, 'A Relict Garden at Linton, Cambridgeshire', *Proceedings of the Cambridge Antiquarian Society*, vol.80 (1991), pp.62-7.

9 Ibid., p.66, citing CA, R59/5/9/166-8.

10 See Timothy Mowl, *Historic Gardens of Oxfordshire* (Stroud, 2007), pp.34-6.

11 We are grateful to Sidney Taylor for driving us out to Catley.

12 CA, R59/5/3/1: a detailed memo book of Sir Thomas Sclater for his Linton estate, post-1670.

13 Ibid.

14 *RCHM*, vol.1, p.135.

15 *RCHM*, vol.2 (1972), p.101.

16 *CGT Gazetteer*, p.69.

17 Ibid., p.160.

18 J C Buckler's view of the mansion before demolition is illustrated in H Avray Tipping, 'Kirtling Tower, Cambridgeshire', *Country Life*, 24 January 1931. We are grateful to Lord and Lady Fairhaven for allowing us access to this private property, and to Fred Waters, head gardener, for an informed tour of the grounds.

19 John Martin Robinson, 'Kirtling Tower, Cambridgeshire', *Country Life*, 1 December 2005.

20 Maggie Campbell-Culver, *The Origin of Plants* (2001), p.139.

21 Tara Selwyn-Jones, 'Labour of Love', *Cambridgeshire Life*, May 2006, p.77.

22 John Nichols, *The Progresses and Public Processions of Queen Elizabeth*, 2 vols. (1788-1805), 2, p.91.

23 *Country Life*, 24 January 1931.

24 Banquet list supplied by Anna Markwell at Kirtling.

25 Mary Hill Cole, *The Portable Queen: Elizabeth I and the Politics of Ceremony* (Boston, Massachusetts, 1999), pp.76-7. We are grateful to Jane Whitaker for sharing with us her doctoral research on the Queen's progresses.

26 J Miller, 'Archaeological Investigations at Kirtling Towers, Cambridgeshire', Cambridge Archaeological Unit, Cambridge University, no.56 (November, 1992), p.3. We are grateful to Samantha Smith of the CAU for making this available for study.

27 Ibid., p.9.

28 Ibid., p.10.

29 Ibid., p.13.

30 Ibid.

31 See Paula Henderson, *The Tudor House and Garden* (2005) pp.77-9.

32 *RCHM*, vol.1, plate 67.

33 Arthur Oswald, 'Sawston Hall, Cambridgeshire – I', *Country Life*, 10 June 1954.

34 *CGT Gazetteer*, p.104.

35 *Country Life*, 10 June 1954.

36 A useful map of the site is given in *RCHM*, vol.1, p.46.

37 *CGT Gazetteer*, p.131.

38 Ibid.

39 CUL, MS. Plans 552.

40 David Watkin, 'Childerley Hall, Cambridge', *Country Life*, 6 November 1969, plate 4.

41 CA, 23/z929.

42 We are grateful to Lee & Laura Hughes for their hospitality at Haslingfield.

43 *RCHM*, vol.1, p.141.

Chapter 3, pages 63-88: Hortus Sociorum and Hortus Magistri – seventeenth-century Cambridge

1 A portfolio of twelve maps, edited by Tony Baggs & Peter Bryan, illustrating the changing plan of Cambridge, was published by the Cambridgeshire Records Society in 2002 and revised in 2012. It is available from the Map Room of CUL.

2 Also included in the above-mentioned portfolio.

3 John Speed, *The Theatre of the Empire of Great Britaine* (1611); the map is dated 1610.

4 Thomas Fuller, *The Church-History of Britain, from the Birth of Christ until the Year 1648* (1655); the map is dated 1655.

5 Included in the Cambridgeshire Records Society portfolio of maps.

6 We are grateful to the King's College Archivist, Dr Patricia McGuire, for information on the structure.

7 Robert Willis & John Willis Clark, *The Architectural History of the University of Cambridge*, 4 vols. (Cambridge, 1886), 1, p.569.

8 Ibid.

9 Gervase Markham, *Country Contentments*, 2 vols. (1615).

10 Ibid., 1, p.108.

11 Willis & Clark, 2, p.54.

12 *English Heritage Register of Parks and Gardens*; hereafter *EHR*.

13 Willis & Clark, 3, p.578.

14 Ibid., 3, p.580.

15 Ibid., 3, p.582.

16 Ibid.

17 Willis & Clark, 2, p.228.

18 *EHR*.

19 *Cantabrigia Depicta: A Concise and Accurate Description of the University and Town of Cambridge* (Cambridge, 1763), p.67.

20 J Le Keux & Thomas Wright, *Memorials of Cambridge: A Series of Views of the Colleges, Halls, and Public Buildings with Historical and Descriptive Accounts*, 2 vols. (1847) 1, pp.89-90.

21 Sanderson was Lucasian Professor of Mathematics (1711-39), Mede was a herbalist and biblical scholar and Cudworth was Master of Christ's (1654-88).

22 *EHR*. The college purchased 300 mulberry trees to support James I's scheme to institute a British silk industry; these were usually white mulberry trees, rather than the *Morus nigra* in the grounds.

23 Willis & Clark, 2, p.719.

24 *The Foreigner's Companion* (1748) p.72; quoted in Willis & Clark, 2, p.720.

25 George Dyer, *History of the University and Colleges of Cambridge* (Cambridge, 1814); quoted in Willis & Clark, 2, p.720.

26 *EHR*. A site inspection failed to find these, though the borders are profuse and may be obscuring them.

27 Willis & Clark, 1, p.27. We are grateful to Dr Roger Lovatt for bringing this reference to our attention.

28 Willis & Clark, 1, p.27.

29 *Cantabrigia Depicta*, p.25.

30 See Pete Smith, 'The Sundial Garden and House-Plan Mount: two gardens at Wollaton Hall, Nottinghamshire, by Robert (*c*.1535-1614) and John (-1634) Smythson', *Garden History*, vol.31, no.1 (Spring, 2003), pp.1-28; see also Karin Seeber, '"Ye Making of Ye Mount", Oxford College's Mount Garden Revised', *Garden History*, vol.40, no.1 (Summer, 2012), pp.3-16.

31 Willis & Clark, 1, p.143.

32 Ibid., 2, p.321.

33 Ibid., 2, p.323.

34 Morris, *The Illustrated Journeys of Celia Fiennes*, p.80.

35 See Timothy Mowl, *Palladian Bridges* (Millstream Books, Bath, 1993), p.13. Etheridge had previously designed a similar, though far larger, wooden bridge to span the Thames at Walton.

36 Willis & Clark, 2, p.638.

37 Ibid., 1, pp.567-8.

38 Ibid., 1, p.96.

39 Paula Henderson, *The Tudor House and Garden: Architecture and Landscape in the Sixteenth and Early Seventeenth Centuries* (2005) pp.186-8; see also Willis & Clark, 2, p.627.

40 Willis & Clark, 2, p.642.

41 Ibid., 2, p.647.

42 Ibid., 2, p.646.

43 Ibid.

Chapter 4, pages 89-112: Canals, avenues and a 'Sweete Prospect' – formal gardens

1 CA, 408/E6.

2 For the precise dating of Wisbech see Howard Colvin, *Essays in English Architectural History* (1999), p.168; for Commonwealth architecture in general and Wisbech in particular, see Timothy Mowl & Brian Earnshaw, *Architecture without Kings: The Rise of Puritan Classicism under Cromwell* (Manchester, 1995), pp.114-16.

3 After Medworth's death the Castle was bought by William Peckover, who removed the northern part of the wall, so that the pleasure grounds could be opened up to the public. It now forms part of Union Place with a war memorial; the Castle was given to the local authority in 1969 and the house is now a museum. See Vera Perrott, 'Preserving the Past', *Cambridgeshire Journal*, April 1999, pp.39-42; also George Anniss, *A History of Wisbech Castle* (Wisbech, 1977).

4 Anniss, *Wisbech Castle*, fig.6. This is a redrawn plan of the Castle taken from a deed acknowledged by Joseph Medworth when he purchased the premises.

5 However, Arthur Oswald suggested in 1947 that there might be another painting of the Castle somewhere in Ely; at this time the painting at Peckover House was in the Museum (*Country Life*, 23 May 1947).

6 Ibid., pp.109-14.

7 See Roy Strong, *The Artist and the Garden* (2000), pp.90-92; also by the same author, *The Renaissance Garden in England*, 1979, pp.39-43.

8 See Timothy Mowl, *Historic Gardens of Oxfordshire* (Stroud, 2007), pp.14-15.

9 Act 2, scene 2.

10 In 1967 the Maze was re-cut, restoring the original pathways, by P M G Dickinson, the Huntingdon historian: *CGT Gazetteer*, p.130.

11 The Maze is in a private garden at Balsham Manor and is not generally open to the public, but arrangements can be made with Jim Potter to view it.

12 See John Harris, *William Talman: Maverick Architect* (1982); see also David Jacques & Arends van der Horst, *The Gardens of William and Mary* (1988), pp.177-80.

13 Timothy Mowl, *Historic Gardens of Wiltshire* (Stroud, 2004), pp.30-41.

14 We were not allowed access for this study.

15 A E Shipley, 'Madingley Hall, Cambridgeshire', *Country Life*, 5 October 1912.

16 *Madingley Hall: A Short History and Description of the Hall and Estate, their Owners and Occupiers* (University of Cambridge, 1976), p.16.

17 We are grateful to Michael and Margaret Braithwaite for their hospitality at the Manor, and for information on the genesis of the house.

18 For an analysis of this design strategy see Caroline Dalton, *Sir John Vanbrugh and the Vitruvian Landscape* (Routledge, London, 2012), p.212.

19 See Peter Willis, *Charles Bridgeman and the English Landscape Garden* (Newcastle-upon-Tyne, 2002).

20 King's College Congregation Book, 1722-78, f.12; quoted in Willis, *Charles Bridgeman*, p.84.

21 Willis & Clark, 1, pp.571-2; the engraving was hanging in the Provost's Lodge in 1886.

22 This axial relationship is shown clearly on Bridgeman's plan for Stowe. Peter Willis attributes the 1739 plan to Bridgeman; see p.110 and plate 117. It is in the Bodleian Library, Oxford: MS. Gough Drawings, a.4, f.46.

23 *Cantabrigia Depicta*, 1763, p.50.

24 S Max Walters, *King's College Fellows' Garden* (Cambridge, 1991), p.6.

25 Willis & Clark, 1, p.572.

26 The survey is preserved at Downing College, Cambridge. We are most grateful to the College Archivist, Dr Kate Thompson, for supplying an image of the survey.

27 For an architectural history of the house see Jeremy Musson, 'Chippenham Park, Cambridgeshire', *Country Life*, 1 January 2004.

28 See Chapter Five of this study.

29 We are grateful to Eustace Crawley for accompanying us on a hair-raising golf-buggy ride around the landscape at Chippenham; it was quite the most memorable of our visits.

30 Morris, *Celia Fiennes*, p.140.

31 Ibid., p.141.

32 Ibid., p.140.

33 The landscape has been the focus of an MA in Garden History dissertation entitled: 'Chippenham Park, Cambridgeshire 1688-1810', by Sarah Hunderby (2009). We are grateful to Eustace Crawley for making a copy of this report available to us.

34 CA 71/P3.

35 Twigs Way, 'The Kitchen Garden at Chippenham Park, Cambridgeshire', *Cambridgeshire Local History Society Review*, New Series, 11 (September, 2002), pp.3-16.

36 This observation is shared by Catriona Campbell in her dissertation on the site for the Architectural Association (June 1998); cited in Hunderby, 'Chippenham Park', p.4.

37 Quoted in Hunderby, 'Chippenham Park', citing CRO 683/A1.

38 CUL, Ms. Plans a.5.

39 RT Gunther, *The Architecture of Sir Roger Pratt* (Oxford, 1928), p.55.

40 Ibid.

41 Ibid.

42 Ibid.

43 ES de Beer (ed.), *The Diary of John Evelyn*, 6 vols. (Oxford, 1955), 3, p.553.

44 Catherine Parsons, 'Horseheath Hall and its Owners', *Proceedings of the Cambridge Antiquarian Society*, vol.41 (1948), pp.1-51; p.6.

45 Ibid., p.7.

46 Excavations have identified some compartments around the site of the Hall; see S N Kemp, 'Archaeology within the Eighteenth Century Gardens of Horseheath Hall, Horseheath, Cambridgeshire. TL 623475', *Cambridgeshire County Council: Archaeological Field Unit Report. No. A148* (1999); also Wayne Cocroft, 'Horseheath Hall, Cambridgeshire – a "Lost" Garden Landscape', in Paul Pattison, David Field & Stewart Ainsworth (eds), *Patterns of the Past: Essays in Landscape Archaeology for Christopher Taylor* (Oxford, 1999), pp.107-14.

47 Gunther, *Roger Pratt*, p.129.

48 Parsons, 'Horseheath Hall', pp.16-17.

49 Gunther, *Roger Pratt*, p.308.

50 Parsons, 'Horseheath Hall', p.27.

51 Ibid., p.29.

52 The Revd William Cole mentions Kent's work in a descriptive list of the pictures at Horseheath: 'In what was called the new drawing-room on the left of the common dining parlour, made by Henry the first Lord Montfort, out of two small rooms at the south-west corner of the hall, there was a most elegant chimney piece all of white marble lined with black marble, supported by two pillars of *giallo antico* (yellow marble) with a frieze of the same, which had at the ends two white marble vases, set in gilded brass, or copper, representing at the ends two vine leaves, all designs by Mr. Kent'. Quoted in Parsons, 'Horseheath Hall', p.40.

53 See Timothy Mowl, *Gentlemen & Players: Gardeners of the English Landscape* (Stroud, 2000), pp.105-23.

54 The design is in a private collection. It is included in John Dixon Hunt, *William Kent: Landscape Garden Designer*, 1987, catalogue no.114.

55 'Archaeology within the Eighteenth Century Gardens of Horseheath', p.9.

56 Ibid., 'Documentary Research', p.5.
57 Parsons, 'Horseheath Hall', p.34
58 BL, MS 58808, f.176.
59 Ibid., p.32.

Chapter 5, pages 113-140: Brown, Woods, Emes and the Fenstanton mystery

1 Catherine Parsons, 'Horseheath Hall and its Owners', *Proceedings of the Cambridge Antiquarian Society*, vol.41 (1948), pp.1-51; p.34.
2 Ibid., p.42.
3 Ibid., p.43.
4 Ibid., p.45.
5 This is now called The Hall, Shudy Camps Park.
6 Fiona Cowell, *Richard Woods (1715-1793): Master of the Pleasure Garden* (Woodbridge, Suffolk, 2009), p.226.
7 Ibid.
8 Ibid.
9 Ibid.
10 Ibid., figure 79.
11 CA, 588/E26.
12 This and subsequent quotations concerning the Madingley commission are taken from CA, 588/E26.
13 *Victoria County History of the County of Huntingdon*, vol.2 (1932), p.280.
14 Ibid., pp.280-81.
15 Dorothy Stroud, *Capability Brown* (1950), pp.72-3.
16 Ibid., p.73.
17 Stroud, *Brown* (1975 edition), p.109.
18 Ibid.
19 This and subsequent financial equivalents have been kindly supplied by Steffie Shields, who read a first draft of this section on Brown at Fenstanton and provided thoughtful and informed comments for which we are grateful.
20 *CGT Gazetteer* states: 'a brick house, now painted, with shaped gables at each end and a porch was the home of Lancelot (Capability) Brown when he obtained the manor from the Earl of Northampton in 1768', p.74.
21 Jane Brown, *The Omnipotent Magician: Lancelot 'Capability' Brown* (Chatto & Windus, London, 2011), p.198.
22 Stroud, *Brown* (1975), p.109.
23 Ibid.
24 Ibid.
25 Information from Steffie Shields.
26 CUL: Ms. Plans x.i, 'A Plan of Fenstanton Town & the Green &c', by John Spyers. We are grateful to Ian and Bronwen Taylor for alerting us to the whereabouts of this plan and for other information regarding what is now known as Fenstanton Manor.
27 Stroud, *Brown* (1950), p.97.
28 Huntingdonshire Archives, 940: Fenstanton Inclosure Map (1810). We are grateful to Esther Bellamy for locating this map.
29 We are grateful to Steffie Shields for this biographical information.
30 Information from Steffie Shields.
31 Stroud, *Brown* (1950), p.97.
32 Stroud, *Brown* (1950), pp.171-2.
33 Ibid., p.172.
34 This is covered by Stroud, *Brown* (1975), pp.181-2; see also Marcus Whiffen, 'Academical Elysium: The

Landscaping of the Cambridge Backs', *Architectural Review*, January, 1947, pp.13-17.

35 CUL, P.I.3.

36 Whiffen, 'Academical Elysium', p.15.

37 Ibid., p.15.

38 The Latin is: '*Nunquam minus solus quam cum solus*'. We are grateful to Christopher Francis for the translation.

39 *CGT Gazetteer*, p.158.

40 Sarah Hunderby, 'Chippenham Park, Cambridgeshire 1688-1810', MA Garden History Dissertation (2009), p.14.

41 Ibid. This correspondence is in the Cambridgeshire Archives, R55/7/27.

42 Ibid., p.16.

43 Vol. 43, p.51; cited in Hunderby, 'Chippenham Park'.

Chapter 6, pages 141-155: 'The present taste for cheerfulness & freedom' – Repton in the county

1 The Red Book is in the Royal Horticultural Society's Lindley Library. We are grateful to Lucy Waitt, Liz Gilbert and Charlotte Brooks at the Lindley for their help and advice. André Rogger, *Landscapes of Taste: The Art of Humphry Repton's Red Books*, 2007, discusses Repton's 'Didactic Excursions into Topographic Drawing' on p.111.

2 For Repton's work at Stoke Edith see Timothy Mowl & Jane Bradney, *Historic Gardens of Herefordshire* (Bristol, 2011), pp.112-25.

3 Michael Hall, 'Island Hall, Cambridgeshire', *Country Life*, 26 February 1998; also information from Christopher Vane Percy.

4 Ibid.

5 Rogger, *Landscapes of Taste*, p.27.

6 Ibid.

7 Humphry Repton, *Sketches and Hints on Landscape Gardening* (1795), Chapter IV, 'Concerning Water', p.70.

8 Dorothy Stroud, *Humphry Repton* (1962) p.41.

9 Auction by Messrs Debenham & Tewson, 18 June 1862; catalogue preserved at the house.

10 A watercolour of the scheme is preserved at the house; we are grateful to David Payne for an informed tour of the grounds.

11 We are grateful to Sir Martin and Lady Lavinia Nourse for making photographs of the Red Book available for study at Dullingham. The original Red Book is now owned by Mark Thompkins at the adjacent Dullingham Park Stud.

12 Stroud, *Repton*, p.165.

13 Humphry Repton, *Observations on the Theory and Practice of Landscape Gardening* (1805), p.137.

14 Stroud, *Repton*, p.165.

15 The house is now a fertility clinic, famous for the pioneering *in vitro* work of Dr Patrick Steptoe and Robert Edwards. We are grateful to Kay Elder for an informative tour of the house and grounds.

16 *CGT Gazetteer*, p.65.

17 See Timothy Mowl & Dianne Barre, *The Historic Gardens of England: Staffordshire* (Bristol, 2009), pp.206-208.

18 A copy of the map is preserved at the house; we are grateful to David and Liz Kendrick for making this available for study.

Chapter 7, pages 156-172: Nineteenth-century diversity and a question of stylistic identity

1 *CGT Gazetteer*, p.131.

2 For Thomas Hope and The Deepdene see David Watkin, *Thomas Hope: Designer and Patron in Regency London*, 2008; for Wilton see Timothy Mowl, *Historic Gardens of Wiltshire* (Stroud, 2004), pp.132-3.

3 See Brent Elliott, *Victorian Gardens* (1986), pp.74-8.

4 Quoted in Elliott, *Victorian Gardens*, p.56.

5 See Christopher Taylor, 'A Late Seventeenth-century Garden at Babraham, Cambridgeshire', *Proceedings of the Cambridgeshire Antiquarian Society*, vol.93 (2004), pp.143-50.

6 *CGT Gazetteer*, p.56.

7 As well as the garden buildings at Tyrells Hall, there is a Regency temple-mausoleum at Duxford Mill, which was brought from Hinxton Hall in 1869. Whether the pillboxes in the grounds at Duxford and at Nine Wells House can be termed garden buildings is debatable, but they are part of the garden history narrative of both sites.

8 CA, City/PB Volume 34, p.187.

9 *Cantabrigia Depicta*, pp.14-15.

10 *A Description of the University Town, and County of Cambridge* (1791), p.26.

11 CA, 588 DR/C68.

12 CA, 124/P10.

13 The architects, Stanton Williams, won the 2012 Sitirling Prize for the building.

14 This description is taken from signage on the site.

15 Ibid.

16 This post-dates 1893, as it is not shown on the sale particulars plan, or in a sketch of the house dated 1892 published in J S Clarke, *An Artist's Rambles in Cambridgeshire* (Cambridge, 1894).

17 CA, 296 SP945.

18 See Timothy Mowl & Diane James, *Historic Gardens of Warwickshire* (Bristol, 2011), pp.179-83.

19 Held at CUL.

Chapter 8, pages 173-197: A solace for the varying moods' – Edwardian gardens

1 Jane Brown, *Newnham College Cambridge: The Making of the Gardens* (Newnham College, Cambridge, 1988).

2 Ibid., p.3.

3 This is preserved in the College. We are grateful to the College Archivist, Anne Thomson, for making this available for study.

4 Brown, *Newnham College*, p.11.

5 Ibid., p.18. Lutyens caused so much offence that his design was not built.

6 Lawrence Weaver, *Houses and Gardens by E L Lutyens*, 1913 (Antique Collector's Club edition, 1981), p.232.

7 Jane Brown, *Gardens of a Golden Afternoon* (1982), p.170. Brown gives no reference for this information.

8 Ibid., p.170. Brown is referring to the 4-volume *Lutyens Memorial*, published in 1950, which comprises the life (volume 1) and the architecture (3 volumes), edited by Christopher Hussey and ASG Butler.

9 *CGT Gazetteer*, p.102.

10 Ibid., p.48.

11 *Madingley Hall Gardens Guide* (Institute of Continuing Education, University of Cambridge, 2008), pp.2-3.

12 HM Baillie Scott, *House and Gardens: Arts and Crafts Interiors*, 1906 (Antique Collectors' Club, Woodbridge, 1995), p.31.

13 Ibid., p.122.

14 Ibid., p.128.

15 Ibid., pp.124-5.

16 Ibid., p.128.

17 Ibid., p.127.

18 Ibid.

19 Ian Macdonald-Smith, *Arts and Crafts Master: The Houses and Gardens of M H Baillie Scott* (Rizzoli, New York, 2010), pp.146-53.

20 Dianne Haigh, *Baillie Scott: The Artistic House* (1995), no pagination.

21 Macdonald-Smith, *Arts and Crafts Master*, pp.208-09.

22 We are grateful to Michael Nedo for information on the house and its owners.

23 See Trish Gibson, *Brenda Colvin: A Career in Landscape* (2011).

24 Christopher Hussey, 'A Fenlandscape Garden I & II', *Country Life*, 18 & 25 March 1954; John Sales, 'Acts of Succession', *Country Life*, 15 September 1994.

25 *Country Life*, 18 March 1954.

26 Ibid.

27 Ibid.

28 Harry, Rée, *Educator Extraordinary: The Life and Achievement of Henry Morris 1889-1961* (1973), Appendix.

29 Ibid., p.14.

30 Ibid., p.72.

31 It has now been moved to the reception area.

Chapter 9, pages 198-222: Railways, sculpture and a flourish of plants – the twentieth century

1 Tessa Wild, *Peckover House, Wisbech* (National Trust, 2006), p.23.

2 Ibid., p.20.

3 An observation shared by Arthur Hellyer, 'Gardenesque in a Victorian Setting: Gardens of Peckover House, Wisbech, Cambridgeshire', *Country Life*, 24 January 1980.

4 Preserved at the Brewery. We are grateful to Nigel and Anne Elgood for their hospitality at Elgood's.

5 We are grateful to Steve Elstub, Head Gardener at Clare College, for this and other information relating to the Fellows' Garden.

6 *Clare College Cambridge* (Clare College & Third Millenium Publishing Ltd., 2009), p.27.

7 Ibid.

8 EN Willmer, 'The Fellows' Garden, Clare College', *Country Life*, 2 September 1971.

9 This and subsequent information is taken from Victor P Whittaker, 'The Willmer Garden: Prof Nevill Willmer and the Garden at 197 Huntingdon Road, Cambridge' (unpublished article, 2009).

10 Ibid., p.1.

11 Ibid., p.2.

12 Jane Brown, *A Garden of Our Own: A History of Girton College Garden* (Girton College, 1999).

13 It was designed by Michael Waterhouse, who had been responsible for the new Library.

14 Brown, *A Garden of Our Own*, p.22.

15 Ibid.

16 Ibid.

17 We are extremely grateful to Andrew Myson, Trinity Hall's Head Gardener, for such an enthusiastic and informative tour of both sites.

18 Alice Ryan, 'Hidden Treasure', *Cambridgeshire Journal* (July, 2011), pp.46-53; p.48.

19 Ibid.

20 Unless otherwise stated, the following quotes are taken from Faith's guide.

21 A good overview of the garden is given by Ursula Buchan, 'Garden of Memories', *Country Life*, 25 Aug 1988.

22 We are particularly grateful to Gavin Smith, Lord and Lady De Ramsey's gardener, for taking us around the gardens.

23 Tony Venison, 'Plots That Triumphed', *Country Life*, 19 September 1991.

24 Ibid., p.116.

25 'When Winter Remakes a Garden', *Country Life*, 23 May 1996.

26 This and other biographical information is taken from an informed guide to the house written in May 2010 by Dame Mary Archer. See also Alasdair Alpin MacGregor, 'Memories of Grantchester', *Country Life*, 29 March 1962.

27 Quoted in the house and garden guide by Mary Archer.

28 Ibid.

Gazetteer

The following is a list of the gardens of significant historic importance which are covered in this book and are open to the public. The individual College gardens are all open at specified times.

Abbreviations

B	Brewery
BG	Botanic Garden
C	Cemetery
H	Hotel, Holiday Accommodation or Bed and Breakfast
M	Museum
NT	National Trust
P	Privately owned but open regularly or occasionally by appointment
PP	Public Park
WV	Wedding Venue

Abbey Park, Ely	PP	
Abbots Ripton Hall	P	
American Cemetery, Madingley	C	www.abmc.gov/cemeteries/cemeteries/ca.php
Anglesey Abbey	NT	www.nationaltrust.org.uk/anglesey-abbey
Cherry Hinton Hall	PP	www.cherryhintonhall.com
Chippenham Park	P	www.chippenhamparkgardens.info
Denny Abbey, Waterbeach	M	www.dennyfarmlandmuseum.org.uk
Docwra's Manor, Shepreth	P	www.docwrasmanorgarden.co.uk
Dullingham House, Newmarket	P	
Elgood's Brewery, Wisbech	B	www.elgoods-brewery.co.uk
Great Abington Hall	WV	www.abingtonhall.co.uk
Harston Park House	H	www.thecoachhousebedandbreakfast.co.uk
Hemingford Grey Manor	P	www.greenknowe.co.uk
Hilton Maze	PP	
Island Hall, Godmanchester	P	www.islandhall.com
Madingley Hall	H	www.madingleyhall.co.uk
Peckover Hall, Wisbech	NT	www.nationaltrust.org.uk/peckover-house
Shepreth Crossing House	P	
University Botanic Garden	BG	www.botanic.cam.ac.uk
Wandlebury Ring	PP	
Wimpole Hall	NT	www.nationaltrust.org.uk/wimpole

The Gardens

Not all gardens shown are open to the public

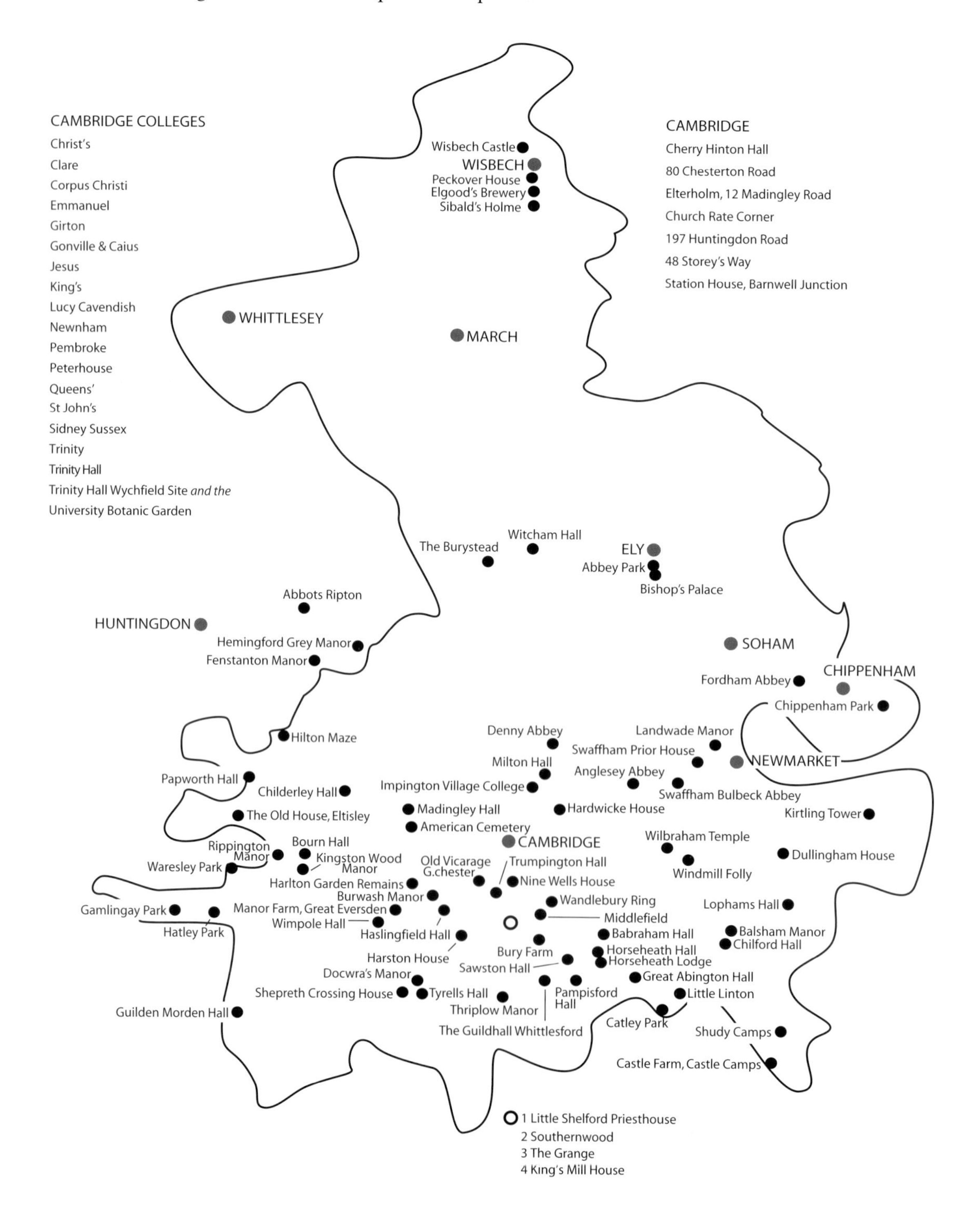

Index Page numbers in **bold** refer to illustrations and captions, **colour** refers to colour plate numbers